Conscientious Objection: Is This for You?

Discerning a Claim and Documenting It with Selective Service

TEACHER'S RESOURCE GUIDE
(Accompanies PowerPoint and DVD Presentations)

Curt Torell, Ph.D.

Conscientious Objection: Is This For You?
Discerning a Claim and Documenting It with Selective Service

TEACHER'S RESOURCE GUIDE

By Curt Torell, Quaker House Board Member and Treasurer
In Collaboration with Lynn and Steve Newsom, Quaker House Co-Directors

Copyright © 2016

Published by:
Quaker House of Fayetteville, NC
223 Hillside Avenue
Fayetteville, North Carolina 28301-4829
www.quakerhouse.org; **910-323-3912**

All Rights Reserved: 2016
ISBN-13: 978-1537741642; ISBN-10: 1537741640

"I wouldn't have known that conscientious objection existed if it wasn't for my Meeting."

- A CO letter writer when asked about
her experiences in Friends Meeting
learning about conscientious objection

Quaker House is a manifestation of the Friends' Peace Testimony. Based in Fayetteville, NC, home of Ft. Bragg, Quaker House provides counseling and support to service members who are questioning their role in the military; educates them, their families, and the public about military issues; and advocates for a more peaceful world. 910-323-3912

The GI Rights Hotline offers free, accurate, non-directive information about issues of conscience, discharge, medical, psychological, and other regulations. 877-477-4487

Military & Veterans' Domestic Violence, Sexual Assault, and Moral Injury Counseling. 904-274-3571

Table of Contests

INTRODUCTION

AGENDAS, LESSON PLANS, AND FIELD TRIP

OPENING EXERCISES AND OTHER ACTIVITIES

REFERENCE HANDOUTS

APPENDICES

POWERPOINT SLIDE PRESENTATION HARDCOPIES

SUPPLEMENTARY MATERIALS (not with curriculum)

Conscientious Objection: Is This for You? PowerPoint Slide Presentation. Download from
    www.QuakerHouse.org under "Resources" tab.
U.S. Postal Office Selective Service Registration Form (See Sample in Handout #11)
    Every U.S. Postal Service should have these two or three page brochures
The Military Enlistment Document (Full, Official Document; Not Excerpts as in Handout #6)
    Go to http://www.dtic.mil/whs/directives/forms/eforms/dd0004.pdf
Sgt. Abe Truth and Recruitment Military Enlistment Document and Letter to Parents.
    Download at www.Quakerhouse.org
Desmond T. Doss DVD/video. Go to www.desmonddoss.com for *The Conscientious Objector: A True
    Story of an American Soldier*
Taped Interviews of CO Letter Writers: *Excerpts from Our CO Letters* and *Reflections on Writing Our
    CO Letters*. Available on DVD from www.Quakerhouse.org
For more info, contact Quaker House Directors, qpr@quaker.org or 910-323-3912

Preface

Background

Several years ago at a Quaker Yearly Meeting workshop on conscientious objection young Friends were asked why they signed up for the session. Their response was universal, "I know conscientious objection is a part of the Quaker peace testimony, so I figured I should learn something about it!"

The session was lively and engaging. The young Friends learned about conscientious objection, explored their beliefs, role-played them before a "Mock Draft Board," and understood how they could start articulating and documenting their convictions.

Given this enthusiasm, a similar workshop was offered to adults the following year. When asked why they took the workshop, the response was equally surprising: "I've been trying to get our Meeting to teach our young people about conscientious objection, but no one is interested."

These two occasions are typical, even in peace churches. Often people are puzzled about our work. "Why conscientious objection? We don't have a draft!" The reason is simple: **Our endless wars make Selective Service—the precursor to a draft—very real, AND discerning a soul-searching conviction at adulthood's threshold about participation in war, or the testimony of peace, is critical.** Unfortunately, this sense of urgency is not part of our public purview. Why?

First, while Selective Service registration **is an obligation for virtually every 18-year-old male** living in the United States (and perhaps in the future will include women), few people are aware of this process, its ramifications, and the lack of a procedure to formalize a conscientious objector (CO) claim. **Within 30 days of their 18th birthday, men must register, or they could face a felony charge, imprisonment, and/or stiff fine.** While these penalties have not been applied for decades, the consequences now are much broader, more subtle, and more indirect, targeting a person's opportunities, rights, and eligibility. Today, for example, non-registration jeopardizes getting a state driver's license, state and federal educational assistance and employment, and citizenship for undocumented immigrants.

In past years, young men registered by filling out a card from the U.S. Post Office, but in today's electronic world, registration is seamless and hidden. In most states and territories it is automatic when getting a driver's license. Moreover, today's All-Volunteer Force makes it easy for teens, especially those who have economic or educational opportunities, to avoid military service and never even think about it. Conscientious objection is a moot point. **Yet, according to current Selective Service law, were a draft reinstated, such as in response to a national emergency, a young person would have as little as nine days to initiate a CO re-classification.** Even then, it would have to be granted by a local draft board. While no one can officially make a CO claim unless drafted, it is important to prepare for that situation in advance. Also, long-held beliefs, if documented, are more persuasive. Registering without a statement against war and the use of violence makes our young people complicit in and vulnerable to its perpetuation. This curriculum is a reminder that Selective Service, while dormant now, is a giant ready to be awakened.

Secondly, conscientious objection and the principles of nonviolence are fading away from the ethos of many young people. Conscientious objector voices from World War II and the Korean and Vietnam wars are long forgotten. For teens and young adults especially, developing and articulating beliefs about their personal participation in war is vital. It takes a concentrated effort, both from the individual and from his or her faith or support community. Discerning, deciding, and documenting a stance on conscientious objection at the time of Selective Service registration begins this process for them in a formal way.

Recently, **a third, and completely unintended, reason emerged about the importance of this work: it is peace training that changes lives!** In particular, for the past 15 years, since my youngest son turned 18 and registered for Selective Service, our Friends Meeting has been helping teenagers, both men and women, articulate and document a claim for conscientious objection. Teens compose a "CO letter" and read it before the Business Meeting. Every letter is unique, highly personal, and deeply moving. Each time, all those listening are overwhelmed with the eloquence, sincerity, and depth of conviction as these teens speak against violence and the tragic futility of war. If a draft is reinstated, these testaments and the Meeting's witness to them will become documentation before a potential draft board. **But beyond this, the process helped these teens crystallize fundamental beliefs about conscientious objection, nonviolence, and the testimony of peace.** Then, after recent interviews with many of them now in their 20s and early 30s, we discovered a more profound and lasting impact. These CO letters helped frame convictions that became a part of them as they entered the adult world and interacted with others in nonviolent ways. And, the letters affected their parents and other adults in the Meeting.

This curriculum, then, was written for three reasons:
1. To create an awareness, preparation, and documentation for participating youth should a draft be reinstated;
2. To develop consciousness about conscientious objection; and
3. To provide training in peace education that has lifelong consequences.

What makes this curriculum different?
Several peace groups offer materials for teens who are considering conscientious objection. The curriculum in this packet, however, is distinctive in several ways:
- **It is comprehensive, blending both instructive and experiential formats.** It contains a full range of information, definitions, and procedures to document a CO claim. It includes exploratory aspects—activities, worksheets, sample letters, stories, and role-playing. These elicit deep feelings, prompt thought-provoking discussion, and encourage individual soul-searching. They expose, illuminate, and clarify values; build confidence; and promote resilience in the face of challenges from others who advocate violence.
- While individuals can use the curriculum for its informative content, **it is designed for teaching in groups.** The agendas, PowerPoint presentation, videos, activities, letter writing exercises, reference handouts, and supplementary materials are for group use.
- **It is both for teens and for their faith or support communities.** An 18-year-old should not bear the full brunt of Selective Service, just as it is unfair to expect service members to carry the weight of war solely on their shoulders. A conviction as a conscientious objector is a collective and communal enterprise.
- **It emphasizes writing a CO letter** to one's faith or support community as well as traditional methods to seek and lay claim for a CO exemption.
- **It is part of a lifelong training in peace.** This process has a long-range impact that frames and crystallizes views about nonviolence as these young people become adults.

Curt Torell, Quaker House Board Member and Treasurer

READ ME FIRST: Overview of Materials

The PowerPoint Slide presentation is the core of the entire curriculum. The *Teacher's Resource Guide*, the PowerPoint Notes Pages, and the two videos form an integrated package designed for multiple uses, audiences, venues, time allocations, and facilitators. The information, activities, and methods can be used by teachers, counselors, parents, and teens as they approach their 18th birthdays and must register with Selective Service. We recommend that these steps be taken proactively to coincide with that first official contact with Selective Service, and we include women. While registration is now seamless, hidden, and even embedded in most state driver's license applications, Selective Service still has an infrastructure ready to reactivate a draft should Congress and the President deem it necessary.

This curriculum originated within Quaker circles, and, while those vestiges remain, it is now directed to any faith or support community. Here is a synopsis of each component:

PowerPoint Presentation (Download from www.QuakerHouse.org under "Resources" tab.)

The PowerPoint slides cover three areas:

- Selective Service and a potential draft;
- Conscientious objection; and
- Discerning, deciding, and documenting a CO (conscientious objector) position.

Some slides refer to specific handouts or exercises in the *Teacher's Resource Guide*. Each slide has an accompanying "Notes Page" with either extensive background material or instructions for that particular slide. The Notes Pages are at the end of the *Guide* and also can be accessed through the electronic version of the PowerPoint. It is assumed that facilitators are familiar with how to use PowerPoint, access Notes Pages, show a slide show presentation, and print slides onto handouts, six per page and in black and white or grayscale.

Though designed as part of an overview, the PowerPoint can be split into two shorter pieces. The *Lesson Plans for Teens* (Plan A and Plan E) use the shorter versions.

Teacher's Resource Guide

Introduction: The *Table of Contents* lists the agendas, exercises, reference handouts, and supplementary materials in this *Guide*. The *Preface* and *Acknowledgements* explain the context and reasons for the curriculum, and they highlight what distinguishes these materials from those published by other groups.

Agendas and Lesson Plans: *Agenda #1, An Overview*, is the basic workshop for teens, adults, or both. It is a fast-paced 1½ to 1¾ hour workshop spanning the full range of curriculum but with minimal detail or depth. It is used in conjunction with the PowerPoint presentation, and it combines instruction with exercises that engage the group. The one-page *Agenda* in the *Guide* is for participants, and the list of *Handouts and Topics They Reference* should be photocopied on its back. The handouts go into a "CO folder" given at the beginning of the session. Following these two documents in the *Teacher's Resource Guide* is a longer *Annotated Version* of the agenda for facilitators.

Agenda #2, An Abbreviated 45-Minute Overview, omits the exercises, videos, and discussion, leaving only the lecture portion. For both teens and adults, it is a good introduction, but it relies on additional workshops for deeper understanding and discussion.

Agenda #3, A 45-Minute Sampling for Adults Using Videos, features the videos, briefly introduces some of the printed materials, and eliminates the PowerPoint presentation. The videos portray the impact of this program as expressed by those who wrote CO letters and by their parents and other adults. This agenda is particularly useful as an introduction for a faith or support community considering this curriculum.

The next section includes *Six 50-Minute Lesson Plans for Teens*. These cover material in more depth and spread out over time. Discerning and articulating a CO position is challenging and complex. Young people benefit most with time, sensitivity, and a safe place to discuss beliefs and inner feelings. These lesson plans provide that kind of interaction and nurturing.

Opening Exercises and Other Activities: The next section in the *Guide* includes exercises and activities that prompt exploration and discussion within teen groups. They can be used as opening exercises with little discussion or as part of the *Lesson Plans* for longer periods and with greater focus.

Reference Handouts: The *Reference Handouts* provide the detail that often cannot be covered during a session. Some delve deeply into a subject area; others illustrate documents or letters; and a few list procedural steps. The materials are formatted to print onto one or two pages as stand-alone handouts.

Appendix: The *Appendix* includes material that goes beyond the *Reference Handouts*, such as detail on Selective Service, conscientious objectors over history, 35 actual CO letters, sacred scripture on peace, a resource and contact list, a bibliography, and the Notes Pages for the PowerPoint Slides. The 35 CO letters are personal, unique, and useful to read by both teens and adults.

Supplementary Materials: Some materials not included in the curriculum but needed for the workshops are listed, along with where to find them, at the end of the *Table of Contents*.

Videos

Two different videos can be used within sessions or independently. Both were done as post-interviews with over a dozen past CO letter writers who did this between 0 and 14 years ago. *Excerpts from Our CO Letters* runs 14½ minutes with the writers reading portions of their letters. *Reflections on Writing Our CO Letters* portrays their experiences when writing the letters and the impact it had on them since then. It runs 18 minutes with their reactions, and then six more with adult comments.

Three Important Disclaimers

First, should a draft be reinstated, declaring and documenting a CO conviction as outlined in this curriculum is no guarantee that a draft board will grant a CO status. The process will be unique for each person; will vary from one board to another; and could follow a new set of laws, procedures, and Supreme Court interpretations. However, laying such a claim now as suggested in this curriculum will proactively affirm a well-thought-out, personal conviction and give the claimant discernment developed over time that others would not have.

Secondly, we do not advocate conscientious objection simply so a person can avoid service or even, as some feel, a patriotic duty. Service to others and one's community is a cornerstone of our faith whether it is done locally, nationally, or globally. Even if granted an exemption, the CO is required to perform alternative service for an equivalent period of time.

Thirdly, our work is spirit-led, and we feel obligated to offer our teens a time to search their souls and inner beings about whether they can be part of a war machine and an instrument of violence. With Selective Service registration so hidden, we feel exposure to this curriculum is a necessary part of young person's maturation or "rite of passage." If not, the decision is made for them.

Additional Information and Assistance

Questions or comments on these materials can be addressed to Curt Torell, Quaker House Board Member and Treasurer, or Lynn and Steve Newsom, Quaker House Co-Directors, at qpr@quaker.org or 910-323-3912.

Acknowledgements

The seminal book, <u>Guide to the Draft</u> by Arlo Tatum and Joseph Tuchinsky, represents the wisdom of post-World War II experiences from which other peace groups grew, expanded, and became branches of the same tree. It was with pleasure that I met Arlo Tatum at a workshop in 1971, took the course *Draft and Conscience* taught by Prentice Pemberton, and worked in a draft counseling office while attending seminary in the early 70s. Dr. Pemberton and Mr. Tatum passed on their devotion to conscientious objection and the methods they used to document such a claim. They laid the seeds of my interest in this work.

Since that time, information about conscientious objection and steps to document a claim are universally represented by several groups. They include CC&W (Center on Conscience and War), CCCO (Central Committee on Conscientious Objection, now dissolved), AFSC (American Friends Service Committee), FGC (Friends General Conference), Mennonites, and Church of the Brethren, to name a few. Their efforts have been steadfast and are much appreciated. To make this curriculum more readable and because many of these methods are standardized, direct citations of them are omitted. Instead, references are used extensively in the *Brief History of COs and Selective Service*, *Contacts and Resources*, and *Bibliography*, which all appear in the *Appendix*.

Special appreciation goes to the Chapel Hill Friends Meeting, NC, and particularly to its young people who wrote CO letters and shared their convictions with the entire Meeting; Alice Carlton and Bob Gwyn who helped form COG (the Conscientious Objection Guidance Committee, which later became NC Choices for Youth); John Hite (the Meeting's youth leader who guided many of our young people through their CO letters); Marnie Clark, Jan Hutton, Pam Schwingl, Emilie Condon, Ruth Zalph, Naveed Moeed, Andrew Meriwether, and other members of the Meeting for their suggestions and editing; Susan Lees, member of Fayetteville Friends Meeting for her eagle-eye review of the final manuscript; representatives from FGC (Friends General Conference); and to Quaker House including its past Director Chuck Fager, the current Co-Directors Lynn and Steve Newsom, and the Board, especially Bill O'Connor, Jennie Ratcliffe, and Margaret Rowlett. And lastly, much appreciation goes to my wife, Patty, and my three sons who support and inspire my devotion to a more peaceful world.

Curt Torell, Quaker House Board Member and Treasurer

At Quaker House, conscientious objection is very much alive, but not among teens at registration time. It is with service members who enlisted, were trained to demonize the enemy and kill reflexively, were sent to war where they became part of its horrors, faced the nightmares and guilt, and then realized they could never fully recover. Many suffer from moral injury, a type of inner trauma that wounds the soul. As Maria Santelli, Director of Center on Conscience & War, says, it is "a natural response to a very unnatural experience….But conscience always comes back. Conscience is the law that has been inscribed by God on the human heart." Some service members go AWOL (absent without leave); many self-medicate; and too many others commit suicide. A few seek a conscientious objection discharge, a long and arduous process within the Armed Forces. These transformations of the heart or spirit are the most moving cases our GI Rights Hotline counselors deal with—humans whose fundamental being or soul was shaken and who realized they can no longer be part of war.

Living in Fayetteville, NC, home of Ft. Bragg, the military base with the largest number of service members, we see life in the military from a perspective different from those who live in civilian towns. As clinical psychologist Paula Caplan in the *Washington Post* recently coined, "We are a war-illiterate nation." Despite our endless wars, shared sacrifice is absent from our general population with only 1% of our population serving in the military and no noticeable or extra burden on taxpayers, especially those in the wealthiest brackets. We have a "great divide" between the naïve 18-year-old who unknowingly is registered into the Selective Service System (SSS) and service members who learn through personal experience what participation in war and its preparedness can do to one's soul and family. As Selective Service registration is "out of sight, out of mind" so are the consequences of wars insulated from the rest of us.

Therefore, Quaker House is publishing this curriculum for two reasons: to stand by teens and young adults who choose to declare a position on conscientious objection and to amplify and nurture the Testimony of Peace, not just for Quakers but for all faith and support groups. We hope more people and their communities will take up this task and breathe new life into conscientious objection, nonviolence, and a more peaceful world.

Lynn and Steve Newsom, Quaker House Co-Directors

The Quaker House Mission Statement
Quaker House is a manifestation of the Friends' Peace Testimony. Based in Fayetteville, NC, home of Ft. Bragg, Quaker House provides counseling and support to service members who are questioning their role in the military; educates them, their families, and the public about military issues; and advocates for a more peaceful world.

"When I saw the definition of a CO,
I realized I wanted to claim it."

- From a CO letter writer on his experience
learning about conscientious objection

AGENDAS, LESSON PLANS, AND FIELD TRIP

Agenda #1: An Overview, 1 hour and 45 minutes
Conscientious Objection: Is This for You?
Discerning a Claim and Documenting It with Selective Service

I. <u>Introduction and Welcome (25 min.)</u>
- A. Welcome, appreciation, and introductions (See PowerPoint Slide #1)
- B. Individual expectations: What do you know about conscientious objection and Selective Service? What led you to this workshop? What's your interest in this subject? What do you want to learn or walk away with?
- C. Purpose/Objectives (Slide #2)
  1. Information: Selective Service, the draft, conscientious objection
  2. Exploration: Help teens discern if they have an inclination in this area and, if so, help them articulate a testimony of peace
  3. Procedures: Review what can be done to start substantiating (or documenting) a CO position; review "CO folder" contents
- D. Method of session
  1. Instructive: Overview in PowerPoint; specific details in handouts
  2. Experiential: Simulations, worksheets, exercises, activities, letter writing
  3. Interactive: Reactions, discussion, personal documentation
- E. Two approaches: A safeguard, and a testimony to peace (Slide #3)
- F. Context and disclaimers (Slide #4)
- G. Three criteria for a conscientious objection status (Slide #5)
- H. Show one of two videos (Slide #6) OR do an Opening Exercise (below)

Opening Exercises*: If a video is used, quickly review some exercises (Slide #6)* **(5 min.)**

II. <u>What is Selective Service, the Draft, and Conscientious Objection? (20 min.)</u>
- A. PowerPoint slide show (Slides #7-27)
- B. Discussion, reactions, reflections

III. <u>Documentation, Procedures, and Simulated Role-Playing (50 min.)</u>
- A. Compose an initial response to Worksheet Form 22 (Slide #28)
- B. Discussion, reactions, and possible additions to Worksheet Form 22
- C. PowerPoint slide show and handouts (Slides #29-37)
- D. Defend your position: Role-play before a Mock Draft Board (Slide #38)
- E. Reactions, reflections, and discussion

IV. <u>Discussion, Summary, and Closure (5 min.)</u>
- A. Review, reflection, and contact information (Slide #39-40)
- B. Final exam, feedback, and wrap up (Slide #41-42)
- C. Thank you for attending (Slide #42)

Handouts and Topics They Reference

KEY: **CO** = Conscientious Objection
SS = Selective Service, the Draft, and the Military
DD = Discerning and Deciding about a Conscientious Claim
Let = Writing CO Letters
Doc = Documentation and Support

OPENING EXERCISES AND OTHER ACTIVITIES

REFERENCE HANDOUTS

Some Other Useful Handouts, But Not To Copy, Are in the Appendix:

Agenda #1: An Overview, 1 hour and 45 minutes
Conscientious Objection: Is This for You?
Discerning a Claim and Documenting It with Selective Service

Annotated for Facilitators

Facilitators' notes are in italics after each section of the agenda. More expanded comments are on the Notes Pages of each PowerPoint slide.

Preparation: This lesson uses the PowerPoint presentation, file folders for each person, many handouts, U.S. Postal Office Selective Service forms, and pens or pencils. Photocopy the following (or use *Teacher's Resource Guides* for all) and put in this order into the file folders:

- The one-page *Agenda #1* with the *Handouts and Topics They Reference* on its back.
- The *PowerPoint Slides* with six slides per page, printing in black and white OR grayscale, copying back to back. Staple. Print out from the PowerPoint print menu.
- All fifteen of the *Reference Handouts*, printed back to back, as listed on the *Handouts and Topics They Reference* page. Staple them together.
- All nine *Opening Exercises and Other Activities* printed back to back and stapled together as one set.
- Recopy *Exercise #4, Worksheet Form 22* as a separate page with nothing on the back. This is used as an exercise, an example of tri-folding, and sent in the mail. Using this single sheet keeps the *Worksheet* with the *Exercises* clean for future use.
- Lastly, get enough *U.S. Postal Office Selective Service Form* for each person and put one in the back of each folder.

This "CO folder" becomes the participant's personal source of reference and documentation.

I. <u>Introduction and Welcome (25 min.)</u>
    A. Welcome, appreciation, and introductions (See PowerPoint Slide #1) (5 min.)

Start on time. Welcome everyone. Express appreciation to those attending and to those who helped arrange the workshop. Pass around a sign-up sheet with names, email addresses, and/or phone numbers. Mention that while the workshop specifically addresses conscientious objection and how to document a claim, it also has a longer range value that teaches a "conscientious commitment to peace" that changes lives.

Say some introductory remarks about why the workshop is being held, such as:
- *Over the years, an understanding of conscientious objection, especially among teens, seems to be fading from our consciousness. Many people feel that since we do not have a draft, the subject is not important. Yet, the testimony of peace is just as significant now as ever.*
- *Is the new "NORMAL" an "endless wars on terrorism?" Is the general population oblivious of its impact? As clinical psychologist Paula Caplan says "we are a war-*

illiterate nation." We have a divide between the civilian and military populations: wars are fought elsewhere. Physical, emotional, and spiritual casualties on both sides are largely hidden from our view; the connection between the costs of war and the depletion of resources that could fill human needs is rarely emphasized.

- *Selective Service Registration, required of 18-year-old males, and likely women in the future, is obscure and automatic, DESPITE its consequences as the precursor to a draft. (More later.)*
- *Our teens are not conscious of a need either to document a conscientious objection claim or to articulate their views about peace as they enter into their adult years. As a consequence, they are ill-prepared.*
- *Faith or support communities have an opportunity to prepare our teens, share the stories of service members affected by war, and seek not just to heal the scars of war but also work "to prevent the occasions that bring about war," as George Fox, the founder of Quakerism, said. In other words, we need to be teaching peace.*
- *This curriculum focuses mostly on developing a statement or CO letter but also includes standard procedures for documenting a CO claim at registration time. These methods are similar to those used by other faith and peace groups. (See "What makes this curriculum different" in the "Preface.")*

B. Individual expectations: What do you know about conscientious objection and Selective Service? What led you to this workshop? What's your interest in this subject? What do you want to learn or walk away with? (5 min.)

To guide what is most important to cover, ask participants to share their interests, expectations, and experiences with conscientious objection. The teens attending may want to make a CO claim; a parent may want to begin this process with a son or daughter; adults may wish to shepherd this process in their faith or support communities.

C. Purpose/Objectives (Slide #2) (1 min.)
1. Information: Selective Service, the draft, conscientious objection
2. Exploration: Help teens discern if they have an inclination in this area and, if so, help them articulate a testimony of peace
3. Procedures: Review what can be done to start substantiating (or documenting) a CO position and review the "CO folder" contents

Stress that this session is an OVERVIEW introducing a broader range of materials but with little depth. Detail is provided in the handouts listed on the back of the agenda and with a key as to what subjects they reference. Also, because they have a copy of the PowerPoint slides, the presentation can be viewed quickly.

You may wish to leaf quickly through what is in the CO folders. Don't spend time reviewing each piece; just show them what is there so they can refer to them afterwards.

D. Method of session (1 min.)
1. Instructive: Overview in PowerPoint; specific details in handouts

2.   Experiential: Simulations, worksheets, exercises, activities, letter writing

3.   Interactive: Reactions, discussion, personal documentation

Mention that the agenda parallels the PowerPoint presentation and various slides refer to handouts that expand a particular subject. Add that while this session is a broad, quick overview, follow up sessions go into detail and use different teaching formats.

E.   Two approaches: A safeguard (Conscientious Objection to War) and a testimony to peace and nonviolence (Conscientious Commitment to Peace) (Slide #3)

This curriculum originated as a safeguard to provide documentation for teens inclined to make a CO claim should a draft ever be reinstated. Over the years, it became evident that the process, done with both young men and women, had tremendous long-range benefits: it helped them articulate a view on nonviolence, the testimony of peace, and a way of living. The first approach we call a Conscientious Objection to War; the second is a Conscientious Commitment to Peace and Nonviolence. Refer to the Handout "Long-Range Benefits of Writing CO Letters." Also mention 18-to-24-minute video, "Reflections on Writing Our CO Letters," that can be shown in a future session.

F.   Context and disclaimers (Slide #4)

Read this slide, which is self-explanatory. It lays a foundation for all that is presented. The PowerPoint "Notes Page" says more.

G.   Three criteria for a conscientious objection status (Slide #5) (1 min.)

While these three criteria are covered in more detail later in the presentation, they are brought to the foreground for emphasis. They are the most important and fundamental learnings of the workshop, and they are on the final exam.

H.   Show Video (Slide #6) OR do an Opening Exercise (below) (18 min.)

Depending on time and interest, show the group one of the two videos ("Excerpts from Our CO Letters" or "Reflections on Writing Our CO Letters") OR the group can do one of the three exercises mentioned on PowerPoint Slide #6. The "Excerpts" video is 15 minutes; "Reflections" is 18 minutes (24 if the adult portion at the end is used). The exercises can be done in less time. Discussion is encouraged, but time is limited.

For any of the three exercises, follow the instructions at the top of each page.

*If more time is allotted, also use the **Violence vs. Nonviolence Brainstorming** exercise. This is an excellent way to get the group to think about these concepts.*

Whatever is chosen, this is a good way to loosen up the group and introduce the subject. The video, though a passive time of listening, highlights the distinctive aspect of this curriculum, which is writing the CO letters. If it is used, the exercises can be mentioned later without doing them. On the other hand, the exercises do get the group up, active, and participating.

Opening Exercises*: If a video is used, quickly review the exercises (Slide #6) (5 min.)*
   Since the video replaces the exercises, just introduce the exercises, without doing any, so the group knows what is available and can use them in future sessions.

II. <u>What is Selective Service, the Draft, and Conscientious Objection? (20 min.)</u>
  A. PowerPoint slide show (Slides #7-27) (15-20 min.)

  Cover the slides ranging from "Part I: Selective Service System" through "Scripture vs. The Military Enlistment Document." Go quickly, reminding them that detail is in the handouts. Stop on the slide "Exercise: Worksheet Form 22."

  B. Discussion, reactions, reflections (0-5 min.)

  Ask for any questions or comments. A lot of material was presented. Remind them that detail is in the handouts. Be aware of the time, and move on if necessary.

III. <u>Documentation, Procedures, and Simulated Role-playing (50 min.)</u>
  A. Compose an initial response to Worksheet Form 22 (Slide #28) (10 min.)

  This is a natural break from the instructive part of the PowerPoint Presentation. Have participants take out the last single sheet in their CO folder. Don't use the one in the Exercise section of the Guide so that it can be kept clean for later use.
  Follow the directions on the PowerPoint Slide. Questions 2 and 3 are more important so if time is running short, tell them to skip #1. Have them take ten minutes to start this Worksheet. Point out that such deep questions are difficult to answer. The purpose of the exercise is to <u>begin</u> thinking about and documenting beliefs, not to finalize a statement. After the workshop, participants can add more to their worksheets or use the two page version in the Appendix.

  B. Discussion, reactions, and possible additions to Worksheet Form 22 (5 min.)

  First, ask participants how it felt to think about, respond, and write their responses. Assure them that this is difficult, but it is a good start. Then, ask for someone to share his or her responses. Encourage them to add more comments on the form as the workshops continue. Direct them to the bottom of the Handout "Suggestions to Build Documentation and Worksheet Form 22 Tips" for helpful hints on filling out this form.
  THEN using this form, demonstrate **Tri-folding***. Except for this case, photocopy the form and keep the original. With the printed portion on the inside, fold the copy in thirds as if it would be inserted into a regular 4⅛ x 9½m legal-sized envelope, and then staple it shut. Self-address and stamp the outside, then send it in the U.S. mail. When delivered back, keep it unopened and place it along with the original in the CO folder. The copy will have a postal service postmark date over the stamp proving when this was done (make sure the date is*

legible). This documents a timeline in case a local draft board accuses you of fabricating evidence at the last minute. These steps are written out at the top of the Handout "Three Fundamental Ways To Document a CO Claim." Use tri-folding to date and document any form, statement, or letter in your CO folder.

C.   PowerPoint slide show and handouts (Slides #29-37) (15 min.)

Return to the PowerPoint slides starting from "How Do You Register as a CO" and running through "A Checklist of Procedures." Then, stop at "Can you defend your position?"

D.   Defend your position: A Mock Draft Board Role-play (Slide #38) (20 min.)

This is the role-playing portion. For sample questions, refer to Exercise #9, "Sample Questions a Draft Review Board Might Ask."

Set up a role-play with a three-person Mock Draft Board. The board could be adults, the facilitators, or a combination of them along with the younger participants.

The Mock Draft Board is intended to simulate an experience, almost to the extreme. Its purpose is to bring out both dynamics and content. It is NOT meant to embarrass, offend, or discourage, but rather to illustrate the difficulty, and sometimes anxiety, of expressing deeply personal views to strangers.

Ask for a volunteer to be the CO applicant (or the person in the hot seat). The applicant will have two minutes to explain his or her case. Then, immediately start drilling the person with questions such as, "Why do you want to be a CO?" As the person responds, look for holes, inconsistencies, hesitations, uncertainties, or other possible weaknesses, and then interrupt the person with a probing question to that effect. To be true to the role-play, some members of the board can be rude and disrespectful; others seemingly nice (like "good cop/bad cop"). For example, one member might appear sympathetic and say, "What if I can guarantee you a nice safe desk job stateside? Would you drop your CO claim then?" The simulation is intended to illustrate how some local board members might have a completely different, biased set of views that could challenge and frustrate the applicant from expressing his or her own. While set up to defend and justify, the core of the CO's task is simply to speak honesty and with integrity.

Use an "angel" (any person) who can come in at any time and whisper help to the one in the hot seat who might be stymied or struggling to frame an answer.

At the end of each role-play, congratulate the person in the hot seat and "process" what happened. Ask the person in the hot seat: What was this like? How did you feel? What did you feel comfortable with? What was difficult? Where did you need better insight to respond? How did you feel about the Mock Draft Board members? When done, ask everyone else to give this person a round of applause.

Then turn to the board and ask similar questions. Emphasize what the person did well to build confidence. Finally, ask for the audience's reactions. Underscore positives.

If time permits, get another volunteer. NOTE: teens generally love this exercise. It may need more time. If several teens attend this workshop, consider a separate session to do this in more detail. (See "Lesson Plan C for Teens" as well as its Debriefing section VI.C. for more questions.)

E.   Responses, reflections, and discussion (combined with above)

IV. <u>Discussion, Summary, and Closure (5 min.)</u>
A.   Review, reflection, and contact information (Slides #39-40) (2 min.)

These two slides begin the wrap-up and review. Aside from what is listed and where to get additional information, share what your own faith or support community will do. Encourage people to contact Quaker House for assistance or questions.

B.   Final exam, feedback, and wrap up (Slides #41-42) (2 min.)

Use the "Let's Review" slide as a final exam. Tell everyone that this as a "group" exam with open notes. Help as needed. Repetition is a good way to reinforce information presented earlier.

The "Wrapping Up" slide encourages those present to document their attendance by having one of the presenters sign and date their Agenda Handout, then put it back in their CO folder.

If time permits, quickly go through each of the other papers in the CO folder. This also is another good review of the material.

C.   Thank you attending (Slide #42)

Thank participants for their time and patience. Announce follow-up steps.

Agenda #2: An Abbreviated 45-Minute Overview
Conscientious Objection: Is This for You?
Discerning a Claim and Documenting It with Selective Service

Facilitators' notes are in italics after each section of the agenda. More expanded comments are on the Notes Pages of each PowerPoint slide.

This agenda is **the same as Agenda #1 but omits all the experiential portions**, i.e., the video, opening exercises, Workshop Form 22 questionnaire, and Mock Draft Board. **These are crossed out ~~crossed out~~ in the agenda below.** This session is entirely a lecture relying solely on the PowerPoint presentation. Details are in the handouts provided in the CO folder.

Preparation: Use the same preparation and tips as in the *Agenda #1 Notes for Facilitators*. Instead of doing the exercises as called for in *Agenda #1*, simply point them out and have participants do them on their own or as homework. Tell them that this agenda is a truncated version with certain sections omitted. The adjusted times appear below.

I. Introduction and Welcome (5 min.)

A. Welcome, appreciation, and introductions (See PowerPoint Slide #1)

B. Individual expectations: What do you know about conscientious objection and Selective Service? What led you to this workshop? What's your interest in this subject? What do you want to learn or walk away with?

C. Purpose/Objectives (Slide #2)
1. Information: Selective Service, the draft, conscientious objection
2. Exploration: Help teens discern if they have an inclination in this area and, if so, help them articulate a testimony of peace
3. Procedures: Review what can be done to start substantiating (or documenting) a CO position and review "CO folder" contents

D. Method of session
1. Instructive: Overview in PowerPoint; specific details in handouts
2. Experiential: Simulations, worksheets, exercises, activities, letter writing
3. Interactive: Reactions, discussion, personal documentation

E. Two approaches: A safeguard and a testimony to peace (Slide #3)

F. Context and disclaimers (Slide #4)

G. Three criteria for a conscientious objection status (Slide #5)

~~H. Show one of two Videos (Slide #6) OR do an Opening Exercise (below)~~

Tell the participants that two videos are available: "Excerpts from Our CO Letters" and "Reflections on Writing Our CO Letters." They can be shown at a future session.

Refer participants to the exercises in the CO folder mentioning that they can be done in future sessions.

II. **What is Selective Service, the Draft, and Conscientious Objection? (20 min.)**
    A.   PowerPoint slide show (Slides #7-27)
    B.   Discussion, reactions, reflections

III. **Documentation, Procedures, & Simulated Role-playing (15 min.)**
    A.   Compose an initial response to Worksheet Form 22 (Slide #27)
    B.   Discussion, reactions, and possible additions to Worksheet Form 22

This section is omitted entirely. It can be done at any future session.

As above, only mention the Worksheet Form 22 and how it is used in the longer Agenda #1. Urge them to take the Worksheet with them, fill it out, photocopy, tri-fold, and send it to themselves.

    C.   PowerPoint slide show and handouts (Slides #28-37)
    D.   Defend your position: Role-play before a Mock Draft Board (Slide #38)

Similarly, the Mock Draft Board is omitted. It can be done in later sessions. Refer them to the Exercise Handout #9 with the draft board questions on it.

    E.   Reactions, reflections, and discussion

IV. **Discussion, Summary, and Closure (5 min.)**
    A.   Review, reflection, and contact information (Slides #39-40)
    B.   Final exam, feedback, and wrap up (Slides #41-42)
    C.   Thank you attending (Slide #42)

Talk about any plans to expand this curriculum and provide follow up sessions, either with teens and/or adults. Point out that the "Teacher's Resource Guide" includes other agendas, as well as a series of more in-depth lesson plans for teens.

Agenda #3: A 45-Minute Sampling for Adults Using Videos
Conscientious Objection: Is This for You?
Discerning a Claim and Documenting It with Selective Service

Facilitator notes are in italics after each section of the agenda.

This agenda is for adults and interested teens in faith and support communities as a <u>sampling</u> of the curriculum, its impact, and its benefits. The videos express the powerful words of teens who wrote CO letters then talked about what it meant to them. After the video(s), the facilitator can simply preview the materials that are part of the curriculum. Except for a printed copy of the slides, the PowerPoint presentation is not used at all.

Preparation: Use either or both of the videos. Have at least one set of handouts (as outlined in preparation section of *Agenda #1*). The facilitator can refer to these, have sets for everyone, or photocopy the *Table of Contents* for everyone so they can see the materials available. Be familiar with the *PowerPoint Presentation*.

I. <u>Introduction and Welcome (10 min.)</u>
A. Welcome, appreciation, and introductions

Start on time. Welcome everyone. Express appreciation for those attending and those who helped arrange the workshop.

B. Purpose and overview of session

This session is for faith or support communities that are considering the curriculum, so the session is simply a quick exposure and introduction, which the videos do. Mention that while the workshop specifically addresses conscientious objection and how to document a claim, it also has a longer range value that teaches a "conscientious commitment to peace" that changes lives.

Say the same introductory remarks as in Agenda #1, such as:
- *Over the years, an understanding of conscientious objection, especially among teens, seems to be fading from our consciousness. Many people feel that since we do not have a draft, the subject is not important. Yet, the testimony of peace is just as significant now as ever.*
- *Is the new "NORMAL" an "endless wars on terrorism?" Is the general population oblivious of its impact? As clinical psychologist Paula Caplan says we are "a war-illiterate nation." We have a divide between the civilian and military populations: wars are fought elsewhere. Physical, emotional, and spiritual casualties on both sides are largely hidden from our view; the connection between the costs of war and the depletion of resources that could fill human needs is rarely emphasized.*

- *Selective Service Registration, required of 18-year-old males, is obscure and automatic, DESPITE its consequences as the precursor to a draft. (More later.)*
- *Our young people are not conscious of a need either to document a conscientious objection claim or to articulate their views about peace as they enter into their adult years. As a consequence, they are ill-prepared.*
- *Faith or support communities have an opportunity to prepare our teens, share the stories of service members affected by war, and seek not just to heal the scars of war but also work "to prevent the occasions that bring about war," as George Fox, the founder of Quakerism, said. In other words, we need to be teaching peace.*
- *This curriculum focuses mostly on developing a statement or CO letter but also includes standard procedures for documenting a CO claim at registration time. These methods are similar to those used by other faith and peace groups. (See "What makes this curriculum different" in the "Preface.")*

Then say that the video(s) will be shown, followed by discussion, then give a quick review of the PowerPoint and other handouts that can be used in later sessions.

C.   Three criteria for a conscientious objection status

Emphasize the three main criteria for qualifying as a CO:
1. *Must be <u>conscientiously opposed to participating in any war and all war</u>. Opposition is not political or selective. It is against any and all war. No such thing as a "just war."*
2. *The objection must be based upon <u>moral, ethical, or religious belief</u>. Old law (belief in Supreme Being) changed to religious training and belief.*
3. *The claim must be <u>sincere or deeply held,</u> or play a significant role in one's life. Not only must this position be truly you, but you must be able to <u>document</u> it, which is explained in the curriculum.*

D.   Context and disclaimers

Declaring and documenting a CO conviction as outlined in this curriculum is no guarantee that a draft board will grant a CO status, but it will demonstrate a greater degree of sincerity and give the claimant a clearness developed over time that others would not have. See the other disclaimers from Slide #4 and its Notes Page.

II.   The Videos: (18-24 min.)
A.   Show one or both of the videos

If time limits the showing of only one video, use "Reflections on Writing Our CO Letters." Its first 18 minutes features the letter writers and can be stopped there. The next 6 minutes includes parent and adult comments. "Excerpts from Our CO Letters" pulls from over a dozen letters and lasts 14½ minutes. If later is not used, read a sample letter or two from the handout "Two Sample CO Letters."

B.   Discussion, reactions, reflections

What themes emerged? What unexpected comments did the teens make? How might your faith or support community support your teens in this regard?

III. <u>Overview of the Curriculum (10 min. or less depending upon length of video)</u>
A. Purpose, methodology, and results

The purpose of the full curriculum is to provide:
1.   *Information on Selective Service, the draft, conscientious objection;*
2.   *Exploration that helps teenagers discern if they have an inclination in this area and, if so, help them articulate a testimony of peace; and*
3.   *Procedures that present what steps can be taken to start substantiating (or documenting) a CO position.*

The method is:
1.   *Instructive - Overview from the PowerPoint presentation; specific details from handouts;*
2.   *Experiential - Simulations, worksheets, exercises, activities, letter writing;*
3.   *Interactive - Reactions, discussion, personal documentation.*

The result is twofold. It is a potential safeguard should a draft ever be reinstated, and it helps teens (men and women) discern and articulate a testimony of peace!

B.   Overview of each component

The curriculum has three major components. They just saw one or both of videos. The PowerPoint provides an overview of information. It also contains "Notes Pages" that give the facilitator additional information for each slide. The "Teacher's Resource Guide" has agendas, exercises and activities, detailed reference handouts, and a copy of the Notes Pages that accompanies the PowerPoint Presentation. The "READ ME FIRST" section at the beginning of the "Guide" gives a description of each.

    Next, go through the handouts that are part of the standard CO packet. The purpose is just to show what is available, not to read each one. The Appendix has more material, including 35 actual CO letters. The Table of Contents lists everything.

IV. <u>Discussion, Summary, and Closure (5 min.)</u>
A. Questions and comments
B. Thank you for attending

Ask for questions or comments; thank everyone for participating; announce any next steps.

Conscientious Objection: Is This for You?
Discerning a Claim and Documenting It with Selective Service

Six 50-Minute Lesson Plans for Teens
Annotated for Facilitators

These six 50-minute lesson plans, while based on the previous agendas, give teens more time to absorb information, discern their beliefs, and discuss them with others. The basic 1-hour 45-minute PowerPoint workshop (*Agenda #1*) is split into two: the first part in *Lesson Plan A* and the remaining in *Lesson Plan E*. The sessions in between delve more deeply into the exercises, activities, and role-plays. As mentioned in the introduction of this *Guide*, discerning and articulating a belief about conscientious objection is not easy, either for teens or adults. A safe space, time, and supportive environment are needed to nurture and explore.

Lesson Plan A
Getting Started: Basic Information and Worksheet Form 22

Preparation: Use the same preparation as described in the annotated version of *Agenda #1* so that everyone has all the materials in their CO folders. Tell the teens to keep their folders and bring them to each session. Have the equipment ready to run the PowerPoint Presentation. Facilitators may wish to refer to the instructions and explanations in the three *Annotated Agendas #1-3* and from the corresponding *Notes Pages* in the *PowerPoint Presentation*. Refer to these particular exercises and handouts in the CO folder. Have extras available.

- *Exercise #1: Could You Chant This at Boot Camp Then Do It Later?*
- *Exercise #2: Cadences and Jody Calls*
- *Alternative Exercises are:*
    - ✓ *#3: Violence vs. Nonviolence Brainstorming*
    - ✓ *#5: Meaningful or Inspiring Quotes*
    - ✓ *#6: Could You—Would You? Some Real-Life Military Decisions*
- *Exercise #4: Worksheet Form 22*
- *Handout #1: Long-Range Benefits of Writing CO Letters*
- *Handout #14: Suggestions to Build Documentation and Worksheet Form 22 Tips*

I. Introduction and Welcome (15 min.)
A. Welcome, appreciation, and introductions (See PowerPoint Slide #1)

Explain that this lesson is the first in a series of six. Specifically, they are to help each person discern if he or she is a conscientious objector and, if so, how to articulate and document that AND generally they focus and think about nonviolence and peace. As an introduction, this lesson presents the most information. Future ones will be full of exercises, activities, role-playing, and writing down beliefs. The entire curriculum has three components: a PowerPoint presentation, two videos, and a range of handouts, including activities and exercises to help explore beliefs and reference materials that provide information about Selective Service, conscientious objection, and ways to make a CO claim.

This lesson covers the first two-thirds of the PowerPoint, i.e., from the beginning slides through Part III and ending with the Exercise on Worksheet Form 22. Lesson Plan E finishes the PowerPoint slides, starting after the Worksheet and covering documentation.

    B.   Some opening questions
        1.   What do you know about Selective Service?
        2.   Are you registered for Selective Service?
        3.   Do you have a state driver's license and what does that have to do with Selective Service?
        4.   What do you know about conscientious objection?

Listen to their responses. Explain that these are some of the questions that will be addressed in this lesson.

    C.   Purpose and Objectives (Slide #2)
        1.   Information: Selective Service, the draft, conscientious objection
        2.   Exploration: Help teens discern if they have an inclination in this area and, if so, help them articulate a testimony of peace
        3.   Procedures: Review what can be done to start substantiating (or documenting) a CO position and review "CO folder" contents

Stress that this first lesson is an overview of Selective Service and conscientious objection. A later session will finish the PowerPoint portion on how to document a claim. Their CO folder contains detailed handouts. The handouts will be covered in future sessions.

    D.   Method of session
        1.   Instructive: Overview in PowerPoint; specific details in handouts
        2.   Experiential: Simulations, worksheets, exercises, activities, letter writing
        3.   Interactive: Reactions, discussion, personal documentation

As stated above, the first and fifth sessions (Lessons A and E) are instructive and cover the most information. The other lessons are more experiential and interactive.

    E.   Two approaches: A safeguard (Conscientious Objection to War) and a testimony to peace and nonviolence (Conscientious Commitment to Peace) (Slide #3)

This curriculum originated to be a safeguard in case the draft is reinstated and to provide documentation for teens inclined to make a CO claim if drafted. Over the years, it became evident that the process, done with both young men and women, had tremendous long-range benefits: it helped them articulate a view on nonviolence, the testimony of peace, and a way of living. The first approach we call a Conscientious Objection to War; the second is a

Conscientious Commitment to Peace and Nonviolence. Refer them to the Handout "Long-Range Benefits of Writing CO Letters" in their CO folder. Also mention that an 18-24-minute video, "Reflections on Writing Our CO Letters," can be shown in a future session. The first 18 minutes is from past CO letter writers, and the final 6 minutes, which can be cut if time is short, has responses from adults and parents.

F.   Context and disclaimers (Slide #4)

Read this slide, which is self-explanatory but worth emphasizing. See the accompanying Notes Page in the PowerPoint presentation.

G.   Three criteria for a conscientious objection status (Slide #5)

While these three criteria are covered in more detail later, they are emphasized here. This is the most important and fundamental concept of the workshop.

H.   Do an opening exercise (Slide #6)

For this lesson, the best choice is probably Exercise #1, "Could You Chant This at Boot Camp Then Do It Later?" Have them pull the Exercise from their CO folder and read the chant out loud. Tell everyone to pretend that they at boot camp. The facilitator is the drill sergeant. Have everyone stand up, form a single file, and march around the room. Make sure they march in step with the cadence and repeat until ordered to stop. As drill sergeant, bark orders, and tell them to chant louder ("I can't hear you!"). If you have good rapport with the group, pick on some individuals, tell them do push-ups if they are slacking. Get into the role.
After they get a taste of the exercise, have everyone sit down and talk about their experience. How did it feel? What did the marching and chanting try to do to them as individuals and as a group? Note: When this exercise was done in the past, some teens protested that this doesn't happen at boot camp. Yes, it does! The chant is real (see the citation referenced on the Exercise sheet). Point out some of the other chants in Exercise #2, "Cadences and Jody Calls."
The other three exercises are good also. See the top of each exercise for instructions.
If time permits, the "Violence vs. Nonviolence Brainstorming" exercise can be done after any of the other three. This is an excellent way to get the group to think about these concepts.

II.   What is Selective Service, the Draft, and Conscientious Objection? (20 min.)
A.   PowerPoint slide show (Slides #7-27) (15-20 min.)

Cover the slides ranging from "Part I: Selective Service System" through "Scripture vs. The Military Enlistment Document." Go quickly. Detail is in handouts. Stop on the slide "Exercise: Worksheet Form 22."

B.   Discussion, reactions, reflections (0-5 min.)

Ask for any questions or comments. A lot of material was presented. Remind them that detail is in the handouts. Be aware of the time, and move on.

III. <u>Worksheet Form 22 (12 min.)</u>
    A.   Compose an initial response to Worksheet Form 22 (Slide #28) (10 min.)

This is a natural break from the instructive part of the PowerPoint Presentation. Have participants take out the last single sheet in their CO folder. Don't use the one in the Exercise section of the Guide so that it can be kept clean for later use.

Follow the directions on the PowerPoint Slide. Questions 2 and 3 are more important so if time is running short, tell them to skip #1. Have them take ten minutes to start this Worksheet. Point out that such deep questions are difficult to answer. The purpose of the exercise is to <u>begin</u> thinking about and documenting beliefs, not to finalize a statement. After the workshop, participants can add more to their worksheets or use the two page version in the Appendix.

    B.   Discussion, reactions, and possible additions to Worksheet Form 22 (2 min.)

First, ask the teens how it felt to think about, respond, and write their responses. Assure them that this is difficult, but it is a good start. Then, ask for someone to share his or her responses. Encourage everyone to add more comments on the form as the workshop continues. Let them know that the bottom of the Reference Handout "Suggestions to Build Documentation & Worksheet Form 22 Tips" has helpful hints on filling out this form.

*THEN, using this form, demonstrate **Tri-folding**. In most cases, photocopy the form and put the original in the CO folder, but for this example, use the original. Fold this in thirds with the printed portion on the inside as if it would be inserted into a regular $4\frac{1}{8}$ x $9\frac{1}{2}$ sized envelope. Staple it shut. On the outside self-address, stamp, and send it in the U.S. mail. When delivered back, keep it unopened and place it with the original in the CO folder. The copy will have a U.S. Postal Service postmark date over the stamp (make sure it is legible) proving when this was done. This protects you in case a local draft board accuses you of fabricating evidence at the last minute. These steps are at the top of the Handout "Three Fundamental Ways To Document a CO Claim." Use tri-folding to date and document any form, statement, or letter.*

IV. <u>Discussion, Review, Homework, and Closure (3 min.)</u>
    A.   Reflection

What did they learn? What was new or most interesting? Any questions?

    B.   Review

As a review, ask them to name the three criteria for being a CO.

    C.   Homework and Closure

Have them take their Worksheets home and add comments to them. Refer them to the bottom portion of the Handout "Suggestions to Build Documentation and Worksheet Form 22 Tips." Ask them to bring their Worksheets along with their CO folder to the next lesson.

Tell them the next lesson will focus on some of the other exercises. They will have more time to share and discuss.

Lesson Plan B
Exploring Your Beliefs: Activities and Discussion

Preparation: Refer to these exercise handouts in the CO folder. Have extras available.
- *Exercise #1: Could You Chant This at Boot Camp Then Do It Later?*
- *Exercise #2: Cadences and Jody Calls*
- *Exercise #3: Violence vs. Nonviolence Brainstorming*
- *Exercise #5: Meaningful or Inspiring Quotes*
- *Exercise #6: Could You—Would You? Some Real-Life Military Decisions*
- *Exercise #7: Before You Enlist, Consider This: Words from the Homefront*

This lesson is particularly important. Our government and the Pentagon have shielded the American public from war's devastating effects both on the civilian populations in war-occupied countries and on our U.S. service members deployed there. Paula Caplan, a clinical psychologist, recently coined the term "a war-illiterate nation" to describe the civilian disconnect and our ignorance about the trauma that service members experience as a result of combat training, deployment, and separation from family. Since Quaker House is located in Fayetteville, NC, home of Ft. Bragg, the largest U.S. Army base in terms of personnel, it sees firsthand "on the homefront" the trauma that our veterans and their families experience. These exercises are intended to alert our youth about these consequences that too often remain hidden from the general public. Time should be allowed for plenty of discussion, reaction, exploration, questioning, and soul-searching of new ideas and perspectives.

I.   Introduction and Welcome (5 min.)
A.   Welcome

Welcome new members and give them their CO folders. Show them the PowerPoint handout and the slides that were presented last session.

This lesson starts with expanding participant comments on the Worksheet Form 22 and is followed by other exercises and activities for deeper exploration and discussion.

B.   Review

Remind the group that this is the second of a series of lessons, that the last session was mostly didactic, and that the remaining ones will be more experiential. Emphasize the two reasons for this curriculum mentioned in Lesson A: a safeguard in case a draft is ever reinstated and a chance to articulate a testimony of peace versus war.

Ask them what they remember specifically from the previous lesson. If no one mentions it, ask them to cite the three criteria for being a conscientious objector.

C. Purpose of Lesson B

    1.   Add more individual comments on Worksheet Form 22
    2.   Explore and discuss reactions to some exercises and activities

Pick up with the Worksheet Form 22, then explore the other three exercises. See the top of each for instructions.

If time permits, the "Violence vs. Nonviolence Brainstorming" exercise can be done after any of the other three. This is an excellent way to get the group to think about these concepts.

II. <u>Worksheet Form 22 (10 min.)</u>
A. Share comments written last week or added since then
B. As a group, discuss their responses to the questions
C. Add more responses to the form

Take time to listen to concerns and questions. Encourage everyone to continue editing and adding comments to their Worksheets throughout all the lessons.

III. <u>Exercises and Activities (Pick One or Two) (30 min.)</u>

Pick one or two of the exercises below. Exercises #1 and #2 may have been done during Lesson A. Any of these exercises not chosen can be done at another time.

A. Exercise #1: "Could You Chant This at Boot Camp Then Do It Later?" OR Exercise #2: "Cadences and Jody Calls"

If not done previously, this exercise is a good, quick activity that is both physical and provocative. These are actual "Jody Calls" that depict the training at boot camp.

B. Exercise #3: Violence vs. Nonviolence

This exercise takes the longest gets the group thinking about these concepts and dialoguing with each other. Read the instructions on the top of the exercise. If ample time is allotted, this exercise can also be done after any of the others.

C. Exercise #5: "Meaningful or Inspiring Quotes"

Refer to Exercise #5 in their CO folder. Let the group read over the quotes and ask everyone to pick one or two that particularly speaks to them. Then ask them to share it and why it was meaningful to them. If time permits, ask them if they know of any other quotes, poems, songs, movies, books, or people who have been an inspiration for peace to them. If they can't remember the exact quote or passage, encourage them bring it to the next lesson. Remind people to write their meaningful pieces on their Worksheet Form 22.

D.   Exercise #6: "Could You—Would You?"

Refer to Exercise #6 in their CO folder. Go around the room and have each person read a statement while everyone else fills in the columns at the left and the right. The statements follow a sequence. When finished with the whole list, ask, "At what point could you no longer do what is asked of you and why?"

Encourage discussion, not argument. Listen and honor each person's opinion. Remind participants that responses are personal opinions with no "right" or "wrong" answers. Instead of disagreeing, ask a person why he or she feels a particular way. Be open and accept another's differences as a way of understanding that person.

This exercise helps clarify whether someone is a Class 1-A-O (part of the military but exempt as a combatant) or Class 1-O (not part of the military but does alternative service). Not all service members are called into combat duty, but everyone is part of the whole system. For some, however, participation in any part of the armed forces is contributing to war and the killing of others. The expression "tooth-to-tail" describes this: for every soldier on the front line, a dozen others are behind that person providing supplies, weapons, ammunition, intelligence, or whatever is needed for that combatant to perform his or her duty on the battlefield.

Discuss this exercise as needed. Remind them that on the Worksheet they must decide between Class 1-A-O Class 1-O.

D.   Exercise #7: Before You Enlist, Consider This: Words from the Homefront

The Quaker House Directors, GI Rights Hotline Counselors, and Domestic Violence in the Military Counselor all talk with service members, veterans, and family members who have been traumatized by war and combat training. This exercise speaks to some of these issues that are generally unknown to, and even hidden from, the civilian world. Have the group do some home research on Moral Injury.

IV. **Discussion, Summary, and Closure (5 min.)**
   A.   Review, reflection, and feedback

Close with any additional questions or comments. Ask for feedback. What was most helpful? What in particular did they learn about themselves?

   B.   Exam questions

Ask again for the three criteria of being a CO.

   C.   Next session

Announce that the next session will be a Mock Draft Board where they will role-play before hypothetical draft boards.

Lesson Plan C
Testing Your Beliefs: Mock Draft Boards

Preparation: Refer to these exercise handouts in the CO folder. Have extras available.
- *Handout #2: Overview of Selective Service and Conscientious Objection*
- *Handout #3: U.S. Supreme Court Rulings, Congressional Legislation, and Law*
- *Exercise #8: Western Union Mailgram, Report for Induction (SSS)*
- *Exercise #9: Sample Questions a Draft Review Board Might Ask*

This is another form of affective learning. Lesson B opened up perspectives. This lesson, through role-playing, puts teens in the position of defending themselves. The lesson elicits deep feelings, prompts lively group discussion, and encourages individual soul-searching. The role-plays expose, illuminate, and clarify values; build confidence; and promote resilience in the face of challenges from a future draft board. It is essential to support and nurture this process in a safe, trusting, and open environment.

I. Introduction and Welcome (5 min.)
A. Welcome, introductions, and overview

Welcome anyone new. Give a CO folder. Meet afterwards to review material presented in the previous two sessions.

B. Session overview
1. Review Handout #2: *Overview of Selective Service and Conscientious Objection* and Handout #3: *U.S. Supreme Court Rulings, Congressional Legislation, and Law*
2. Mock Draft Board simulations or role-plays

After reviewing the three criteria for conscientious objection and some key Supreme Court rulings, this session is devoted entirely to role-playing before a Mock Draft Board. It is a simulation meant to be fun and in a safe setting but at the same time to provoke some anxiety and uncertainty.

C. Context of why draft boards are important

If a draft is reinstated and based on the current Selective Service Law, all 18-25-years-olds will be randomly assigned a lottery number between 1 and 366 corresponding to each of the year's birthdates. Those with low lottery numbers will be sent Induction Notices, see "Western Union Mailgram, Report for Induction (SSS)," and those who wish to be conscientious objectors will be required to request re-classification as such and appear before a local draft board. Boards allot a brief amount of time to substantiate such a claim, though applicants can submit written documentation to help bolster their case. This was covered in the PowerPoint presentation in the first lesson when discussing Selective Service. Reference can be made to the PowerPoint handout in their CO folders, and more suggestions for documentation will be covered in a future session.

So, this lesson is an opportunity to experience and practice what a local draft board might be like. It will give a better sense of what is needed now to crystallize and document views should an appearance be necessary in the future.

II.   Criteria for Conscientious Objection; Supreme Court Interpretations (10 min.)

   A.   Refer to Handout #2: *Overview of Selective Service and Conscientious Objection* and Handout #3: *U.S. Supreme Court Rulings, Congressional Legislation, and Law*

These are in the CO folders, but have extra copies just in case.

   B.   Read and briefly discuss

While this was covered in the first PowerPoint presentation, read the three sections of Handout #2 that talk about conscientious objection, and then read all of Handout #3 (the interpretations and rulings). Either the facilitator can read them, or let each participant read a section. These definitions and rulings help guide what should be presented to a local draft board. Their decisions (and a possible appeal) are based on these laws, so understanding fundamental criteria and interpretations is paramount.

III. Choosing Inductees (Who will go before the Local Draft Board) (5-15 min.)

Two different methods can be used choose who will go before the draft board. Decide based upon time and sensitivity to the group. The Induction Notice Exercise takes more time but it is more instructive and reflective of reality.

   A.   Volunteers

The simplest, fastest, and least threatening is to ask for volunteers.

   B.   Simulate the actual process by using Induction Notices

Though it may take more time, use the Induction Notices, see "Western Union Mailgram, Report for Induction (SSS)." It is the most realistic way of choosing who would come before the draft board, and it also portrays through its no-nonsense directives how life in the military will begin.

As preparation, copy (back-to-back) enough Induction Notices for the group. Write a random number between 1 and 366 on the top of each of them. Choose a range of numbers that reflects the actual number in the group. For example, if you have 10 people, select 1, 36, 72, 108, etc. up to 330. If only three in the group, pick 1, 120, and 240. Pass out the Induction

Notices to everyone, women included. The number on the Notice corresponds to the order before the Mock Draft Board.

    1.   *Have each person read the paragraph from the notice that begins with each these phrases (the Notice uses bold font at its beginning of each):*
        a.   "This is your order to report_____"
        b.   "If you are found qualified for military service_____"
        c.   "If you believe you qualify for reclassification_____"
        d.   "Read the important information provided with this order. If you fail to obey this order_____"
        e.   The last sentence from the paragraph titled, "What to Bring" which is "Do not bring family, friends, pets, weapons/knives, non-prescription drugs, large sums of money or expensive jewelry."
        f.   "You may file a claim for postponement or reclassification_____" (to end of paragraph).
    2.   *Ask for reactions, impressions, and comments.*
        a.   What do think about the general tone of this notice?
        b.   What number did you draw? Was it high or low?
        c.   How do you feel about the number you drew? Did it make a difference?
    3.   *Explain that a person could have as few as 9 days to request/file for reclassification.*
    4.   *Pick those inductees with the lowest lottery numbers to appear first before the draft board.*

IV. Defending Your Position: Mock Draft Board Role-Plays (25 min.)
    A.   Set up and explain the intention of the role-play

This is the role-playing portion. For sample questions, refer to the Exercise #9 "Sample Questions a Draft Review Board Might Ask."

The Mock Draft Board is intended to simulate an experience, almost to the extreme. Its purpose is to bring out both dynamics and content. It is NOT meant to embarrass, offend, or discourage, but rather to demonstrate the difficulty, and sometimes anxiety, of expressing deeply personal views to strangers. While the role-play is set up to defend and justify, the core is simply to speak honestly and with integrity.

Set up the role-play with a three-person Mock Draft Board. The three might be invited adults, the facilitators, or a combination of adults and teens. Arrange chairs with the applicant facing the three board members. You might want to place a desk in front of the board with the applicant sitting in a lone, or exposed, chair.

Use an "angel" (any person) who can come in at any time and whisper help to the one in the hot seat who might be struggling to frame an answer.

Explain that while the applicant is responding to the Board's questions, others should take note of the dynamics that emerge, including both content and emotional reactions. They will be asked to share their reactions and impressions after the role-play. The facilitators might consider having someone actually take notes of questions and answers during the role-play. Another option is to videotape the interview, though that takes more time.

B. Do the role-plays

Ask for the volunteer applicant or person selected through an Induction Notice to sit "in the hot seat." Tell the applicant that he or she will have two minutes to present his or her case. Then, immediately start drilling the applicant with questions, starting with perhaps, "Why do you want to be a CO?" As the applicant responds, look for holes, inconsistencies, hesitations, uncertainties, or other possible weaknesses, and then interrupt with probing questions to that effect. To be true to the role-play, some members of the board can be rude and disrespectful; others seemingly nice (like "good cop/bad cop"). For example, one member might appear sympathetic and say, "What if I can guarantee you a nice safe desk job stateside. Would you drop your claim for CO then?"

In another role-play, consider asking the candidate only one simple question, "Why are you claiming status as a CO?" Then, don't say anything. Let the applicant just talk. This puts the applicant on the spot knowing he or she has only a few minutes to give all the information that would determine his or her claim. When the claimant is finished, have someone on the board simply say, "Do you have anything else to say? Or "thank you very much; next applicant."

C. Debrief

At the end of each role, congratulate the person in the hot seat (with applause). Then, "process" what happened:

Ask the applicant:
1. *What was this like and how did you feel to be "put on the hot seat?"*
2. *What was easy or comfortable? What was difficult?*
3. *Where did you feel you needed better insight or preparation? What did you want to say, or didn't know how to say it?*

Next, ask the Draft Board similar questions:
1. *What was this like and how did it feel to be on the Draft Board?*
2. *In what ways did the applicant present a strong case? Why?*
3. *Where did you feel the applicant needed better insight, preparation, or presentation?*
4. *What in particular made you feel this applicant was sincere?*

Lastly, debrief the full group:
1. *What were your emotional reactions towards the board and towards the applicant?*
2. *What did you feel the applicant did particularly well? Give specific examples.*
3. *What are some other ways the applicant could have answered?*
4. *In what ways do you need to prepare yourself better before going in front of a draft board?*

D. General discussion

Refer back to the Handouts and review the criteria and rulings that might apply to any of the role-plays. Ask for any other comments or questions.

V. Closing Comments, Homework, Next Session (5 min.)

A. Review and reflection

Summarize the session. Congratulate those who were in the hot seat. Remind everyone that if a draft is ever reinstated and anyone wants to make a claim for conscientious objection that your faith or support community can help with practice sessions and give you suggestions. Also stress that this curriculum is specifically designed to start teens thinking about this question and prepare documentation that would strengthen a CO's case.

B. Announce the next session: CO Letters

The next lesson will go over writing CO letters, present a standard format to use, and incorporate comments from the Worksheets into those letters.

C. Homework

In preparation for that lesson, ask teens to add more comments to their Worksheet Form 22. Refer them to the bottom portion of Handout: "More Suggestions to Build Documentation and Worksheet Form 22 Tips." When they feel that their Worksheet is complete, encourage them to tri-fold and send a copy to themselves. They may want a facilitator to sign and date the Worksheet as further documentation, especially from a third party.

Lesson Plan D
Articulating Your Beliefs: CO Letter Writing

Preparation: Have teens bring their Worksheets Form 22 and any drafts of CO letters. Bring writing paper, pens or pencils, newsprint, tape, and magic markers. Refer to these exercise handouts in the CO folder. Have extras available.

- *Handout #5: Scripture vs. the Military Enlistment Document*
- *Handout #6: Excerpts from Military Enlistment/Re-enlistment Document*
- *Handout #8: A Template or Generic Letter Documenting a CO Claim*
- *Handout #9: Two Sample CO Letters*
- *Thirty-five additional CO letters are in the Appendix for those interested*

I.   Introduction and Welcome (5 min.)
   A.   Welcome everyone
   B.   Purpose of session
       1.   Articulate personal beliefs
       2.   Learn a basic format for a CO letter
       3.   Write a first draft of a CO letter

This session pulls together everything from the previous three sessions, culminating in a first draft of a CO letter. Answering the questions on the Worksheet Form 22 and responding to the Mock Draft Board questions can be both intimidating and soul-searching, but writing those beliefs in a narrative is the next step.

II.   Review of Moral, Ethical, and Religious Beliefs (10 min.)
   A.   Some scripture passages

The PowerPoint presentation has a slide contrasting the military enlistment document to some key scriptural passages from the Bible (Hebrew and New Testament) and the Qur'ān. This is also copied as the Handout "Scripture vs. the Military Enlistment Document." Distribute this along with the Handout, "Excerpts from Military Enlistment/Re-enlistment Document" and/or the Quaker House Sgt. Abe Poster (download from www.Quakerhouse.org)

The Appendix of the Teacher's Resource Guide also has a longer listing of scriptural passages on peace and nonviolence from the three Abrahamic texts. Many of these can be translated into moral and ethical frameworks.

   B.   Group sharing of individual beliefs

By now, everybody should have notes on their beliefs and how they acquired them. They can rely on their Worksheet comments or what they learned from the previous exercises, activities, or role-plays. If the handout, "Suggestions to Build Documentation Workshop Form 22 Tips" was not used previously, then review this.

Post two pieces of newsprint, one for beliefs and the other on how they were acquired. Label the top of each accordingly, and ask the group to share their responses.

Sharing as a group builds confidence and strengthens personal views.

C. Discussion

Take some time to discuss. Offer encouragement, reinforcement, and praise.

III. Writing a CO Letter (30 min.)
A. A basic format or structure for the CO letters

Start out in the full group. Distribute and review the handouts: "A Template or Generic Letter Documenting a CO Claim" and "Two Sample CO Letters." Explain that while every person's letter is unique, it should address the three key criteria for being a CO (which they should certainly know by now). Read the first handout.

Talk about the overall format of the letter. Note how it frames the three criteria.

Then, read the two sample letters, but remind everyone not to be influenced by them or paraphrase someone else's beliefs. Each letter must be personal. Examine the letters closely. How do these letters fit the standard format? Do they meet the three criteria? How are they different? What makes them believable and sincere?

B. Draft a CO letter

Have each person start writing a CO letter. Emphasize that writing this letter can be both easy and difficult. On the one hand, it is difficult to discern and then articulate one's beliefs. That was the reason for the exercises. On the other hand, whatever rings true to an individual, regardless of what those beliefs might be, cannot be disputed by another. The CO letter is not an academic research assignment with right or wrong answers. It is a unique articulation of one's inner beliefs about personal participation in war. Those are the correct answers.

C. As a full group, ask for volunteers to read a letter, then discuss

After a person reads a letter, ask everyone else to say what they found particularly strong and convincing. Suggest where the writer might say more, illustrate, or revise to make a statement more powerful. In what ways does the letter meet the three criteria and/or the Supreme Court interpretations?

IV. Summary and Next Steps (5 min.)
A. Benefits of writing a letter

Pass out the Handout, "Long-Range Benefits of Writing CO Letters." Point out that writing this letter has two benefits: it provides future documentation should a draft ever be reinstated (a conscientious objector to war), and it helps articulate a belief in nonviolence and

the testimony of peace that has long term benefits (a conscientious commitment to peace). Everyone's beliefs crystallize and mature over time, but this letter serves as a reminder to the writer about what he or she believed at this particular point in time.

Should a draft ever be reinstated and a person must go before a local draft board, this letter written at age 18 shows the board the early thought of the applicant. The person's views will inevitably mature or crystallize, and he or she will probably want to write a stronger statement in the future. Nevertheless, the two documents together will show a trend or evolution over time that represents the sincerity of the deeply held beliefs.

B. Extra help

Offer additional help to anyone who wants it. Consider forming what Quakers call a Clearness Committee to bring personal "clearness." Have the letter writer select a group of two or three others from his or her faith or support community, young or older, who would meet and help him or her explore beliefs by discussing, asking questions, or recommending readings and other activities that would illuminate these beliefs further. These people can also write Letters of Support (see Handout #12).

It is always helpful to have someone else edit a piece of writing, whether a committee is used or not. Few people can catch their own errors and typos.

Lesson Plan E
Declaring Your Beliefs: Documentation and Support
Some Procedures for Registering a CO Claim

Preparation:

If not already in everyone's CO folders, pick up from a U.S. Postal Office enough official Selective Service Registration forms for each teen. Have the following handouts available or make sure they are in the CO folders:

- *Handout #7: Three Fundamental Ways to Document a CO Claim*
- *Handout #10: Suggestions for Faith and Support Communities*
- *Handout #11: Sample Selective Service System (SSS) Registration Form*
- *Handout #12: Change of Information Form and a Suggested Reply*
- *Handout #13: Letters of Support*
- *Handout #14: Suggestions to Build Documentation and Worksheet Form 22 Tips*
- *Handout #15: Sample Letters to Independent Agencies or Repositories*

I. Introduction and Welcome (5 min.)

A. Welcome everyone

B. Purpose of session is to review the procedures to document a CO claim

This session picks up from where the PowerPoint presentation from Lesson Plan A stopped at "Exercise: Worksheet Form 22." It covers the various ways to document a claim for conscientious objection. An alternative is to omit the PowerPoint presentation and simply review the handouts listed above.

Make sure everyone has copies of the handouts.

II. Documentation (30 min.)

A. Review methods for documentation

Return to the PowerPoint slides starting from slide #29, "How Do You Register as a CO," and running through to slide #38, "Can You Defend Your Position," the Mock Draft Board role-play. Review the handouts from above or as they are referenced in the PowerPoint. The slides after the Mock Draft Board will be part of the Summary at the end of the lesson.

B. Discussion

Take some time to discuss and share as a full group.

III. Action Steps (10 min.)

A. Review the handout *Suggestions for Faith and Support Communities*

Review this handout and discuss how the faith or support community can help.

B.   Develop individual action plans

Take some time to help people decide their next steps and what they need to accomplish them.

IV. Summary and Next Steps (5 min.)
A.   Wrap up

As a final review, go over the last four PowerPoint Slides from #39 "Did We Miss Anything?" to #42 "War is not the answer."

B.   Extra help

Refer those interested in more information to the Appendix: "Contacts and Resources" and the "Bibliography." The Internet also has plenty of resources. Encourage them to contact Quaker House for assistance or questions. Provide names of contact people within each person's faith or support community.

Lesson Plan F
Bringing in Your Faith or Support Community

Preparation: Consider the agenda options listed below and find some volunteers to help. The Reverse Mock Draft Boards and Panel Discussions are the most powerful. Review the instructions on running the Mock Draft Boards from Lesson Plan C. Have teens bring the rough drafts of their CO letters. Bring copies of these exercises and handouts:

- *Exercise #9: Sample Questions a Draft Review Board Might Ask*
- *Handout #8: A Template or Generic Letter Documenting a CO Claim*
- *Handout #13: Letters of Support*

I. Introduction and Welcome (5 min.)
    A. Welcome everyone
    B. Purpose of session: Integrate learning with the wider faith or support community
    C. Options (pick one):
        1. A "reverse" Mock Draft Board
        2. Panel discussion with previous COs and veterans
        3. CO letter writing assistance

By pulling in key members of the faith or support community, this session reinforces previous ones. Three agenda options follow.

II. Option 1: "Reverse" Mock Draft Board (40 min.)
    A. Background information and set up
    B. Role-Play
    C. Debrief and Discussion

This lesson resembles Lesson Plan C, the "Mock Draft Board." The difference is that roles are reversed: the adults are now the CO applicants and the "Mock Draft Board" members are the teens. This lesson can also be done during an adult religious education class or forum instead of during the teen youth group time.

This lesson gives teens the opportunity to hear the answers from older, seasoned members of the faith or support community. But it also informs adults about the pressures, complexity, and emotional impact this process on the teens. Many will appreciate the challenge to articulate personal, deeply held views. Remember that while set up to defend and justify, the focus is to speak honestly and with integrity.

Explain the context of this lesson to the adult members. Say, for example, that previous lessons for teens centered on defining conscientious objection, reviewing legal definitions and interpretations, and knowing how to document a position.

See Lesson Plan C, section I.C and sections IV.A.C for instructions and debriefing.

III. Option 2: Panel Discussion of Previous COs or Veterans (40 min.)

A.   Introduce panel members

Many faith and support communities have members who were COs during past wars (some even from the current wars) or veterans who since realized the futility of wars and the emotional costs on veterans and their families. Ask if they would be willing to help with this session. Contact a local Veteran's for Peace Association to see if they have members willing to participate. This lesson illustrates the topic of peace in a very personal and real way.

B.   Panel presentations

Have the guests talk about their experiences. Some sample questions are:
1   *How did you come to your decision to claim conscientious objection?*
2.   *What was your experience with others (friends, local draft board, government authorities, religious leaders, military personnel, etc.)?*
3.   *As a veteran who now questions the validity of war, what changed your mind?*
4.   *As a service member, how did training and/or combat affect you?*
5.   *What was it like to leave active duty and re-acclimate to civilian life?*
6.   *In hindsight, what would you have done differently, if anything?*
7.   *What advice do you have for our teens now?*

C.   Discussion

Thank the presenters, especially acknowledging any personal discomfort they may have experienced. Open the floor for questions, comments, and discussion.

IV. Option 3: CO Letter Writing and Letters of Support (40 min.)
A.   Introduce the volunteer mentors from the faith and support community
B.   Help teens with their CO letter drafts; have adults write their own letters with the teens; ask adults to write Letters of Support for teens they know well

This is a worthwhile activity if teens struggled at all writing their CO letters. Depending upon the number of adult volunteers and teens in the group, pair adults and teens in one-on-one dyads or mix in small groups.

C.   As a full group, as for volunteers to read a letter, then discuss

IV. Summary and Next Steps (5 min.)

Except for a possible field trip, this concludes the curriculum. Make sure everybody knows who they can contact for further help. Thank everyone for their attentiveness.

Field Trip
Visiting a Military Base, Museum, or Quaker House
(Optional, dependent upon locality and availability)

If possible, arrange a trip to a military base or military museum. Talk with some military personnel, preferably different people who can speak either to the advantages or disadvantages of military service. Visit their base chapel or places of worship and observe any stained-glass windows, pictures, or other symbols on the walls. At the end of the visit and/or interviews, discuss these questions as a full group:

1. In what ways was violence represented, glorified, or under-represented?
2. Did the museum/base reflect or display casualty figures; destruction to individual soldiers and their families; or the devastation to civilian homes, lives, or environment?
3. What is the effect of the military culture on new recruits or veteran soldiers?
4. In what ways is the military town different from a civilian community?
5. What effect does the base have on the town in which it is located?
6. In what ways did your own bias and past focus on COs affect your perspective of this visit?
7. How was religion and war reflected in places of worship?

One place to visit is Quaker House, Fayetteville, NC home of Fort Bragg and the 82nd Airborne and Special Operations Museum. Contact Co-Directors, Lynn and Steve Newsom at www.quakerhouse.org or call 910-323-3912.

A sample "Worksheet, Scavenger Hunt, and Focus Questions" with "Answer Sheet" is in the Appendix. This can be used when visiting the 82nd Airborne and Special Operations Museum in Fayetteville or adapt this to most any military museum around the country.

> "The enemies look like people
> and the people look like enemies."
> - Anonymous service member, *19 Soldiers Reveal the
> One Thing Nobody Tells You about Going to War*

OPENING EXERCISES AND OTHER ACTIVITIES

EXERCISE #1: Could You Chant This at Boot Camp Then Do It Later?

War dehumanizes the enemy using demeaning cultural slurs. For the Iraqi and Afghanistan Wars, the Arab world, religion, and family are ridiculed. This exercise is from a soldier's account of his boot camp experience, as told in the DVD *Ground Truth*. It depicts exploits such tactics. It may evoke strong reactions among participants.

While the exercise is not intended to offend, the chant definitely does. If people get upset, the exercise should be stopped, or skipped altogether. Let any person sit out or not participate because of the exercise's impact. The facilitator will need to de-brief the group at the end of the exercise. Forewarn anyone in an adjoining room who might overhear this exercise.

Instructions: Have everyone, as a group, chant this actual marching cadence used during a U.S. boot camp for the Iraqi War. If the room space is big enough, march while chanting. The facilitator should be familiar with the chant. Participants can hold and read from their papers.

Setup: This is a simulation of your first day at Boot Camp. The facilitators is the Drill Sergeant who starts by commanding that everyone standup and form a single line. Order them to march in place, repeating the chant below. Then, order them to march around the room in rhythm and to the chant. The Drill Sergeant may embellish with slurs and degrading remarks.

After the "recruits" get a taste of the exercise (usually in 5 minutes or so), have them sit down and talk about the experience. See the questions at the end.

			kill							
		lage;	♪E							
Bomb	the	vil-	♪D	the	Throw some na-					square.
♪C	♪C	♪C		♪C	♪C	♪C	♪C		the	♪C
				peo-					in	♪B
			♪A	ple.			palm	♪A		
			♪G				♪G			

Here's the whole cadence:

Bomb the village; kill the people,	→	Throw some napalm in the square.
Do it on a Sunday morning.	→	Kill them on their way to prayer.
Ring the bell inside the school house,	→	Watch those kiddies gather round
Lock and load with your 240.	→	Mow those mother f‛ers down.

Some Debriefing Questions:
1. What emotions does this exercise bring up in you?
2. Did you put aside emotions and simply repeat the cadence in unison along with the group? What effect did chanting with a group have on you?
3. What did you feel about your fellow boot campers reciting this chant? In what ways, if any, did you separate or distinguish yourself from them?
4. How would this chant, over time under conditions at boot camp, mold you or your buddies' cultural opinion of the Islamic faith?
5. Why do you think this chant is used?

EXERCISE #2: Cadences and Jody Calls
Other Examples of Boot Camp Cadences

I went down to the market where all the women shop
I pulled out my machete and I begin to chop
I went down to the park where all the children play
I pulled out my machine gun and I began to spray.

See the kiddos playin' in the playground
Lock and load a .50 CAL round
And as I gently pull back on my trigger
I see their skanky bodies hit the ground

What's the spirit of the bayonet?
Kill, kill, kill without mercy!

What makes the green grass grow?
Blood! Blood! Blood!
Bright red blood makes the green grass grow!

Bomb the village
Kill the people
Throw some napalm in the square
Do it on a Sunday morning
Kill them on their way to prayer
Ring the bell inside the schoolhouse
Watch the kiddies gather round
Lock and load with your 240
Mow them mother(*)uckers down

Run run Iraqi run,
Pull the trigger let's have some fun,
Die die Iraqi die.

Postscript: Does military training affect the mind and personal judgment? The U.S. soldier, Robert Bales, convicted of murdering sixteen Afghan villagers in 2012 said three years later while in prison that he lost compassion for Iraqis and Afghans over the course of his four combat deployments. *My mind was consumed by war....I planted war and hate for the better part of ten years and harvested violence....After being in prison two years, I understand that what I thought was normal was the farthest thing from being normal....Over my past two years of incarceration, I have come to understand there isn't a why; there is only pain.* Over his combat tours he came to hate *everyone who isn't American,* becoming suspicious of local residents who might be supportive of those fighting Americans. *I became callous to them even being human; they were all enemy. Guilt and fear are with you day and night. Over time your experiences solidify your prejudice.*

37

EXERCISE #3: Violence vs. Nonviolence Brainstorming
Adapted from <u>Alternatives to Violence Project, Basic Manual</u> and from Deborah Bromiley.

Purpose: This is a simple exercise to get group members thinking consciously about their perceptions of violence, nonviolence, and then their differences. Examples should include several dimensions of both: physical, emotional, psychological, spiritual, personal, group, societal, internal, external, direct, indirect, active, passive, etc. Approximate length of the exercise is 30 minutes.

Materials: Newsprint and several magic markers.

Setup: Post two pieces of newsprint with the word "Violence" on the top of one paper and "Nonviolence" on the top of the other.

Instructions: Explain to the group that they will brainstorm examples of violence and nonviolence. The rule of brainstorming is that words and phrases are said without censorship or criticism. Ideas are neither good nor bad, and some said even in jest may trigger a deeper thought in another person. If someone disagrees with an idea, do not to argue or negate. Instead of reacting, just throw out another idea.

Start with the "Violence" list. Ask, "What comes to your mind when you think about violence?" Scatter the group's words and phrases over the newsprint. If needed, prompt the group with the different dimensions of violence as listed in the first paragraph above (in the Purpose section). Get a list of about 25 or so items. Use a second piece of newsprint if necessary.

When the group exhausts its suggestions, ask them sit in silence for about 20 or 30 seconds to review the list. Then, ask everyone to come up to the list and with a magic marker circle the three words or phrases that are the most important to them (or what "speaks to them") when they think about violence. Items can be circled by more than one person.

When everyone is finished and returns to their seats, have them look over the list again, and reflect on what they see. Then, have them turn to the person next to them and share which words or phrases they circled and the reason why they chose them.

When they finish discussing, repeat the exercise using the "Nonviolence List."

Discussion: When that is completed, have the group "process" the exercise.

1. What did you notice about the words and phrases on the Violence list?
2. What did you notice about the words and phrases on the Nonviolence list?
3. What differences did you notice between the two lists or in what was circled?
4. Why did you pick the particular words or phrases that you chose?
5. What did you learn from your partner about what he or she chose?
6. What general reactions or thoughts did you have from this exercise?

EXERCISE #4: Worksheet Form 22: Claim for Conscientious Objector
Adapted and Edited from Selective Service System Form 22

1. **Describe your beliefs that are the reasons for your claiming conscientious objection to combatant military training and service or to all military training and service. Check either box and explain your reasoning:**

☐ 1. I claim exemption <u>ONLY</u> from training and service as a combatant member of the Armed Forces (Class 1-A-O). (*Author's note: this person is inducted into the military but does not train with, carry, or use a weapon.*) **OR**

☐ 2. I claim exemption from <u>ALL</u> training and service as a member of the Armed Forces (Class 1-O). (*Author's note: this person remains a civilian and does alternative service instead.*)

_____
_____
_____
_____
_____
_____
_____
_____
_____
_____

2. **Describe how and when you acquired your beliefs. Your answer may include such information as the influence of family members or other persons; training, if applicable; your personal experiences; membership in organizations; books/readings which influenced you.**

_____
_____
_____
_____
_____
_____
_____
_____
_____
_____
_____

3. **Explain what most clearly shows that your beliefs are deeply held. You may wish to include a description of how your beliefs affect the way you live.**

_____
_____
_____
_____
_____
_____
_____
_____
_____
_____
_____

EXERCISE # 5: Meaningful or Inspiring Quotes
Pick a quote and say why you picked it. Or, share your own quote.

The Golden Rule from Several Faiths

Hinduism: *This is the sum of duty; do naught onto others what you would not have them do unto you.*

Judaism: *What is hateful to you, do not do to your fellow man. That is the entire Law; all the rest is commentary.*

Buddhism: *Hurt not others in ways that you yourself would find hurtful.*

Confucianism: *Do not do to others what you would not want them to do to you.*

Taoism: *Regard your neighbor's gain as your gain, and your neighbor's loss as your loss.*

Christianity: *Do unto others as you would have them do unto you.*

Islam: *No one of you is a believer until he desires for his brother that which he desires for himself.*

Bahá'í: *Blessed is he who preferreth his brother before himself.*

U.S. Presidents and Military Commanders

John F. Kennedy, 35th U.S. President: *War will exist until that distant day when the conscientious objector enjoys the same reputation and prestige that the warrior does today.*

Jimmy Carter, 39th U.S. President, 2002 Nobel Peace Prize winner: *War may sometimes be a necessary evil. But no matter how necessary, it is always an evil, never a good. We will not learn to live together in peace by killing each other's children.*

Robert E. Lee, Commander, Confederate Army: *What a cruel thing is war: to separate and destroy families and friends, and mar the purest joy and happiness God has granted us in this world; to fill our hearts with hatred instead of love for our neighbors, and to devastate the fair face of this beautiful world.*

Dwight Eisenhower, 5-Star Army General, World War II Supreme Commander of the Allied Forces in Europe, 34th U.S. President: *I hate war as only a soldier who has lived it can, only as one who has seen its brutality, its futility, its stupidity.... There is not glory in battle worth the blood it costs....When people speak to you about a preventive war, you tell them to go fight it. After my experience, I have come to hate war....War settles nothing....The problem in defense is how far you can go without destroying from within what you are trying to defend from without.*

Leaders and Proponents of Peace

Vijaya Lakshimi Pandit, Indian Diplomat: *The more we sweat for peace, the less we bleed in war.*

Lucretia Mott, 19th Century Quaker Abolitionist: *If we believe war is wrong, as everyone must, then we must also believe that by proper efforts on our part it can be done away with.*

Dorothy Day, Catholic Worker: *I really only love God as much as I love the person I love the least....Love casts out fear, but we have to get over the fear in order to get close enough to love them.*

Eleanor Roosevelt, First Lady and Diplomat: *It isn't enough to talk about peace. One must believe in it. And it isn't enough to believe in it. One must work at it.*

Howard Zinn, WWII Vet and Historian: *Historically, the most terrible things—war, genocide, slavery—have resulted from obedience, not disobedience....How can you make a war on terror, if war itself is terrorism?*

Albert Einstein: *It is my conviction that killing under the cloak of war is nothing but an act of murder....Peace cannot be kept by force, it can only be achieved by understanding....The pioneers of a warless world are the (youth) who refuse military service.*

Deng Ming-Dao, Taoist Monk, 2400 BCE: *If you go personally to war, you cross the line yourself. You sacrifice ideals for survival and the fury of killing. That alters you forever. That is why no one rushes to be a soldier. Think before you want to change so unalterably. The stakes are not merely one's life, but one's very humanity.*

Leo Tolstoy, from <u>War and Peace</u>: *The aim of war is murder; the methods of war are spying, treachery, and their encouragement, the ruin of a country's inhabitants, robbing them or stealing to provision the army, and fraud and falsehood termed military craft. The habits of the military class are the absence of freedom, that is, discipline, idleness, ignorance, cruelty.*

Martin Luther King, Jr.'s address at SCLC Ministers' Leadership Training Program: *On some positions, Cowardice asks the question, 'Is it safe?' Expediency asks the question, 'Is it politic?' And Vanity comes along and asks the question, 'Is it popular?' But Conscience asks the question 'Is it right?' And there comes a time when one must take a position that is neither safe, nor politic, nor popular, but he must do it because Conscience tells him it is right.*

Elise Boulding, from her book <u>Cultures of Peace, The Hidden Side of History</u>: *Current research on violence in contemporary societies suggests that high levels of aggression in the civil society are associated with recent participation of that society in war. The socialization for aggression involved in the preparation for and fighting of wars has subsequent effects on civilian behavior. In short, wars produce socialization for aggression as well as socialization for aggression producing war.*

Leo Tolstoy, Letter to Peace Conference, Non-Commissioned Officer: *Armies will only be diminished and abolished when people cease to trust governments, and themselves seek salvation from the miseries that oppress them, and seek that safety, not by the complicated and delicate combinations of diplomatists, but in the simple fulfillment of that law, binding upon every man, inscribed in all religious teachings, and present in every heart, not to do to others what you wish them not to do to you—above all, not to slay your neighbors....And the will of God is not that we should fight and oppress the weak, but that we should acknowledge all men to be our brothers and should serve one another.*

Daniel A. Seeger, plaintiff, U.S. Supreme Court case striking Supreme Being clause: *Personally, when I first filed my claim for conscientious objection back in the late 1950's, I felt somewhat diffident about my own action. While my sense was overpowering that entering the military and getting trained to kill people would be deeply and profoundly wrong. I was...awed by what seemed to be a universal consensus that war is often an inevitable necessity. After fifty years of observation, I am more than ever convinced that all military endeavors are utterly immoral and monumentally foolish, and I would probably be much more acerbic expressing a conscientious claim today, and perhaps, therefore, less successful in gaining the sympathy of people who disagree with me, including judges and other government officials.*

Maria Santelli, Director, Center on Conscience and War: *Our government, our media, our schools, and even our churches take great pains to obscure the reality of war and military service. So sometimes people don't know what they're getting themselves into, and they find themselves in a crisis of conscience. This 'crisis of conscience' is the realization that their actions are in opposition to their moral and ethical beliefs, or the conscience. In the military a crisis of conscience means that a service member faces the choice of either violating orders or violating their conscience of killing. This type of* *trauma, this wound to the soul, is not characterized by fear for one's life. It is characterized by inner conflict, moral injury—a natural response to a very unnatural experience.*

The science of military training is intensive and laser-focused, and it has a name: it's called Killogy. Its primary purpose is to get an otherwise psychologically healthy individual to kill by rote— reflexively, without thinking, without filtering through the conscience. It is designed to circumvent human nature; to fire reflexively....But conscience always comes back. Conscience is the law that has been inscribed by God on the human heart.

<u>Service Members and Veterans Who Had a Change of Conscience</u>

Sgt. Timothy John Westphal, U.S. Army, Iraq War Vet: *I just remember thinking to myself, I just brought terror to someone else under the American flag and that's just not what I joined the Army to do.*

A Pentagon official on why the Pentagon censored graphic footage from Gulf War (of an Iraqi soldier being sliced in two by helicopter fire): *If we let people see that kind of thing, there would never again be any war.*

Desmond T. Doss, the first CO (Class 1-A-O) to get the Medal of Honor during WWII: *There were other important jobs to be done other than having to take life. I was willing to go to the front lines to save life but not to take life.*

Jeremy Hinzman, U.S. Army Vet of Afghanistan war; denied CO status then moved to Canada rather than deploy to Iraq: *If you kill a bunch of people, you have to live with it. When you put someone in your sights and pull the trigger, you cross a line.*

Clifton Hicks, Iraq Vet, U.S. Army, filed for CO status and refused to return to Iraq: *My actions in the past and at present have well proven that I am not a coward, for a coward will never do what he believes to be right when those around him say that he is wrong, he will simply be bullied into submission....I intend to live my own life in a way that will affirm the lives of others, not destroy them.*

Pablo Paredes, U.S. Navy, refused to board a ship ferrying soldiers to Iraq: *I don't want to be a part of a ship that's taking 3,000 Marines over there, knowing a hundred or more of them won't come back. I can't sleep at night knowing that's what I do for a living....I think it's no accident that some of the [soldiers] who have come out more vocal [against the Iraq War] have been Latinos. There's this conflict inside of us just because of the history of what the U.S. military has done in our countries that makes us question things.*

Stephen Funk, U.S. Marine, refused to fight in the Iraq War, re-classified as CO: *The purpose of military training is to churn out non-thinking killing machines, and being forced to shout 'Kill, Kill, Kill' every day is a major stress on the mind, body, and soul....Boot camp is the exact opposite of civilized training. You are praised for being violent and for stupidity....I don't believe it is right to kill people and would never shoot at someone....You don't have to be a cog in the machinery of war. Everyone has the unconquerable power of free will.*

Camilo Mejia, U.S. Army, Iraq War Vet, served in jail upon refusing to return to Iraq: *I saw an innocent man decapitated by our machine gun fire. I saw a soldier broken down inside because he killed a child....We weren't preventing terrorism or making Americans safer....I realized that I was part of a war that was immoral and criminal, a war of aggression, a war of imperial domination....By putting my weapon down, I chose to reassert myself as a human being....Behind these bars I sit a free man because I listened to a higher power, the voice of my conscience....There is no higher freedom that can be achieved.*

Victor Agosto, U.S. Army, Iraq vet, refused to deploy to Afghanistan: *There is no way I will deploy to Afghanistan. The occupation is immoral and unjust. It doesn't make the American people any safer. It has the opposite effect. I came to oppose it the way a lot of people did. I thought about it, read books. Then I began seeing the role I played in the imperialist framework. I came to realize that the wars really don't do what the stated reasons are, which is to make us safer. Both [Iraq and Afghanistan] occupations fuel the insurgencies in those countries. We are creating 'terrorists' and we are killing so many innocent people.*

Agustín Aguayo, Mexican-born U.S. Army medic, Iraq Vet, CO: *Before I left for Iraq I searched deep within me. I concluded that if I go over there I can't take a life....I'm definitely a conscientious objector. I'm not willing to cross that line, no matter what I can't take a life. I want to bring young people awareness....We don't educate them about the realities of war. They don't hear what it is like to kill someone, to see a friend die, to hurt another human, to be in an occupied country, shooting someone at close range....[I saw] what happens to regular soldiers, the hate, the racism, the total disrespect for humanity that develops. Soldiers who return from Iraq need a lot of psychological care.*

Logan Mehl-Laituri, CO application quoted in his Moral Injury book <u>Reborn on the Fourth of July</u>: *I am opposed to participation in combatant training and service because I believe that all life is sacred, that no single human life is worth more or less than any other....War is wrong, and contributes to the degradation of both the oppressor and the oppressed....I have learned that the unconditional love that the New Testament describes applies to everyone; your neighbor and your enemy (Lk 6:27-28; Mt 5:44-45), and in no way can loving them be confused with killing them. I value all human life....I hope to be an example of Christ's infinite love....Love is the overriding message of the entire Bible...*

Admiral Gene La Rocque, WWII Naval Officer and member Joint Chiefs of Staff: *In World War II, I had been in 13 battle engagements....In that 4 years, I thought, what a hell of a waste of a man's life. I lost a lot of friends....You lose limbs, sight, part of your life—for what?...Since World War II, we began to use military force to get what we wanted in the world. That's what military is all about. For about twenty years after the war, I couldn't look at any film on World War II. It brought back memories I didn't want to keep around. I hated to see how they glorified war. In all those films, people get blown up with their clothes and fall gracefully to the ground. You don't see anybody being blown apart. You don't see arms and legs and mutilated bodies. You see only an antiseptic, clean, neat way to die gloriously. I hate it when they say, "He gave his life for his country." Nobody gives their life for anything. We steal the lives of these kids. We take it away from them. They don't die for the honor and glory of their country. We kill them.*

I was in Vietnam. I saw the senseless waste of human beings. I saw this bunch of marines come off this air-conditioned ship. Nothing was too good for our sailors, soldiers, and marines. We send 'em ashore as gung ho young nineteen-year-old husky nice-looking kids and bring 'em back in black rubber body bags.

A service member's CO application: *I am seeking separation from service instead of reclassification as a noncombatant (1-A-O) because I do not believe violence, war, and bloodshed are in line with my personal, professional, and spiritual beliefs. Violence begets more violence. As a noncombatant medic I would be maintaining combat effectiveness. I would be contributing to the violence and the psychological problems that come from fighting. I would be contributing to something I no longer believe in. If I am fixing someone up who will go do something I think is immoral, I would be sharing in the guilt. In my heart, I know violence is a sin. For me, sin is separation from God's will in my life; anything that distracts me from God's voice. I no longer want to be a soldier, because a soldier's main job is to make war and kill for no other reason except that he or she is ordered to by some person of higher rank.*

EXERCISE #6:
Could You–Would You? Some Real-Life Military Decisions

In the left column, write a number 1 thru 5, according to the scale or range below, to represent the extent of your feeling or value:

1	2	3	4	5
I would do this, and feel OK about it				This would be difficult, and I'd feel badly

Then put an N in the right column for anything you could NEVER do, this despite direct military orders to do so.

Answer: 1 2 3 4 or 5	*Could You —Would You?*	Put N for anything that you would NEVER do
	1. Serve on active duty and be stationed in the United States or abroad* (*taken from mailed promotional brochures, paid for by the United States Army, © 2007)	
	2. Enlist for duty in the U.S. Army with the promise of a civilian skills bonus of up to $5,000, a Thrift Savings Plan Matching Fund Program, technical training in one of more than 150 careers, up to $72,900 for college tuition, and an education bonus of up to $6,000.* (*brochure)	
	3. Elect for the two year enlistment option and be eligible for an enlistment bonus of up to $15,000 and up to $36,864 for College with the Montgomery GI Bill and Army College Fund.* (*brochure)	
	4. Serve in the Army Reserve, train near home and serve when needed, get a civilian skills bonus of up to $20,000, participate in the Thrift Savings Plan Matching Fund Program, get technical training in one of more than 120 careers, get up to $10,000 to repay qualifying student loans, and earn an education bonus of up to $4,000.* (*brochure)	
	5. Give your life in the service of your country or fellow soldiers.	
	6. Go to boot camp for six weeks, getting up early each morning then to bed late; undergo rigorous physical and mental conditioning and emotional stress; march, obey all orders, and act on behalf of the unit first; and learn to use a rifle, fight hand-to-hand, and execute other combat maneuvers.	
	7. Deliver food and medical supplies to Iraqi or Afghanistan citizens affected by war.	
	8. Load supplies from a military base in the United States onto cargo planes headed for Iraq, Afghanistan, or any other war zone.	
	9. Learn Arabic to be an interpreter in Iraq, Afghanistan, or other country.	
	10. Fly a plane into a remote mountain outpost in Afghanistan to deliver needed food, clothing, and other supplies to troops stranded in their fight against the Taliban or other terrorist designated group.	
	11. Fly, from a computer terminal on an aircraft carrier somewhere in the Indian Ocean or from an air-conditioned room in Nevada, the *Predator* drone airplane, which provides aerial surveillance and logistical support (overhead visual imaging) of suspected terrorist or insurgent ground movement of forces, weapons, or supplies.	

	12. Inventory supplies arriving from the United States and/or other foreign markets to your post in Iraq, Afghanistan, or other warzone.	
	13. Repair a bridge over the Tigris River in Iraq, linking vital supply lines for both military and civilians.	
	14. Guard a convoy of supplies driving from a port in Kuwait to a remote military strip in Northern Iraq.	
	15. Fly, from a computer terminal somewhere in Colorado, the *Reaper* drone airplane, which provides logistical attack support (fires weapons and drops bombs) during troop movement and engagement.	
	16. Load 500-pound bombs and cluster bombs onto planes and helicopters to be used on suspected insurgent areas.	
	17. Guard an entry post into Baghdad's Green Zone with orders to use your weapon on any person who does not stop for inspection.	
	18. Drive a truckload of ammunition and arms to be used in an imminent attack on a Sunni community, suspected of harboring Iraqi insurgents.	
	19. Not tell anyone that your best friend in your unit went berserk when he stormed into a house and killed five scared children hiding in a corner.	
	20. Upon your lieutenant's order, as a sniper open fire on a wounded Iraqi insurgent crawling from a burning car before it explodes.	
	21. Open automatic fire, along with the rest of your unit, spraying a group of houses suspected of being a source of insurgent gun fire, knowing that civilians might still be hidden within.	
	22. Barge down the door of a family's home in Afghanistan along with a platoon of heavily armed soldiers ready to shoot anything that moves, corralling women and children into one room and men into another.	
	23. Execute three prisoners—all hooded, hands bound, clearly broken and kneeling at your feet—who are suspected of detonating a road side bomb that just blew up two friends in your unit.	
	24. Shackle, by wrists between the legs and close to the floor, a hooded, 15-year-old Taliban prisoner, stripped naked, for a period of two days.	
	25. Drop 500-pound bombs and cluster bombs into insurgent areas.	

_____ Add right column numbers total   Add total number of *N's* _____

Examples from previous wars would be:
- ✓ Fly a helicopter under Viet Cong fire to rescue wounded or stranded troops, and lay down fire to secure entry & exit.
- ✓ Rescue 2,000 Jews in a concentration camp in Poland.
- ✓ Provide medical services to troops wounded in Pacific Island campaigns. Treat wounds, e.g. loss of limb or mental function.
- ✓ Deliver needed supplies to troops trapped in the freezing Battle of Bulge campaign, the last desperate stance of Germans against Allied troops.
- ✓ Drop fire bombs on Dresden, Germany, killing tens of thousands of people.
- ✓ Drop the atomic bomb on Hiroshima knowing it could kill 200,000 civilians yet believing it would save thousands of American soldier lives from invading Japan. Some historians claim Japan was ready to surrender before the bomb.
- ✓ Can the group think of others?

EXERCISE #7: Before You Enlist, Consider This
Words from the "Homefront," Lynn and Steve Newsom, Quaker House Co-Directors

With fifteen years of war behind us and no end in sight, our service members today are facing the possibility of being deployed over and over again. One child had his parent home only three of his ten years. The All-Volunteer Army (AVF) is getting burned-out. The troops are depleted by war. They are worn out, wounded in body and mind, and too often involuntarily discharged with less-than-honorable discharges, depriving many of promised medical benefits.

With the condition of the AVF, could we very well be looking at the return of the draft, if an increase in troops is needed? Regardless, it is important that all youth understand what military life is like.

First of all, a service member gives up certain individual rights and must conform to a military culture. Being a part of a strong unit is of utmost necessity to the military. Service members must go where they are told to go, do what they are told to do, and above all, not appear weak. If soldiers do appear weak, they are vulnerable to bullying and harassment by their superiors and peers. For that reason, doubts, fears, and mental difficulties are repressed.

Because of the frequency of deployments, our service members are returning home in large numbers with Post Traumatic Stress Disorder (PTSD), Traumatic Brain Injury, and/or Moral Injury. Over 500,000 veterans were diagnosed with PTSD in 2013. Often service members hide their injuries for fear of losing rank or being involuntarily discharged without the medical benefits that keep them going. Many fear being thought of as "damaged." They just want to go home and be left alone.

War damages the soul. We are taught throughout our lives that murder is immoral, and then, once in the military, we are ordered to kill in the line of duty. Participating in combat, soldiers face killing and wounding not only the "enemy" but also innocent civilians. They witness others in their company being killed or wounded. They will most likely handle body parts after explosions. They will witness the destruction and devastation of villages and towns. They are taught "reflexive-fire" shooting: learning to kill without thinking about it. As quoted in the *Company Command* section from the May 2005 issue of Army Magazine: "Every Soldier in our Army must be able to close with and destroy the enemy. If we aren't able to hit what we shoot at under all conditions in combat, we will not be successful, and we will sustain casualties" (http://cc.army.mil/pubs/armymagazine/docs/2005/cc_05-05-reflexivefire.pdf).

The result of these experiences is an injury to the soul, called moral injury. Veterans do not fully recover from this invisible wound. They can be haunted by their experiences for the rest of their lives. Remorse, regret, sorrow, and depression are common. The suicide rate currently among veterans is 22 a day, and more Vietnam veterans have died from suicide than from combat. Alcoholism and drug abuse, domestic violence, and sexual assault are escalating in the military and with veterans. The Veteran's Administration is unable to handle the large numbers of veterans who need help and 238,000 veterans have died while waiting to be helped.

Do you really want to be a part of this? Watch YouTube clip *The Human Cost of War: IVAW, Jacob David George:* https://www.youtube.com/watch?v=XzeUj1bXJy0

EXERCISE #8: Western Union Mailgram (SSS)

Give everyone an induction notice, each with a different random number evenly distributed between 1 and 366. Cut off for induction is 100. Lesson Plan C has instructions. Bold print inserted by author.

SELECTIVE SERVICE SYSTEM NORTH SUBURBAN, IL 60197	Western Union MAILGRAM

GEORGE FOX   2 QUAKER WAY   ANYWHERE, USA 00001

ORDER TO REPORT FOR INDUCTION

DATE
SEL. SER. NO.   INDUCTION ORDER NO.
SOC. SEC. NO.   LOCAL BOARD NO.
RSN   STATE CODE

THIS IS YOUR ORDER TO REPORT FOR AND SUBMIT TO EXAMINATION AND INDUCTION INTO THE ARMED FORCES OF THE UNITED STATES. BY DIRECTION OF THE PRESIDENT, YOU HAVE BEEN CLASSIFIED 1-A (AVAILABLE FOR UNRESTRICTED MILITARY SERVICE) AND ARE DIRECTED TO REPORT, WITH THIS ORDER, TO THE MILITARY ENTRANCE PROCESSING STATION (MEPS) LOCATED AT:
            (ADDRESS)
ON: (DATE)   AT: (TIME)

YOU MAY REPORT TO ANOTHER MEPS IF IT IS CLOSER TO WHERE YOU ARE NOW. MEPS ADDRESSES MAY BE OBTAINED FROM ANY SELECTIVE SERVICE AREA OFFICE, ARMED FORCES RECRUITING OFFICE OR MILITARY INSTALLATION.

IF YOU ARE FOUND QUALIFIED FOR MILITARY SERVICE, YOU WILL BE INDUCTED IMMEDIATELY INTO THE ARMED FORCES AND GO DIRECTLY TO TRAINING. WHEN YOU ARE INDUCTED, YOU WILL BE RECLASSIFIED 1-C (MEMBER OF THE ARMED FORCES). IF YOU ARE NOT INDUCTED, YOU WILL BE SENT HOME.

IF YOU BELIEVE YOU QUALIFY FOR A RECLASSIFICATION OR A POSTPONEMENT OF INDUCTION, CONTACT THE SELECTIVE SERVICE AREA OFFICE LOCATED AT:
            (ADDRESS)
PRIOR TO THE DATE YOU ARE TO REPORT FOR INDUCTION. SEE PAGE 2.

THE TRAVEL WARRANT ENCLOSED IS TO BE USED ONLY BY YOU FOR YOUR TRANSPORTATION TO THE MEPS. IF NO TRANSPORTATION IS AVAILABLE, CONTACT THE AREA OFFICE LISTED ABOVE IMMEDIATELY.

READ THE IMPORTANT INFORMATION PROVIDED WITH THIS ORDER. IF YOU FAIL TO OBEY THIS ORDER, YOU MAY BE REPORTED AS A SUSPECTED VIOLATOR OF THE MILITARY SELECTIVE ACT AND, IF CONVICTED, SUBJECT TO IMPRISONMENT FOR UP TO FIVE YEARS, A FINE OF UP TO $250,000, OR BOTH.

BY DIRECTION OF THE PRESIDENT:
      DIRECTOR OF SELECTIVE SERVICE   SSS FORM 252

HOW TO TRAVEL TO MEPS

TAKE THE ATTACHED TRAVEL WARRANT TO A BUS OR TRAIN TICKET AGENCY WHO WILL ISSUE YOU A TICKET TO THE CITY WHERE THE MEPS IS LOCATED. WHEN YOU ARRIVE IN THAT CITY ASK THE AGENT FOR DIRECTIONS TO THE MEPS. IF YOU COME BY CAR, ARRANGE TO HAVE IT RETURNED HOME. RESIDENTS OF ALASKA ... TRAVEL BY LAND, SEA, OR AIR.... YOU ARE STRONGLY ENCOURAGED TO USE THE TRAVEL WARRANT AND NOT TRAVEL BY CAR.

WHAT TO BRING

COMFORTABLE CLOTHING AND TOILET ARTICLES FOR THREE DAYS WHICH CAN BE CONTAINED IN A TRAVEL BAG NO LONGER THAN 9" X 13" X 24" AND ALL OF THE FOLLOWING THAT APPLY TO YOU: BIRTH CERTIFICATE, SOCIAL SECURITY CARD, DRIVER'S LICENSE, LAST SCHOOL RECORD, DOCTOR'S STATEMENT AND HOSPITAL RECORDS IF YOU HAVE A HISTORY OF PHYSICAL OR MENTAL DISORDER, EYEGLASSES OR CONTACT LENSES, PRESCRIPTION DRUGS YOU TAKE, RECORDS OF COURT DECISIONS THAT AFFECT YOUR STATUS, PROOF OF MARITAL STATUS IF OTHER THAN SINGLE, CHILDREN'S BIRTH CERTIFICATES, PRIOR MILITARY SERVICE RECORD (DD FORM 214). DO NOT BRING FAMILY, FRIENDS, PETS, WEAPONS/KNIVES, NONPRESCRIPTION DRUGS, LARGE SUMS OF MONEY OR EXPENSIVE JEWELRY.

ATTENTION ALIENS

IF YOU ARE AN ALIEN AND HAVE LIVED IN THE UNITED STATES FOR LESS THAN ONE YEAR, THIS IS YOUR ORDER TO FURNISH PROOF OF YOUR STATUS. SEND THE PROOF TO THE AREA OFFICE SHOWN ON THIS ORDER WITHIN TEN DAYS FROM THE DATE THE ORDER WAS ISSUED AND DO NOT GO TO THE MEPS. IF YOU HAVE LIVED IN THE UNITED STATES OVER ONE YEAR, DISREGARD THIS PARAGRAPH.

POSTPONEMENT AND RECLASSIFICATION INFORMATION

YOU MAY FILE A CLAIM FOR POSTPONEMENT OR RECLASSIFICATION AT ANY TIME PRIOR TO THE DATE YOU ARE SCHEDULED TO REPORT FOR INDUCTION. INFORMATION IS AVAILABLE FROM ANY SELECTIVE SERVICE AREA OFFICE, OR THROUGH INFORMATION BOOKLETS FURNISHED FOR REGISTRANTS AT ALL U.S. POST OFFICES, CONSULATES AND EMBASSIES. DO NOT REPORT TO THE MEPS AFTER YOU HAVE FILED A CLAIM IN WRITING WITH YOUR AREA OFFICE. YOU WILL BE ADVISED BY THE AREA OFFICE OF ADDITIONAL INFORMATION YOU NEED TO PROVIDE IN SUPPORT OF YOUR CLAIM, AND THE PROCEDURES TO BE FOLLOWED FOR SUBMITTING DOCUMENTATION.

EXERCISE #9: Sample Questions a Draft Board Might Ask*

Bible passages from *New Revised Standard Version*; Qur'ān from *The Meaning of The Holy Qur'ān* by 'Abdullah Yūsuf 'Ali

From Worksheet Form 22:

1. What beliefs have led you to claim conscientious objection to <u>combatant</u> military training and service OR to <u>all</u> military training and service? (from *Worksheet Form 22, Question #1*)
2. How and when did you acquire these beliefs? (from *Worksheet Form 22 Question #2*)
3. What shows most clearly that your beliefs are deeply held? How do you think your beliefs affect the way you live? (From *Worksheet Form 22, Question #3*)

Some Challenging, and Sometimes Biased, Questions about Religious Belief:

4. Are you a member of a church, synagogue, mosque, or other faith community? How long have you been a member? If not a member, why not? How often do you attend?

5. What does your faith group or support community say about participation in wars?

6. Many faith communities support participation in war. Why don't you agree?

7. Is there something in the Bible and/or the Qur'ān that forbids you to defend your country?

8. How do you explain this Hebrew scripture: *Fracture for fracture, eye for eye, tooth for tooth (Lev 24:20)*, or where Jacob's two sons, avenging their sister, *took their swords and came against the city unawares, and killed the males (Gen 34:25)*, or *You give chase to your enemies, and they shall fall before you by the sword (Lev 26:7)*? Or in the New Testament: *And the one who has no sword must sell his cloak and buy one (Lk 22:36), Give to the emperor the things that are the emperor's (Mk 12:17), Let every person be subject to the governing authorities (Rom 13:1)*, and *I have not come to bring peace, but a sword (Matt 10:34)*? Or in the Qur'ān: *And slay them wherever ye catch them (2:191), Tumult and oppression are worse than slaughter (2:217), I will instill terror into the hearts of the Unbelievers: smite ye above their necks and smite all their fingertips off them (8:12)*?**

**Taken out of context, these verses are chosen knowingly to represent the opposite of each religion's loving essence.

9. What about your friends or peers, less spiritually led? Should they fight and not you?

10. Are you really expressing just a personal moral code, with nothing to do with religion?

11. If you think all human life is precious, what about killers like Saddam Hussein, Osama bin Laden, or other terrorists? Was there "that of God" in Hitler, Stalin, or Mussolini?

12. If you thought God was telling you to defend your country, what would you do? What do you say to those who believe they are answering God's call by serving in the military?

13. How about early Catholic doctrine, confirmed today, approving "just" wars? What about Islamic jihad? Did you ever sing the song, "Onward, Christian Soldiers?"

14. How do you explain all the wars recorded in the Hebrew scripture or in the Qur'ān?

15. What good does it do just to pray for those who would attack us and do nothing else?

16. Why is it wrong for our military to prevent evil from happening to others?

17. "Islamic terrorists" like ISIS want to rule the world. Will you let that happen?

*Adapted from Tatum, Arlo, ed., *Handbook for Conscientious Objectors*, Central Committee on Conscientious Objection: Printed by PDQ Printing Co., Philadelphia, PA, 1971.

Other General Questions:

18. Why didn't you put in a claim for CO before, instead of now when you just got drafted?

19. Why did you register under Selective Service initially if its purpose is to raise an army?

20. Do you object to others being drafted, or just yourself?

21. Would you have fought in World War II to stop the genocide of Jews and stop Hitler from world domination? What about Rwanda, Darfur, Somalia?

22. This local board needs to fill 100 slots in the armed forces by the end of the month. What gives you the right to claim this CO exemption knowing that, if granted, we will just go one slot deeper to 101 and someone else will take your place?

23. If we could assure you that you could get a desk job, just doing administrative paperwork, would you give up this CO claim and just go into the military? By staying out of combat, would you be willing to change your request from 1-O to 1-A-O?

24. Are you against all wars, or only this war in Syria, Iraq, or Afghanistan?

25. If someone in your family had been killed on 9/11, would you feel differently?

26. If someone held a gun against your child's/mother's/father's head ready to shoot, and you also had a gun, would you shoot the criminal to protect your family member?

27. Do you have any duty at all to your community and nation? Is it wrong to defend your country's interests? Why? Why accept the benefits of a country you won't protect?

28. What do you think happens to people like you in China, Iraq, North Korea, Russia, etc.?

29. Should we let dictators oppress their people, build weapons of mass destruction, and practice genocide? If not, what should we do about them?

30. Should Israel defend itself with its military? Should Palestinians defend themselves? Why?

31. If a nation suffers unprovoked attack, should it not defend itself?

32. How can you restrain an army except by a more powerful army?

33. If everyone held your views, our country might be destroyed by chemical, biological, and eventually nuclear weapons. What do you think about that?

34. Do you realize that by not helping our army, you are, in effect, encouraging the terrorists?

35. If you don't believe in participating in war, how do you expect us to stop terrorism? What method would you use to resist evil?

36. What will you do if your CO application is denied? Are you willing to go to jail?

37. Do you play electronic games that are violent or warlike, forcing you to kill enemies? How do you reconcile this activity with your application for a conscientious objector?

38. Why should you avoid military service when so many other brave men and women have given their lives to protect your freedom?

"The conscientious objector is relieved from the obligation to bear arms in obedience to no constitutional provision, expressed or implied; but because, and only because it has accorded with the policy of Congress thus to relieve him."

- Justice Sutherland, U.S. Supreme Court in United States v. Schwimmer, 1929

REFERENCE HANDOUTS

Long-Range Benefits of Writing CO Letters
A Summary of Comments from Past CO Letter Writers
See video *Reflections on Writing Our CO Letters (written 0-14 years ago)*

Past CO letter writers had the following to say about writing their letters, some of them from up to 14 years ago:

1. The writing of CO letters solidified and crystallized my beliefs and convictions on conscientious objection, nonviolence, and the Peace Testimony:
   ✓ By learning about the Selective Service System and conscientious objection;
   ✓ By discussing my beliefs with peers and members of my faith community;
   ✓ By putting these down on paper (articulating my beliefs);
   ✓ By understanding it at a personal level; and
   ✓ By having the support of my faith community.

2. The writing of the CO letter served as a guide for me during subsequent years in that:
   ✓ I identified myself as a conscientious objector;
   ✓ The letter served as a benchmark on what my beliefs were/are;
   ✓ The process of writing the letter gave me a chance to reflect back when faced with new situations that tested my beliefs;
   ✓ The letter gave me talking points when discussing nonviolence and peace, especially with those who disagreed with me; and
   ✓ At 18 I was more passionate and viewed life in finite terms (yes or no, black or white). Now I view the world more realistically, but the convictions I had at 18 are still at my core beliefs.

3. It made me feel both welcomed into and a part of my faith community:
   ✓ By the attention, focus, education, and support of my faith community given to us as teens, particularly in explaining conscientious objection, Selective Service, the registration process, and its implications. I would not have known about this otherwise.
   ✓ By the overwhelming support of my faith community when I read the letter and how they embraced both me and what I said. They signed the letter, put it in their "lockbox" to save for years to come, and they minuted the letter and the event in their official record of business. At the same time, it was nerve-wracking to go before all of them.

4. It prepared me in case of a possible draft or, at least:
   ✓ It established a record or initial documentation of my conscientious objector convictions.
   ✓ It got me thinking proactively about conscientious objection and a possible defense of my convictions, especially should a draft ever be reinstated.

5. I felt I had a choice to say "yes" or "no" when presented the information about conscientious objection and,
   ✓ I am glad that I made the choice to do so.
   ✓ I hope and wish that others are made aware of this information, both on the Selective Service System and what conscientious objection is all about.

Overview of Selective Service and Conscientious Objection

Introduction

Currently, the U.S. has no draft, but it does have a Selective Service System (SSS) where all 18-year-old men (and, possibly in the future, women) must register within 30 days prior to their 18th birthday or 29 days after it. Failure to do so is a felony with a fine up to $250,000 and five years in jail. While these penalties have not been applied for decades, the current deterrent is a loss of opportunities, rights, and eligibility: federal college student aid (Solomon Amendment), federal job training and employment (Thurmond Amendment), veteran's dependent benefits, and, if not U.S. born, citizenship. In almost all states and territories, registration is automatically linked to getting a driver's license; for the majority, it is required. Many states also tie registration to state employment, state educational assistance, and enrollment in state colleges. Unfortunately,

> Laws that deny education, employment, or other opportunities amount to an unacceptable burden upon those individuals who cannot in good conscience register...Penalization without prosecution or conviction...penalizes people in ways that are unrelated to their alleged offense (for which they have not been charged) [and] runs counter to our fundamental system of law and our notion of justice (Center on Conscience & War).

What is the Selective Service System?

The Selective Service System is an independent agency within the Executive branch of the Federal Government. Its director is appointed by the President and confirmed by the Senate. It is NOT part of the Defense Department. It was formed by the Military Selective Service Act (MSSA) of 1948 with minor amendments since then. Selective Service has a twofold mission: (1) to deliver manpower to the Armed Forces in time of emergency and (2) to administer an Alternative Service Program for Conscientious Objectors.

In essence, it is a draft "ready to go." In non-draft times, it is a registry that holds the name, address, birthdate, and social security number of young men (possibly women in the future) eligible and ready for military induction. If Congress declares a war, Selective Service transforms into a federal system that drafts young men (and possibly women) into the military. The system will include a lottery selection, induction notices, re-classifications and deferments, local draft boards, and procedures right up to the time of induction, when the person shifts from civilian to military jurisdiction.

Who must register?

Almost every 18-year-old male must register, and during the fall of 2016 Congress included provisions to include women, though it did not pass yet. Surprisingly, registration includes the disabled; those confined in prison, hospitals or other medical institutions; and noncitizens who are permanent or seasonal residents (agricultural workers), noncitizens in refugee or asylum status, undocumented noncitizens, and dual nationals (See *Selective Service: Who Must Register?* in the Appendix).

Who Is a Conscientious Objector (CO)?

A person who, by deeply held moral, ethical, or religious beliefs, opposes participation in war.

Three Legal Requirements for Conscientious Objection Under Current & Past U.S. Law

1. The CO must be *conscientiously opposed to participating in any war and all war.*
   Opposition is not political or selective. It is against any and all war. No 'just' war.
2. The objection must be based upon *moral, ethical, or religious belief.*
   The old law's *belief in a Supreme Being* was changed to *religious training and belief.*
3. The claim must be *sincere or deeply held;* or play a significant role in one's life.
   Not only must this position be truly yours, but you must be able to <u>document</u> it.

Two Types of Conscientious Objectors (Class 1-A-O and Class 1-O)

In the military: *Class 1-A-O* claims exemption **ONLY** from training and service as a combatant in the armed services. Though inducted into the military, the individual is exempt from training, carrying, and using a weapon. He or she might serve as a medic, chaplain, or in other noncombatant functions.

Not in the military: *Class 1-O* claims exemption from **ALL** training and services in the military. This person would NOT be inducted into the military but would perform two years of civilian alternative service, i.e., in a mental hospital, schools for handicapped, rehabilitation, etc.

Other *objectors*, <u>not recognized</u> by Federal Law, are: (1) tax resisters who object to their tax dollars paying for war, (2) selective or political objectors who refuse to fight in an 'unjust' war, but will for a 'just' war, (3) nuclear pacifists who are against developing or using nuclear weapons, and (4) non-cooperators with the draft who either don't register (absolutists) or would not comply with an induction notice by either ignoring it or leaving the country.

Non-registration: the "Absolutist"

Some men, called "absolutists," decide not to register. They consider conscription itself a part of the war process. To them, complicity with registration is a first step towards war. Non-registration is illegal, a felony under current law, and consistently seen by the courts as outside the definition of a conscientious objection. It may jeopardize future eligibility for federal and state aid, training, employment, and citizenship for immigrants. Some absolutists are quiet about non-registration, attract little attention, and hope consequences will pass them by. Others make their refusal a public and vocal act of civil disobedience.

This curriculum <u>does not</u> cover non-registration. Instead, this *Guide* is aimed specifically for the 18-year-old who decides to register AND to make a claim for conscientious objection. Those who wish to learn more about non-registration can Google "not signing up for Selective Service" and find materials, some from the Selective Service System itself. A strong proponent of the absolutist position is Edward Hasbrouck. See his article *The Draft, Draft Registration, Draft Resistance and "Selective Service"* found at https://hasbrouck.org/draft/nojoke.html.

Why Start Documentation Now?

Official procedures for filing a CO claim at registration time do not exist, so the steps outlined in this curriculum are necessary to lay a foundation. In a declared state of emergency, a draft can be instituted at once. Should Congress pass a draft, however, it would more likely take about 180 days. Twenty-year-olds in a given calendar year probably would go first. An induction notice could give someone as little as nine days to request a CO status. So anyone considering a CO reclassification should prepare in advance (See Handout: *Three Fundamental Ways to Document a CO Claim*). Not only does it provide a paper trail supporting a claimant's sincerity before a local draft board, but it helps the claimant over a period of time crystallize his or her deeply rooted beliefs and convictions about nonviolence and participation in war.

U.S. Supreme Court Rulings, Congressional Legislation, and Law

Discussing moral, ethical, or religious beliefs is difficult. These sections from the U.S. Constitution, the Military Selective Service Act, and U.S. Supreme Court cases provide the legal basis and interpretation for conscientious objection. They also show a broadening of the CO definition within current Congressional law, but that law can change. (Bold used by author.)

U.S. Constitution, Article I, Section 8: The Constitutional basis of conscription

*The Congress shall have the Power To ... provide for the common Defence and general Welfare of the United States...To declare War...**To raise and support Armies**...To provide and maintain a Navy...To provide for calling forth the Militia...To provide for organizing, arming, and disciplining the Militia...*

Amendment I of the Bill of Rights to the U.S. Constitution

Congress shall make no law respecting an establishment of religion, or prohibiting the free exercise thereof... The Bill of Rights limits the government's ability to restrict an individual, but the Constitution says <u>nothing</u> about conscientious objection.

U.S. v. Schwimmer (1929): Affirming that conscientious objection is not a "right"

*The conscientious objector is relieved from the obligation to bear arms in obedience **to no constitutional provision**, expressed or implied; but because, and only because it has accorded with the policy of Congress thus to relieve him.* Conscientious objection is not a "right," but it is granted and defined by Congress through legislation (Military Selective Service Acts) and interpreted by the U.S. Supreme Court.

Sicurella v. U.S. (1955): Violence in self-defense is OK

It is OK to believe that violence may sometimes be justified in self-defense, or in the defense of your family, or to protect a friend from attack.

U.S. v. Seeger (1965): Definition of *religious training and belief* was expanded

The 1917 Draft Law exempted only members of a *well-organized religious sect or organization...whose existing creed or principles (forbid) its members to participate in war in any form.* During the 1930s, the Court ruled that the government's duties to ensure military readiness outweighed the rights of individuals to refuse. In 1940, Congress passed the Selective Service Act recognizing individuals who *by religious training and belief were opposed to participation in war in any form.* In 1948, to narrow the CO provision, Congress inserted the "Supreme Being" phrase *a belief in a Supreme Being involving duties superior to those arising from any human relation.* In *Seeger*, the **Supreme Court struck down the requirement that a CO must affirm belief in a Supreme Being and derive his claim from that belief**, thus re-broadening the legal definition of who would qualify as a CO. In 1967, *Supreme Being* was deleted from the CO application.

The Court set three criteria:
(1) within *religious training and belief...would come all sincere religious beliefs which are based upon a power or being, or upon faith, to which all else is subordinate or upon which all else is ultimately dependent;*

(2) a sincere and meaningful belief which occupies in the life of its possessor a place parallel to that filled by the God of those admittedly qualifying for the exemption comes within the statutory definition; and

*(3) **does the claimed belief occupy the same place in the life of the objector as an orthodox belief in God holds in the life of one clearly qualified for exemption?*** <u>However,</u> the belief could not be *essentially a political, sociological, or philosophical view or a merely personal code.*

<u>*Welsh v. U.S.* (1970): Does not even need to be *religious*; *moral and ethical* is sufficient</u>

Welsh crossed out *religious;* to him it was based on *moral and ethical* grounds. The Court agreed, including these tests:

(1) if an individual deeply and sincerely holds beliefs which are purely ethical or moral in source and content...occupy...a place parallel to that filled by...God;

*(2) exempts from military service all those whose consciences, spurred by **deeply held moral, ethical, or religious beliefs**, would give them no rest or peace if they allowed themselves to become a part of an instrument of war; and*

(3) the belief upon which conscientious objection is based must be the primary controlling force in the man's life. **Depth and fervency of beliefs were paramount.**

<u>*Gillette v. U.S.* (1971): Not for political, selective reasons; against a particular unjust war</u>

You cannot say you would fight in some wars but not others. The courts said your objection *must amount to **conscientious opposition to participating personally in any war and all war.*** At the same time, you do not have to respond to hypothetical situations either in the past or future, like would you fight in World War II or if invaded from outer space, or know if your views would ever change if put in those circumstances. The court said, *Unwillingness to deny the possibility of a change of mind, in some hypothetical future circumstances, may be no more than humble good sense, casting no doubt on the claimant's present sincerity of belief.*

<u>The Military Selective Service Act, 1950, Section 6(j), as amended by Public Law 112-166, Aug. 10, 2012 (note that phrases in bold are by the author)</u>

*Section 6 (j): Nothing contained in this title shall be construed to require any person to be subject to combatant training and service in the armed forces of the United States **who, by reason of religious training and belief, is conscientiously opposed to participation in war in any form**. As used in this subsection, the term "religious training and belief" does not include essentially political, sociological, or philosophical views, or a merely personal moral code. Any person claiming such exemption from combatant training and service because of such conscientious objections whose claim is sustained by the local board shall, if he is inducted into the armed services under this title (said sections), **be assigned to noncombatant service** as defined by the President, **or** shall, if he is found to be conscientiously opposed to participation in such noncombatant services, in lieu of such induction, be ordered by his local board, subject to such regulations as the President may prescribe, to **perform for a period equal to the period prescribed in section 4(b) such civilian work contributing to the maintenance of the national health, safety, or interest** as the Director may deem appropriate and any such person who knowingly fails or neglects to obey any such order from his local board shall be deemed, for the purposes of section 12 of this title to have knowingly failed or neglected to perform a duty required of him under this title. The Director shall be responsible for finding civilian work for persons exempted from training and service under this subsection and for the placement of such persons in appropriate civilian work contributing to the maintenance of the national health, safety, or interest.*

COs and Selective Service in America (1656 to Present)
Summary Handout - See Appendix for a Detailed Narrative and Sources

The Colonial and Revolutionary Era:
- Conscientious objection came to America in 1656 with the Quakers and later with the Mennonites, Brethren, Amish, Moravians, and other lesser-known peace churches.
- A conscientious objector (CO) exemption was granted according to membership to a peace church, i.e., one's religious denomination.
- Individual colonial or state legislatures that recognized conscientious objection defined it differently while others did not accept it at all.
- No national consensus or federal legislation covered conscientious objection.
- Protection or acknowledgement as a CO often depended upon local community support.
- Noncombatant service, substitutes, or paying fines sometimes fulfilled military service.
- Some COs were abducted into service.

The Civil War:
- The War brought the first federal draft, both in the Union North and Confederate South.
- The North imposed a payment of $300 in lieu of service that went to the War Department or later, after Quakers protested, to a Slave Fund.
- Sometimes men were abducted into service; land/property from those not participating in the war was confiscated, especially as resources and personnel became scarce.
- Those who refused to fight were not treated kindly.

World War I:
- Conscription was universal and with no exemptions, substitutes, or payment in lieu of.
- COs were part of the military system and, if granted, performed noncombatant duty.
- Conscientious objection was granted only to those of traditional peace churches.
- Opposition to war grew from traditional peace churches to other pacifist-minded people including new peace churches, secular pacifists, absolutists, and political objectors.
- COs, especially those who refused military service, were treated harshly and inhumanly.
- Conscientious objection shifted from the quietist stance of individual religious objection to more vocal opposition to war for other reasons—political, philosophical, social, etc.

World War II:
- The criteria for conscientious objection shifted from membership in a peace church to individual conscience based upon religious training and belief.
- A Selective Service System, an independent civilian federal agency, decided deferments at a local board level.
- Alternative service programs performing work of national importance and outside of the military were set up for those who refused being part of the military system.
- Non-religious, political, and selective objectors were still not recognized.
- The bias against COs persisted while some noncombatant COs serving in the military were awarded honors.

The Korean War - Selective Service Before, During, and After:

- The new Selective Service Act of 1948 added the "Supreme Being" clause.
- With some variation and amendments, the 1948 Act serves as the basis of today's Selective Service System.
- The act included student deferments which laid the groundwork for future deferment categories, which later were considered inequitable and unfair.
- While Congress, the Executive Branch, and the wider public remained biased against conscientious objection, the Federal Judiciary became more accommodating.

The Vietnam War:

- Several Supreme Court liberal interpretations, particularly in 1965 landmark Seeger Case, opened up "religious training and belief" to include morals and ethics.
- The Supreme Court ruled against the "Supreme Being" clause, and Congress later dropped it from the Selective Service Act.
- The courts maintained the exclusion against political and selective objectors.
- The period reflected a huge increase in war dissent, particularly among the youth and with an increase in applications for conscientious objection and "draft dodgers."
- Initially, the draft had many deferments that favored the wealthy and well-connected, making the draft open to considerable bias.
- Eventually, a lottery was established to make the draft more "fair" and equitable.
- Nixon ended the draft on Jan. 27, 1973 and allowed the Selective Service Act to expire.
- Presidential amnesties tried to restore the nation's wounds from the thousands who refused to fight, broke the law, or left the country.

From the End of the Vietnam War to 9/11:

- To heal the nation, amnesty was offered by Ford, then another version by Carter.
- Registration was briefly suspended by Ford then reinstated five years later by Carter.
- Reliance on an All-Volunteer Force met enlistment needs for the few limited or minor military engagements between Vietnam and 9/11.
- CO criteria did not change but, without a draft, Selective Service made it a moot point; they provided no administrative mechanism to document a CO claim at registration time.
- A conscientious objection discharge from the military remained possible for those who had a change of conscience about war, but the process was quite difficult.

Post 9/11: The Privatization of the Military:

- Outsourcing to private contractors accelerated.
- Private armed security guards were employed by the Defense and State Departments, USAID, and other agencies taking over roles traditionally held by the military.
- Contractors given immunity but not held accountable to same standards as military.
- Stop-loss orders, repeated deployments, and signature wounds of PTSD (Posttraumatic Stress Disorder), TBI (traumatic brain injury) , and Moral Injury "break" many service members.
- Use of drones, Special Forces, and private contractors shield public awareness of wars making the U.S. "a war-illiterate nation."

Scripture vs. The Military Enlistment Document
(Slide from the PowerPoint Presentation)

Hebrew, Christian, & Islamic Scripture

i. Can you kill, or be part of the killing, of another human being? (*You shall not kill; Love your neighbor; Take no life which Allah hath made sacred; Turn off evil with good.*)

ii. Can you subordinate or give up your obedience to God and place it in the hands of another, i.e., a commanding officer? (*You shall have no other gods before me; No one can serve two masters; Therefore serve me, and Me alone; So invoke not anyone along with Allah.*)

Military Enlistment Document

i. *Many laws, regulations, and military customs will govern my conduct and require me to do things a civilian does not have to do.* Military Enlistment & Re-Enlistment Document, Sec. 9.

ii. You will be *required to obey all lawful orders and perform all assigned duties* and these *laws, and regulations…may change without notice to me.* Sections 9a(1) & 9b, of same.

When God says, "Do not kill" and your command says "Kill," who do you obey?

Logan Mehl-Laituri's book, *Reborn on the Fourth of July: The Challenge of Faith, Patriotism, & Conscience*, provides a thorough and personal discussion of these theological beliefs that stand in contrast to the duties required of a service member. Logan joined the Army, was a forward artillery observer, and became part of the 82nd Airborne Division. After several years, he came to the realization that Christians were obligated not to kill one's enemy. While he could no longer carry a weapon, he did not feel morally obligated to seek discharge from the Army. He eventually applied for conscientious objector status as a noncombatant. His application was essentially dismissed, but he was soon honorably discharged coinciding with the completion of his six years of active duty.

Logan's book and YouTube video (https://www.youtube.com/watch?v=_ZgbI3VmM7E) describe his transformation and struggles with Moral Injury, which is defined as "perpetrating, failing to prevent, bearing witness to, or learning about acts that transgress deeply held moral beliefs and expectations;" "a type of inner trauma that wounds the soul;" or simply "a natural response to a very unnatural experience."

Excerpts from Enlistment/Re-Enlistment Document
These passages are excerpted verbatim from U.S. Armed Forces DD Form 4/1, Oct 2007

8c. The agreements in this section and attached annex(es) are all the promises made to me by the Government. **ANYTHING ELSE ANYONE HAS PROMISED ME IS NOT VALID AND WILL NOT BE HONORED.** *[Author's note: Caps and bold in the original.]*

9. FOR ALL ENLISTEES OR REENLISTEES:
I understand that many laws, regulations, and military customs will govern my conduct and require me to do things under this agreement that a civilian does not have to do. I also understand that various laws, some of which are listed in this agreement, directly affect this enlistment/reenlistment agreement. Some examples of how existing laws may affect this agreement are explained in paragraphs 10 and 11. I understand that I cannot change these laws but that Congress may change these laws, or pass new laws, at any time that may affect this agreement, and that I will be subject to those laws and any changes they make to this agreement. I further understand that:

a. My enlistment/reenlistment agreement is more than an employment agreement. It effects a change in status from civilian to military member of the Armed Forces. As a member of the Armed Forces of the United States, I will be:

(1) Required to obey all lawful orders and perform all assigned duties.

(2) Subject to separation during or at the end of my enlistment. If my behavior fails to meet acceptable military standards, I may be discharged and given a certificate for less than honorable service, which may hurt my future job opportunities and my claim for veteran's benefits.

(3) Subject to the military justice system, which means, among other things, that I may be tried by military courts-martial.

(4) Required upon order to serve in combat or other hazardous situations.

b. Laws and regulations that govern military personnel may change without notice to me. Such changes may affect my status, pay, allowances, benefits, and responsibilities as a member of the Armed Forces **REGARDLESS** of the provisions of this enlistment/ reenlistment document.

10. MILITARY SERVICE OBLIGATION, SERVICE ON ACTIVE DUTY AND STOP-LOSS FOR ALL MEMBERS OF THE ACTIVE AND RESERVE COMPONENTS, INCLUDING THE NATIONAL GUARD. *(Author's Note: "STOP LOSS" was not included in prior versions.)*
a. FOR ALL ENLISTEES: If this is my initial enlistment, I must serve a total of eight (8) years, unless I am sooner discharged or otherwise extended by the appropriate authority. This eight year service requirement is called the Military Service Obligation. Any part of that service not served on active duty must be served in the Reserve Component of the service in which I have enlisted.... Some laws that affect when I may be ordered to serve on active duty, the length of my service on active duty, and the length of my service in the Reserve Component, even beyond the eight years of my Military Service Obligation, are discussed in the following paragraphs.

b. I understand that I can be ordered to active duty at any time while I am a member of the DEP [Delayed Entry Program]. In a time of war, my enlistment may be extended without my consent for the duration of the war and for six months after its end (10 U.S.C. 506, 12103(c)).

Three Fundamental Ways to Document a CO Claim

Since the Selective Service Registration Form has no place to request or indicate a CO classification, the following steps are recommended to decide, discern, and document a claim.

To protect you in case a local draft board accuses you of fabricating evidence at the last minute, **"tri-fold"** all papers and documents related to your CO claim. To "tri-fold," photocopy the form, letter, worksheet, or other statement. Fold the copy in thirds with the printed portion on the inside as if it would be put into a regular 4⅛ x 9½ sized envelope, then staple it shut. On the outside, address it to yourself, stamp it, and send it in the U.S. mail. When you get it back, keep it unopened and put it with the original in your CO folder. Your copy should have a legible U.S. postal service postmark date over the stamp proving **when** it was done. If not, redo and resend.

1. **Write a CO Letter to Your Faith or Support Community** (See *A Generic or Template Letter Documenting a CO Claim, Two Sample CO Letters; U.S. Supreme Court Rulings, Congressional Legislation, and Law; Worksheet Form 22: Claim for Conscientious Objection;* the bottom half of *Suggestions to Build Documentation and Worksheet Form 22 Tips; Sample Letters to Independent Agencies or Repositories,* and then *CO Letters Documenting a Claim* in the <u>Teacher's Resource Guide</u> Appendix)

   Articulating and documenting personal beliefs about conscientious objection is challenging but also at the heart of substantiating a claim. On the one hand, articulating your beliefs can be daunting and using words to describe deep, inner convictions can seem trite. On the other hand, your sincere, personal expression of truth cannot be debated by another person, including an official local draft board. Being honest is what is most important, and that is different and distinctively unique for each person. No letter has to conform to universal or academic principles. It only has to be an expression of your deeply held personal beliefs. No one can refute these, especially if they are honest and sincere.

   Your letter should include the three legal criteria for conscientious objection: a) that you are conscientiously opposed to participation in any and all war, b) that this is based on moral, ethical, and/or religious beliefs, and c) that these beliefs are deeply held or sincere. Rely on the five handouts listed above to get started, but remember that the letter is about your beliefs, not anyone else's. Ask your faith or support community to keep a copy in their official files, minutes, newsletters, lock box, or other records. Remember to "tri-fold" and send the letter to yourself. And finally, you might also want send an additional copy to an outside group, independent agency, or other repository for CO documentation (see Handout).

2. **Use the Selective Service Registration Form and Change of Information Card** (*Sample Selective Service Registration Form* and *Change of Information Form and Suggested Reply*)

   First, within 30 days before or after your 18th birthday, register via the Service Registration Form from the Post Office. Do NOT register online, by phone, or any alternate way set up by Selective Service. These do not allow you to add anything manually. Use the U.S. Postal Office form even if you were registered automatically when applying for a state driver's license, federal or state work permit, education grant, or training program. After filling out the form, write in a blank area in the middle of the form, but <u>not in the margins,</u> "I am a conscientious objector." Then sign and date it. Also, get two witnesses, probably from your faith or support community, to attest to and date your declaration. "Tri-fold" this registration form and send the photocopy to yourself. Send the original to Selective Service.

Second, respond to the Registration Acknowledgment Card sent back from Selective Service. This is a nifty way to get dated documentation from Selective Service that demonstrates your attempt to apply for conscientious objection. After you register, Selective Service will send you a card with two portions: the bottom half is the *Registration Acknowledgment Card* (informally called a draft card) and the top is a *Change of Information Form*. On the left side of the form, almost half way down, the card says, *If any information shown is incorrect, make corrections, sign, and remove this half of card.* Tear off the top half and on the right side write, "This does not acknowledge my declaration as a conscientious objector noted on my Selective Service Registration Form dated _____" (fill in date). Do the same photocopy, tri-fold, and send procedure as before. Though Selective Service might change their protocol in the future, you should get back a letter from them saying that procedures for filing CO claims for registrants are not in place. Keep this letter! It is further documentation—now dated, from Selective Service, and with its official seal—that you asked for this classification.

3. Gather Letters of Support from Others (See *Letters of Support* handout)

Letters of Support are like a job or college recommendation. They are collected from respected people who can attest to your CO beliefs, convictions, and integrity. The person writing the letter does not have to agree with you. In fact, some of the strongest letters are from people who do not hold these beliefs but can vouch that you do!

Letters of Support were especially important during the Vietnam era when the draft was in effect. They gave local draft boards further evidence about a CO claim, this time from witnesses who could attest to the sincerity of the claimant.

Some young adults tend not to ask older adults, like teachers, for *Letters of Support*. But because of transitions from high school to college or job, young adults often relocate and lose touch with these mentors who might have known them well and could speak on their behalf. *Letters of Support* also educate adults who may know little or nothing about conscientious objection, so the process has an indirect, educational or social benefit as well.

Do not be shy about asking adults to write a *Letter of Support* for you. The worst they can do is say "no" and most adults will be glad to help you. The *Letters of Support* handout has recommendations for both you and the adult writing the letter. Share any of your handouts or your CO letter with them to acquaint them with your concerns and position.

Beyond these three fundamental ways to document a CO claim, the Handout: *Suggestions to Build Documentation and Worksheet Form 22 Tips* has more. Update your CO folder as your beliefs become more crystallized. This shows a progression, not a contradiction. Remember that your CO folder is a resource. If you are ever called before a local draft board, you can still select what you want to submit. Remember also that your documentation is no guarantee that you will be given a CO classification, but it will certainly help.

A Template or Generic Letter Documenting a CO Claim

CO letters combine both standard, general language as well as the distinctively unique and personal views of the writer. The context of the letter is that the writer is about to turn 18 years of age (in most circumstances) and is required to register with the Selection Service System. Legally, the letter should state the three main requirements for meeting a CO claim. That is the generic part. However, explaining how the writer meets each of these criteria is highly personal and different for every person. It fits no template. Reasons and beliefs often are quite difficult to discern and articulate. They emanate from deep within a person's heart and soul. Words seem inadequate and even trite. At the same time, these are the writer's beliefs, and whatever rings true for that person is a sincere statement that no other person can refute.

The following is a template to frame the letter. Worksheet Form 22 can help discern a person's beliefs. Actual letters from other teens appear in the Appendix, but remember that the reasons a person meets the criteria for being a CO are unique and individualistic.

<u>A Sample Letter:</u>

(Fill in date)

Dear Members of _____ (fill in the name of the support or faith community):

On _____ (date of birthday), I will turn 18 years old and am required to register with the Selective Service System. On the registration form, I will indicate my status as a conscientious objector. Although the form does not ask for this information specifically, in the event of a future draft I want to record my convictions now. In this regard, I ask that two representatives of this support/faith community serve as witnesses to my testimony. I also request that you keep a copy of this letter and my registration form in a permanent and secure manner.

While my beliefs continue to crystallize, I can state the following:

- I have a deep, firm, and fixed belief against personal participation to war in any form. (*Expand on this in a few sentences or even a few paragraphs explaining why.*)
- This conviction is based upon my moral, ethical and religious training and beliefs. (*Elaborate on these convictions and beliefs documenting the kind of training you received, especially within your support/faith community and/or family household.*)
- I sincerely feel… (*Your claim must be sincere, not just a way to get out of military service. Write a few sentences or paragraphs to substantiate your sincerity, such as "I was raised not to harm others," "No person has the right to take another's life," "I do not act violently towards others and am known among my friends for acting in this manner," "I seek solutions that respect the rights of all others," and "There is that of God in everyone." Talk about how these beliefs play a significant role in your life.*)

Please accept this letter and a copy of my Selective Service registration as a record of my convictions. I thank you for your willingness to stand with me in witness of my beliefs.

Sincerely,
(Your Name)

Two Sample CO Letters

I am writing this letter to inform you of my decision concerning the Selective Service. It is among my core beliefs that violence in any form is wrong, and because of that I am going to file for conscientious objector status when I register. I ask that you support me in my decision.

I believed in peace and nonviolence my whole life. Growing up in the Quaker Community, I was taught never to physically harm another person. Everyone has an inner light, and I have no right to hurt or take away that light.

As I continue to grow, I become more aware of my own true beliefs. Taking into account both ideas taught me and those learned on my own helped me understand what I truly believe. I hold true to the notion that there exists an inner light inside everyone. It is this light that binds us together. Rather than separate individuals, we are small parts of a single entity. To harm another would be to harm myself. To kill another would be to kill a part of myself. I cannot bear to hurt the force holding us all together. I cannot participate in war of any kind or in any way.

As a conscientious objector, there is the option of participating in the military service as a noncombatant, such as a medic or mechanic. Although such duties are less violent than that of a soldier, they are still participating with the act of war. I cannot bring myself to be part of a war in any way, so I cannot be a noncombatant either.

It has taken me a full eighteen years to know myself well enough to truly understand my core values. I put deep thought into my decision, and I know that I am making the correct one. As I try to picture myself in the possible future of the world, I cannot see myself taking the life of another in any situation. The act of violence goes against everything I believe in. If I am to go against my beliefs, then I am to go against myself. No matter how many people may disagree with it, I cannot go against myself. I request that you support me with my decision and help me in filing to be a conscientious objector.

I turned 18 years of age on [date deleted]. This is a time when young men are required to register with Selective Service. I registered as required, but feel it is necessary for me to put forth my beliefs so that they can be known to all.

I am opposed to war. I do not see how in this modern world when we can communicate with others so easily how conflict is needed. We now have the ability to destroy our own world, so how can sensible beings be willing to take such a risk by indulging in conflict?

I believe that everyone should have the right to make his or her own choices in life. War puts people in inhuman situations, placing young men and woman in situations where they must do things that go against what they would consider common decency in any other situation.

Presently for this country, war is conducted in such a fashion that people don't really understand all the horrible results of it. People do not realize how war forces people from their homes, causes great harm to people living near it and participating in it.

The violence that takes place in a war is rooted in anger, and this anger is spread by war becoming a poison to our greater community. I've seen this anger while living in Africa and how it can spread from person to person, as each new person in the chain is hurt. And the anger does not die over time. After a war it is rare that people confront this poison in the population with reason, understanding and compassion and thus it never goes away. It grows in a community until something happens and the community releases the anger back into the world through more violence beginning a cycle of war, diaspora, and hate.

I request that you keep a copy of this letter in your records to document my beliefs.

Suggestions for Faith and Support Communities

Not all faith and support communities are familiar with or endorse a conscientious objection claim. For some, being approached by a young person to help document a claim might be new. However, nurturing and supporting a young person's beliefs should be part of the community's function. Discerning, deciding, and documenting a conscientious objector claim is challenging, especially for young people as they are still forming a belief system. The suggestions below give some guidance.

Building a Peaceful Community

1. In what ways do you teach your youth peace? How do you nurture this seed in your young people? How are the peace testimony, nonviolent conflict resolution, and the value of all human life inculcated in your youth? What is done programmatically in educational programs? How do personal interactions with children model peace? How does your community uphold nonviolence and peace? What peace programs do you support, fund, or participate in? How do these nurture nonviolence in your youth and adults? How do your members witness to peace? Does your community have COs from prior wars and have they shared their experiences with your youth? How do you support parents/guardians as they nurture loving and peaceful environments for their children?

2. Record in your community's newsletters and other publications peace activities or events in which your youth participate. For parents or guardians, start a scrapbook or file that documents your child's experiences or activities that promote peace or nonviolent service.

Specific Suggestions that Support the CO's Claim:

3. Use this CO curriculum regularly as teens approach their 18th birthdays. Listen to them, help them articulate their beliefs, and edit their letters. Promote awareness in the teens and the entire community about conscientious objection and the importance of framing a testimony of peace. At the same time, honor those who choose not to make a CO claim.

4. Set up a special committee or designate a person(s) to oversee this process. Contact those turning 18 years old and offer support and guidance with Selective Service registration.

5. As a community, listen to the young person's statement of belief and support the candidate's convictions. Offer an individual or small group to mentor the young person. Provide, if requested, a type of clearness, advisory, or support committee to help any candidate with logistics or an opportunity to explore internal questions of conscience.

6. Witness the community's response to the CO's declaration, letter reading, or registration form, as in the Handout: *Sample Selective Service System Registration Form*. Write a minute or official recording of the community's support. If possible, publish this minute and the applicant's letter in the community's newsletter. Ensure candidates of ongoing support and maintain contact with them as they move on to college or their early careers.

7. Keep copies of the registrant's Selective Service form, his/her request for support, minutes, official records, and other supporting evidence in a secure place, such as a lock box or safe.

8. Write *Letters of Support*. Have adults write their own CO letters.

   NOTE: *Failure to register for Selective Service is a felony carrying other penalties.* ***Advising someone not to register is also a felony***, *but presenting options and their ramifications is legal.*

Sample Selective Service System Registration Form

Within 30 days of your 18th birthday, register via the Service Registration Form from the U.S. Post Office. **Do NOT register online**, by phone, or any alternate way set up by Selective Service. These do not allow you to add anything manually. Use the U.S. Postal Office form even if you were registered automatically when applying for a state driver's license, federal or state work permit, education grant, or training program. After filling out the form, write in a blank area in the middle of the form, but <u>not in the margins</u>, "I am a conscientious objector." Then sign and date it. Also, get two witnesses, probably from your faith or support community, to attest to and date your declaration. "Tri-fold" this registration form and send the photocopy to yourself. Send the original to Selective Service. (See other tips in the Handout: *Three Fundamental Ways to Document a CO Claim*.)

Register on-line (http://www.sss.gov) or complete this form.

SELECTIVE SERVICE SYSTEM REGISTRATION FORM   DO NOT WRITE IN THIS SPACE
PRINT ONLY IN BLACK INK AND IN CAPITAL LETTERS ONLY

DATE OF BIRTH (MM-DD-YYYY)   SEX (Mark with "X")   SOCIAL SECURITY NUMBER

1⇒ □□-□□-□□□□   2⇒□Male □Female   3⇒□□□-□□-□□□□

***Note: I am a conscientious objector. Martin L. King, Jr., January 15, 2007. (Signed/Dated)*

LAST NAME   SUFFIX: (Mark with "X")   OTHER SUFFIX

4⇒□□□□□□□□□□□□□□□□□□□□   □ □   □□□

FIRST NAME & MIDDLE NAME

□□□□□□□□□□□□□□□□□□□□□

I, M. L. King, Sr, Minister, Ebenezer Baptist Church, witness Martin's conviction. (Signed/Dated)

CURRENT MAILING ADDRESS: STREET ADDRESS & APARTMENT NUMBER

5⇒□□□□□□□□□□□□□□□□□□□□□□□□□

CITY   STATE   ZIP CODE

□□□□□□□□□□□□□□□□□□□   □□   □□□□□

I, Howard Thurman, long-time mentor of Martin, witness his conviction as a CO. (Signed/Dated)

TODAY'S DATE (MM-DD-YYYY)   I AFFIRM THE FOREGOING STATEMENTS ARE TRUE

6⇒□□-□□-□□□□   7⇒ |_____|

SIGNATURE   UPO

Change of Information Form and a Suggested Reply

(Form from Selective Service Site: https://www.google.com/?gws_rd=ssl#q=%22Lindsay+Calvin+Johnson%22)

Change of Information Form

After completing the U.S. Postal Office Selective Service Registration Form, you will get back a "Change of Information Form," as below. On the left side about a third down, just under the bar code, it says in small print, *If any information shown is incorrect, make corrections, sign, and remove this top portion.* The instructions below that say, "Use the top portion of this letter to update and/or correct information. Mark through any mistakes and write the correct information."

Obviously, your claim as a CO will <u>not</u> be indicated on this card. So, to document this again, write in a space suggested below, *This does not show my declaration as a conscientious objector noted on (DATE) on my SS Registration Card.* Remember to sign and date it (to the right of the bar code). Make a copy, tri-fold, and send back. Consider sending return receipt requested.

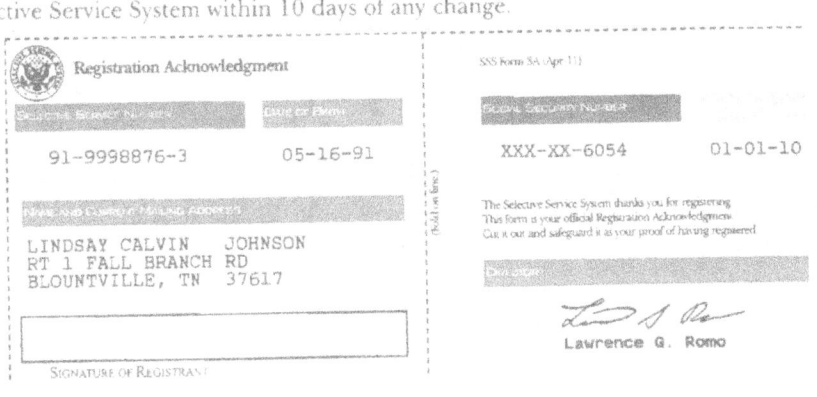

Sample Reply from Selective Service To Your Change of Address Form:

In a few weeks, you will likely get back from Selective Service an official letter like the one below, complete with their seal and documented date, acknowledging your attempt to seek CO status. Put this in your CO folder. This is excellent documentation as it is a dated record from Selective Service about your requested exemption.

(Official SSS Seal)

Selective Service System
P.O. Box 94638, Palatine, Illinois   60094-4638
Telephone... 1-847-688-6888
http://www.sss.gov

April 1, 2007

Martin Luther King, Jr.
2A Nonviolent Way
Some City, Some State 99999

Dear Dr. King:

We are responding to your request for information about conscientious objection.

Classification for conscientious objection is an integral part of Selective Service law, but a person does not register as a conscientious objector. That classification is made only after registration, and only if inductions are authorized by Congress and the President.

One of the qualifications of classifications as a conscientious objector is that a registrant be sincerely opposed to war in any form.

In the event classification is resumed in the future, a registrant will be given instructions on how and where to submit a claim for classification as a conscientious objector. Determination of classification will be made by members of a local board in the registrant's area of residence.

Sincerely,
William F. Delaney
Director, Data Management Center

smo - L006

Author's Note: The last paragraph does not provide a warning that the window to claim a CO exemption may be as little as nine days from the receipt of an induction notice to the date to report for induction.

Letters of Support

Adapted from Central Committee on Conscientious Objection (CCCO), 1981
and Center on Conscience and War (CC&W), 2005

If a draft is resumed, *Letters of Support* from others substantiating your CO claim will be vital. These letters attest to your sincerity. They are like character references and can be as important to a local draft board as your responses at a hearing. They may even be a deciding factor. *Letters of Support* that are consistent with your views and beliefs demonstrate your sincerity and make it difficult for a draft board to question or doubt your claim. The person writing this reference does not have to agree with your position but should be able to say that you are honest and sincere in the views you have. Attesting to your honesty is key. They do not need to demonstrate detailed knowledge about your claim or even agree with it.

A good *Letter of Support* should include the following four areas:

1. How long and in what capacity has the reference (the person writing your letter) known you?

2. Does the reference believe you are sincere in your claim as a conscientious objector, and why?

3. Does the reference feel that your conduct since arriving at this belief is consistent with your claim, and why?

4. Does the reference feel that your claim is based on deeply held moral, ethical, or religious beliefs (however broadly defined), and why? If possible, the reference should describe influences or training in your life that have led to the development of your beliefs. The reference may cite conversations, interactions, or observations of the claimant regarding his or her beliefs.

Letters of Support should be specific. Personal letters detailing your convictions are usually more convincing than general, impersonal ones. Consider giving your reference a brief statement explaining your position, for example your Worksheet Form 22 or the letter you wrote to your support or faith community. You may want to include some handouts or brochures—either from this curriculum, others from Quaker House, CC&W, or other draft counseling agencies—which answer questions and dispel misconceptions about conscientious objectors and Selective Service. Spend as much time with your reference as necessary explaining your views, and be sincere. Developing a relationship with this person, where he or she understands the depth of your convictions, may prove valuable later as he or she might serve as a witness at a possible hearing. In the meantime, you are helping this person understand what a CO is.

You can get supporting letters from teachers, clergy, members of your support or faith community, friends, family, or other people familiar with you. If the reference has some standing in the community, the letter is stronger. The person should know you well, understand your position, and, most importantly, speak to your sincerity. Again, it is not necessary that the person agrees with your beliefs. In fact, some of the best letters are written by persons who disagree with your CO position but who can say that you are truthful and adamant in your own stance.

Here are some other suggestions:

- Letters should be dated and addressed to "Chairman, Local Board" but given to you, not sent to the local board! Selective Service will not accept *Letters of Support* or any material from persons seeking a CO claim until after a draft is resumed and a claim is made. So, keep your letters in your CO folder and be ready to submit them, if needed.

- The letter should be as brief as possible. One page maximum; single-spaced.

- Typed letters and those on letterhead are more impressive, but a neatly handwritten letter is acceptable. Since your local board will consider other claims, it is important that yours be easy and quick to read.

- Members of your community can be invaluable resources and references. They know you in special ways and can lend historical record to accounts that shaped your testimony for peace, nonviolence, and refusal to participate in war.

- Consider asking for a Clearness Committee or small group of people with whom to bounce off your views. Then ask them for documentation that described the process, its benefits, and its support of your convictions.

- Most good CO claims include several supporting letters. Fewer will make your claim seem weak—as if not very many people are ready to stand up for you. You may not feel the need to get many now as a draft is not imminent, but get a few to be safe.

- Be proactive and collect some letters now! With so many transitions from high school, college and/or the workplace, as well as moves to different localities, you should ask people along the way. It is easiest for people to write letters and vouch for your beliefs when they know you now, not several years later or when you have lost touch with them.

- If you receive a letter that is vague, inaccurate, or does not speak to the four main areas points listed earlier, either ask your reference to revise it or do not include it in your final file. It might prove detrimental.

Remember: Keep your letters in your CO file, send yourself a stapled, tri-folded photocopy to get that U.S. Postal date on it. Update and add new references as needed. Do not hesitate to ask a significant person at any time in your life to write a *Letter of Support* for you. You will be surprised how many people are willing to help you.

Suggestions to Build Documentation and Worksheet Form 22 Tips

The third criterion for being a CO is that your beliefs must be deeply held or sincere. Your beliefs are internal but are demonstrated by how you act in the world. For some, that might be quite active and extensive; for others it may be more passive and restrained. In either case, the law looks at documentation, so keeping a *CO File Folder* is encouraged.

Each person is unique and fundamentally different. What is in a person's CO folder will vary accordingly. The beliefs and actions contained in the folder likely will show an evolution, especially as convictions crystallize and mature. Making a statement about conscientious objection, even early in its development, is worth doing.

This section provides examples of how to document beliefs beyond the three fundamental methods. This list is comprehensive with the expectation that each teen will be more selective.

1. **Keep all past, current, and ongoing documentation in your CO folder.** Stay organized and vigilant. Continually update your folder with materials that are dated, signed, tri-folded, and sent to self. Keep everything, even if your initial views change or were not that strong. Showing a progression is common. Here are some specific ideas:

   ✓ Keep a journal with entries about your beliefs, the influences that affect you, how your values run against participation in war, etc.

   ✓ Read peace literature, such as materials by Gandhi, Dorothy Day, M. L. King, Jr., Mother Teresa, Henry David Thoreau, Elise Boulding, Kenneth Boulding, Thomas Merton, Leo Tolstoy, Ang Sang Su Kee, and others.

   ✓ Participate in peace organizations, demonstrations, and rallies.

   ✓ Spread your convictions against war to others, either formally in presentations at school or to your support or faith community, or informally in private discussions.

   ✓ Describe how you "naturally" handle conflict, including specific incidents or actual situations.

   ✓ Gather *Letters of Support* from people who can speak to your convictions. They do not necessarily have to agree with you, but they must attest to your honesty and sincerity.

   ✓ Document attendance at religious services or special events that show how that influenced your training and beliefs.

   ✓ Document participation in retreats, educational sessions, workshops, lectures, etc.

2. **Revise, edit, and expand your answers to *Worksheet Form 22*.** The Church of the Brethren and the Center on Conscience and War (CC&W) give suggestions on how to elaborate on the three questions from this form. Many of these are summarized below:

Question 1: Describe your beliefs which are the reasons for you claiming conscientious objection to combatant military training and service or to all military training and service.

This question asks you to describe, in some detail and as honestly as possible, the basic principles which guide your life. Describe values and beliefs that are of utmost importance to you, such as God, love, truth, etc., and why these are in conflict with participation in the Armed Services. You are asked to formulate your own statement against participation in war. Begin by saying that you are conscientiously opposed to war, and then describe the beliefs that lead you to such opposition. The point of the question is not to have a polished essay but to get you to think, describe, and write about what you believe.

The second part of the question seeks to determine whether you claim noncombatant status in the military or a full exemption from military service. You should specify what it is about noncombatant service that would violate your conscience, if this is the exemption you seek.

Question 2: *Describe how and when you acquired these beliefs. Your answer may include such information as the influence of family members or other persons; training, if applicable; your personal experiences; membership in organizations; books and readings which influenced you.*

Include anything of significance that helped you form your beliefs. Describe a story or incident (or two) about events, either sudden or over a period of time, that have influenced you in the direction of being a CO. Mention any formal religious training if it helped you arrive at your position. If you feel your beliefs were arrived at with no formal training, no need to mention it. Describe the way you were raised, especially if in a nonviolent household that resolved conflict in peaceful ways. If your upbringing was violent or traumatic, discuss how this affected you and framed an understanding and commitment to nonviolence and peace. Describe influences of parents and other family members, clergy, teachers, books, poetry, music, television, movies, and membership in organizations. Be specific. Show that strong influences in your life stimulated you to think clearly and seriously about participation in war.

Specific incidents can be mentioned, such as demonstrations, seminars, or assemblies you attended; experiences and courses in school and college; trips taken; contact with refugees, veterans, or previous COs. These show that your beliefs had substantial formation beyond an academic interest. Obviously, if you have experienced war, be sure to reflect on it.

Avoid giving the impression that your belief is primarily a matter of political consideration, expediency, or merely an arbitrary, personal moral code unrelated to higher values. Unconventional beliefs do qualify, but they will require careful statement. Selective or political objection against a particular was does not qualify.

Question 3: *Explain what most clearly shows that your beliefs are deeply held. You may wish to include a description of how your beliefs affect the way you live.*

This question seeks proof of sincerity, which may be a difficult to substantiate, particularly for young objectors who have had few experiences that demonstrate convictions. Select the best illustrations to show your deeply held beliefs.

Think about community service; church, mosque, or synagogue participation; clubs and sports; or relationships with friends. You can discuss how your future plans are strongly affected by a commitment to those beliefs. Describe kinds of employment you had, or plan to have, which reflect your commitment. Discuss any public expression, written or oral, of your beliefs. Describe your lifestyle, life goals, and how they are an outgrowth of your beliefs. Give examples of peaceful conflict resolution.

Each person is unique, raised differently, and under varied circumstances. Being honest and true to oneself is the key. Writing down beliefs is hard because these are deep inner feelings, but this is also easy because they are your beliefs.

Sample Letters to Independent Agencies or Repositories
Center on Conscience & War and Peace Abbey

Several outside groups, independent agencies, or repositories will hold documentation for a prospective CO. They are a good backup source in case personal files get lost or misplaced. Keep any letters they send back to you, especially if dated, in your CO folder.

The Center on Conscience and War (CC&W) is a long and established group supporting conscientious objection both for teens at Selective Service Registration time and also for those service members in the military who seek a CO discharge. They are also a member of the GI Rights Hotline along with Quaker House. The format of their materials includes a written statement like the Worksheet Form 22 used in this curriculum. Their basic Registration Packet can be found at http://www.centeronconscience.org/images/stories/pdf/basic.pdf. The CO can either complete the forms from their site or write the following letter and attach his or her CO letter with it. Remember to copy, tri-fold, and send everything to self.

Mahatma Gandhi
4 Peaceful Way
Nonviolent Township, State 00001
Today's Month, Day, Year

Center on Conscience & War
1830 Connecticut Avenue, N.W.
Washington, D.C. 20009

To Whom It May Concern:

On (*fill in the date of your 18th birthday*), I will turn 18 years old and am required to register for the draft under the Selective Service code. Due to my beliefs, I wish to indicate a conscientious objector status. I have already declared this conviction to my faith or support community, where my statement is now on record. Enclosed are copies of my letter to them, which outlines my beliefs, and my Selective Service registration form, where I requested a claim as a conscientious objector.

I ask that you would keep a record of this letter, along with the enclosed documents. Any support you can offer now or in the future would be greatly appreciated.

Sincerely,

Applicant's Name

The Peace Abbey is a retreat center in Massachusetts. They will hold the form on the following page in a repository as another form of outside documentation. Information about Peace Abbey can be found at: http://www.peaceabbey.org/programs-projects/conscientious-objectors/. The form can be photocopied from the next page or downloaded from: http://www.peaceabbey.org/wp-content/uploads/2015/04/nationalregistry.jpg.

Remember to tri-fold and send the signed original to The Peace Abbey, PO BOX 216, Sherborn, MA 01770-0216.

The National Registry
For Conscientious Objection

Founded in 1991

The National Registry for Conscientious Objection was created following the war in the Persian Gulf in early 1991. The National Registry provides men and women of all ages with an opportunity to register their objection to personal, national, and international violence. As a concept, conscientious objection was co-opted by the military who gave itself the power to grant or withhold official status as a "C.O." The National Registry reclaims the notion of conscientious objection, and returns it to its original meaning as a way of life (rather than a military or governmental designation). Conscientious objection is not the property of the military, to be handed out or withheld according to the judgement of draft boards or commissioned officers of the armed services. Objection to violence and courage of conscience are characteristics of a life committed to peace.

The National Registry is a national campaign to promote peacemaking as a practical ideal: a way of living in the present that represents our best hope for the future. It seeks to inspire peace and justice in society by inviting peacemakers everywhere to "register" their conscientious objection to violence, and in so doing, to share with others their commitment to a peaceful world. The intent of The National Registry for Conscientious Objection is to emphasize one's absolute dedication to peaceful living and to peaceful resolution of conflict. It is only by committing ourselves to peaceful living that peace will in fact prevail, in our lives and on the planet.

IMPORTANT: This statement should be read silently first and then aloud in the presence of two witnesses who will then sign along with the registrant. Please send the original back to The Peace Abbey, Two North Main Street, Sherborn, MA. 01770 and keep a copy for your personal records.

Affirmation Statement

I hereby affirm that: because of my deeply held beliefs about peace, justice, and nonviolence, I am opposed to the use of violence to settle disputes. Furthermore, I wish to make public my decision not to participate in any group, organization, or agency of government that would require from me acts of violence against a fellow human being.

I sign The National Registry for Conscientious Objection to have my position on peace, justice, and nonviolence duly recorded as a way of life that I embrace and am totally committed to.

Date _____ Printed Name _____

Address _____

_____

Signature

Witnesses: 1. _____

2. _____

Soldiers generally believe that they are doing the right thing. Their sacrifice and suffering needs to mean something honorable....There is a deep need to believe war's cause is just, so we often make up a just cause to justify the great sacrifices made in war's name. People don't know what we do to win wars. We make a science out of dealing in deceit, lies, assassination, and sometimes, plain old murder....We justify eradicating entire races of people in the name of manifest destiny. We create a culture where we glorify the acts of murder and death, and we shame acts of creating life....Many of the infantry soldiers I met...simply enjoy killing people. I heard a lot of jokes and contests to see how many people they killed in grotesque ways. I heard how 'funny' it is when someone is hit by their grenade and explodes into a 'pink mist.'...War is ugly. War's ugliness saturates the hearts of those who fight it. Why is suicide the number one killer of former veterans? Do you think that if these men and women really felt they were being 'noble defenders of the free world' they would want to kill themselves? A soldier has to drink the 'Cool aid' [sic] of thinking themselves as the noble defenders or they will have to face the truth of the reality of war. They'd have to open their hearts to the moral compromises we make in the name of political and economic dominance. The truth may be unbearable. The truth may just lead a soldier to want to commit suicide. I have had a dance with this darkness, and I decided I wanted to live.

- A service member, who Quaker House helped, written after his CO discharge:

APPENDICES

More on Selective Service

The Selection Service System is a Federal agency that holds essential information about all 18-25-year-old males in order to initiate conscription (a draft) at short notice.

- It is an independent, civilian agency within the Executive Branch. Its 2015 annual budget was $21,500,000.
- Its director is appointed by the President and confirmed by the Senate.
- It is NOT part of the Department of Defense.
- It maintains a ready-to-go system of conscription based on law, precedent, and evolving technologies.
- It collects information on 18-25-year-old men.
- It holds this information and checks to its reliability (any persons missing).
- In the event of a national emergency and should Congress and the President decide to reinstate a draft, it is able to deliver manpower quickly to the Armed Forces.
- It administers the Alternative Service Program for conscientious objectors (1-O).

Despite its low visibility, Selective Service is active, complex, and comprehensive. It is the precursor to the draft, drives the entire registration process, and lays the legal context for claiming conscientious objection. In this curriculum, the topic is covered in one Reference Handout (*Overview of Selective Service and Conscientious Objection*) and fifteen PowerPoint slides and Notes Pages (from Slide #7, *Part I: Selective Service System*, through Slide #21, *Part II: Who is a Conscientious Objector*). This Appendix expands on that, referring to the Selective Service and other relevant sites. Their website is sophisticated and detailed, including regulations, definitions, procedures, laws, manuals, reference pages, PDFs, and charts.

The most accurate information about Selective Service is the act itself: *Military Selective Service Act (MSSA)*, 50 U.S.C. App. 451 et seq., amended Public Law 112 - 166, 8/10/12 at: https://legcounsel.house.gov/Comps/Military%20Selective%20Service%20Act.pdf. Next is the Selective Service website with articles *About the Agency* at https://www.sss.gov/About and on *Registration* at https://www.sss.gov/Registration-Info. They link specific topics (subject to change) on the left-hand column. The outline below parallels the PowerPoint presentation.

I. SELECTIVE SERVICE: AN OVERVIEW

Slide #7, *Part I: Selective Service System*
Slide #8, *The Military Selective Service Act(s)*
Slide #9, *The Selective Service System: A Draft Ready to Go*
Reference Handout: *Overview of Selective Service & Conscientious Objection*

A. HISTORY OF SELECTIVE SERVICE
Background of Selective Service, https://www.sss.gov/About/History-And-Records/Background-Of-Selective-Service
B. HOW IS IT DIFFERENT TODAY
Slide #16, *SSS: Same But Different*

How the Draft Has Changed Since Vietnam, https://www.sss.gov/About/History-And-Records/How-The-Draft-Has-Changed-Since-Vietnam

Agency Structure, https://www.sss.gov/About/Agency-Structure

II. REGISTRATION

REGISTER—Online Fillable Registration Forms, https://www.sss.gov/Home/Registration

A. WHY REGISTER?

Why Register?, https://www.sss.gov/Registration/Why-Register

B. WHO MUST REGISTER

Who Must Register, https://www.sss.gov/Registration-Info/Who-Registration

Who Must Register–Chart, https://www.sss.gov/Registration/Who-Must-Register/Chart

Immigrants and Dual Nationals, https://www.sss.gov/Registration/Immigrants-and-Dual-Nationals

Policy from the United States Citizenship & Immigration Services (USCIS) policy on naturalization and Selective Service registration: USCIS Policy Manual - Volume 12 - Part D - Chapter 7 (Current as of 1/7/13), https://www.sss.gov/Portals/0/PDFs/PrinterFriendly/USCIS%20Naturalization%20_%20SSS%20registration%20policy.pdf

Hospitalized or Incarcerated Men, https://www.sss.gov/Registration/Who-Must-Register/Hospitalized-or-Incarcerated-Men

Men with Disabilities, https://www.sss.gov/Registration/Who-Must-Register/Men-With-Disabilities

C. WOMEN AND THE DRAFT (as of January 2016)

Women Aren't Required to Register, https://www.sss.gov/Registration/Women-And-Draft

Backgrounder: Women and the Draft, https://www.sss.gov/Registration/Women-And-Draft/Backgrounder-Women-and-the-Draft

Historical Perspectives On Women and The Draft (Portions from General Accounting Office), http://www.gpo.gov/fdsys/pkg/GAOREPORTS-NSIAD-98-199/html/GAOREPORTS-NSIAD-98-199.htm

D. HOW TO REGISTER

Slide #15, *Ways SSS Suggests to Register*

How to Register, https://www.sss.gov/Registration/How-to-Register

E. FREQUENTLY ASKED QUESTIONS

Frequently Asked Questions about Selective Service, https://www.sss.gov/QA

III. FAILURE TO REGISTER

Overview: What Happens If I Fail To Register? http://www.militarydraftregistration.com/

A. FELONY, FINES, AND JAIL TIME

Slide #10, *Selective Service Registration Law & Threats (Real, but not used now)*

B. LOSS OF FEDERAL BENEFITS, INCLUDING CITIZENSHIP

Slide #11, *What Actually Happens! Solomon & Thurmond Amendments*

Slide #12, *What If I Don't Register? Federal Consequences*

Benefits/Penalties, https://www.sss.gov/Registration/Why-register/Benefits-and-Penalties

C. LOSS OF STATE BENEFITS

Slide #13, *What If I Don't Register? State Consequences: Your Driver's Licenses; "Solomon & Thurmond Penalties*

State/Commonwealth and Territory Legislation, https://www.sss.gov/Registration/State-Commonwealth-Legislation

Other Legislations by States, Territories, and the District Of Columbia, https://www.sss.gov/Registration/State-Commonwealth-Legislation/Other-Legislations

D. THREE STATE DRIVER'S LICENSE LAWS

North Carolina Legislation: SS and State Driver's License, http://www.ncga.state.nc.us/EnactedLegislation/Statutes/PDF/BySection/Chapter_20/GS_20-9.2.pdf

Virginia Department of Motor Vehicles Website, http://www.dmv.state.va.us/drivers/#applying.html

South Carolina Department of Motor Vehicles Supplement for SC Credential SELECTIVE SERVICE REQUIREMENTS 447-SEL (Rev. 9/13), http://www.scdmvonline.com/DMVNew/forms/447-sel.pdf

E. WHAT HAPPENS AFTER AGE 26 FOR THOSE WHO DON'T REGISTER

Slide #14, *What If I Am Over Age 26 and Haven't Registered?*

Men 26 And Older — Born After 1960, https://www.sss.gov/Home/Men-26-and-OLDER

IV. PROOF OF REGISTRATION—ACKNOWLEDGEMENT CARD

Proof of Registration, https://www.sss.gov/Registration/Proof-of-Registration

A. DRAFT CARD

Draft Cards, https://www.sss.gov/About/Return-to-the-Draft/Draft-Cards

B. CHANGE OF ADDRESS OBLIGATION

Change of Information — Address And Personal Information, https://www.sss.gov/Home/Address-Change

C. STATUS INFORMATION LETTER

Status Information Letter, https://www.sss.gov/Registration/Status-Information-Letter

D. REGISTRY (CROSS CHECKING)

Automatic Registration in the United States: The Selective Service Example, Laura Seago, Brennan Center for Justice at New York University School of Law. https://www.brennancenter.org/sites/default/files/legacy/publications/selective%20service.color.FINAL.pdf

V. THE DRAFT

Return to the Draft, https://www.sss.gov/About/Events-after-Draft

A. SPECIALTY DRAFTS

Medical Draft in Standby, https://www.sss.gov/About/Medical-Draft-in-Standby-Mode

B. INDUCTION OR DRAFT PROCESS

Slide #18, *The Draft Process*

Sequence of Events, https://www.sss.gov/About/Sequence-of-Events

C. LOTTERY AND SELECTION PROCESS

The Vietnam Lotteries, https://www.sss.gov/About/History-And-Records/lotter1

Selective Service Lottery, https://www.sss.gov/About/History-And-Records/Selective-Service-Lottery

D. LOCAL BOARDS AND APPEAL BOARDS

Local Boards and Appeal Boards, https://www.sss.gov/Volunteers/Board-Member-Program/Board-Member-Facts

E. CLAIMS, POSTPONEMENTS, RECLASSIFICATION, & APPEALS PROCESS

Postponements, Deferments, Exemptions, https://www.sss.gov/About/Return-to-the-Draft/Postponements-Deferments-Exemptions

VI. DEFERMENTS AND CLASSIFICATIONS

A List of All Deferments and Classifications is in the Appendix

A. DEFERMENTS

Classifications, https://www.sss.gov/Classifications

Non-Citizens and Dual Nationals, https://www.sss.gov/About/History-And-Records/Non-Citizens-and-Dual-Nationals

Affects Of Marriage And Fatherhood On Draft Eligibility, https://www.sss.gov/About/History-And-Records/Effects

Only Sons and Sole Surviving Sons, https://www.sss.gov/About/Return-to-Conscription/Only-Sons-and-Sole-Surviving-Sons

B. COs

Slide #21: *History of COs in America*

Slide #22: *Key U.S. Supreme Court Rulings Since World War II*

Reference Handout: *U.S. Supreme Court Rulings, Congressional Legislation, and Law*

1. DEFINITIONS

Slide #19, *Part II: Who is a Conscientious Objector?*

Reference Handout: *Overview of Selective Service & Conscientious Objection*

Slide #23: *Two Types of COs*

Slide #24: *Desmond T. Doss*

The Courage of Their Convictions: Three Conscientious Objectors and the Heroism that Earned Them Medals of Honor, https://www.sss.gov/Alternative-Service/CO-Story-1

2. HOW TO APPLY

Conscientious Objectors, https://www.sss.gov/consobj

3. ALTERNATIVE SERVICE

Alternative Service Employer Network, https://www.sss.gov/About/Alternative-Service/Alternative-Service-Employer-Network

Alternative Service Program, https://www.sss.gov/About/Alternative-Service

VII. SOURCES AND WEBSITES:

Sources of Information on Selective Service, https://www.sss.gov/About/Sources-of-Information-on-Selective-Service

Selective Service: Who Must Register?

From Selective Service Site, https://www.sss.gov/Registration/Who-Must-Register/Chart

Does every young man have to register when he turns 18? Just about!

Almost all male U.S. citizens regardless of where they live, and documented or undocumented immigrant men residing in the U.S., are required to be registered with Selective Service if they are at least 18 years old but are not yet 26 years old. Men who are 26 years old and older are too old to register. Some requirements are shown below:

Category	Yes	No
All male U.S. citizens born after December 31, 1959, who are 18 but not yet 26 years old, except as noted below:	X	
Military Related		
Members of the Armed Forces on active duty (active duty for training does not constitute "active duty" for registration purposes)		X*
Cadets and Midshipmen at Service Academies or Coast Guard Academy		X*
Cadets at the Merchant Marine Academy	X	
Students in Officer Procurement Programs at the Citadel, North Georgia College and State University, Norwich University, Virginia Military Institute, Texas A&M University, Virginia Polytechnic Institute and State University		X*
ROTC Students	X	
National Guardsmen and Reservists not on active duty	X	
Delayed Entry Program enlistees	X	
Separatees from Active Military Service, separated for any reason before age 26	X*	
Men rejected for enlistment for any reason before age 26	X	
Civil Air Patrol Members	X	
Immigrants**		
Students in Officer Procurement Programs at the Citadel, North Georgia College and State University, Norwich University, Virginia Military Institute, Texas A&M University, Virginia Polytechnic Institute and State University		X

Permanent resident aliens (USCIS Form I-551)	X	
Seasonal agriculture workers (H-2A Visa)		X
Refugee, parolee, and asylee immigrants	X	
Undocumented immigrants	X	
Dual national U.S. citizens	X	
Confined		
Incarcerated, or hospitalized or institutionalized for medical reasons		X*
Handicapped physically or mentally		
Able to function in public with or without assistance	X	
Continually confined to a residence, hospital, or institution		X
Gender Change / Transgenders		
U.S. citizens or immigrants who are born male and have changed their gender to female	X	
Individuals who are born female and have changed their gender to male		X

*Must register within 30 days of release unless already age 26.
NOTE: To be fully exempt you must have been on active duty or confined continuously from age 18 to 26.

Residents of Puerto Rico, Guam, Virgin Islands, and Northern Mariana Islands are U.S. citizens. Citizens of American Samoa are nationals and must register when they are habitual residents in the United States or reside in the U.S. for at least one year. Habitual residence is presumed and registration is required whenever a national or a citizen of the Republic of the Marshall Islands, the Federated States of Micronesia, or Palau, resides in the United States for more than one year in any status, except when the individual resides in the U.S. as an employee of the government of his homeland; or as a student who entered the U.S. for the purpose of full-time studies, as long as such person maintains that status. **NOTE: Immigrants who did not enter the United States or maintained their lawful non-immigrant status by continually remaining on a valid visa until after they were 26 years old, were never required to register. Also, immigrants born before 1960, who did not enter the United States or maintained their lawful non-immigrant status by continually remaining on a valid visa until after March 29, 1975, were never required to register.

Deferments and Classifications

From Selective Service Site, Classifications, https://www.sss.gov/Classifications

Class 1-A: Available for unrestricted military service

Class 1-A-O: Conscientious objector available for noncombatant military service only

Class 1-O: Conscientious objector to all military service

Class 1-O-S: Conscientious objector to all military service (separated/discharged from military service)

Class 2-D: Registrants deferred because of study preparing for the ministry. Last academic year postponement till courses end

Class 3-A: Registrants deferred because of hardship to dependents

Class 3-A-S: Registrants deferred because of hardship to dependents (separated/discharged from military service)

Class 4-D: Minister of religion

Class 1-D-D: Deferment for certain members of a reserve component or student taking military training

Class 4-B: Official deferred by law

Class 4-C: Alien or dual national

Class 4-G: Registrants exempted from service because of the death of his parent or sibling while serving in the Armed Forces or whose parent or sibling is in a captured or missing in action status

Class 4-A: Registrants who have completed military service

Class 4-A-A: Registrants who have performed military service for a foreign nation

Class 4-W: Registrants who have completed alternative service in lieu of induction

Class 1-D-E: Exemption of certain members of a reserve component or student taking military training

Class 1-C: Members of the Armed Forces of the United States, the National Oceanic and Atmospheric Administration, or the Public Health Service

Class 1-W: Conscientious objector ordered to perform alternative service in lieu of induction

Class 4-T: Treaty alien

Class 4-F: Registrants not acceptable for military service

Class 1-H: Registrants not subject to processing for induction

Registration Linked to State Driver's License and Other Opportunities

Penalties and missed opportunities for not registering with Selective Service are the result of federal legislation (1982 Solomon Amendment and 1985 Thurmond Amendment) and similar laws at state levels. Also, in an effort to reach 100% compliance, nearly all states and territories now link registration to obtaining or renewing a driver's license or state I.D. Currently, these penalties do NOT include women, who are not required to register with Selective Service. Men older than 26 who did not register may find themselves ineligible for benefits. They would have to "show by a preponderance of evidence" that failure to register was not knowing or willful.

The following is from the official Selective Service site. The chart is **current as of July 2015**. Details for each state can be found at: https://www.sss.gov/Registration/State-Commonwealth-Legislation for driver's licenses and https://www.sss.gov/Registration/State-Commonwealth-Legislation/Other-Legislations for education and employment.

Federal restrictions on education and employment

"Many state laws mirror, reinforce, or strengthen two federal laws below:

1. The *Solomon Amendment* added Section 12(f) to the Military Selective Service Act in September 1982. Male students who have a requirement to register with Selective Service must satisfy that requirement as an eligibility precondition for receipt of Title 4 federal student financial aid. Title 4 aid includes such need-based programs as Guaranteed Student Loans and Pell Grants.
2. In November 1985, the *Thurmond Amendment* to the Defense Authorization Act established Title 5, U.S. Code, Section 3328, which requires Selective Service registration (of men who are required to register) as a prerequisite for appointment to most federal jobs."

State restrictions on driver's license, education, and employment

"**BACKGROUND:** In an effort to ensure compliance with federal law among young men, many states and territories, and the District of Columbia, have enacted legislation which links Selective Service registration with the process of applying for a driver's license, renewal, or state identification card. As a result of such legislation, in May 2002, the state of Delaware, which enacted driver's license legislation in 2000, became the first state to reach nearly 100 percent registration compliance since Selective Service began compiling this data. In that same year, seven other states increased their compliance rates by 3 percent or more after enacting similar driver's license legislation."

"These laws are simple and inexpensive to implement. They instruct the state's Department of Public Safety or Motor Vehicles to include a consent statement on all applications or renewals for driver's permits, licenses, and I.D. cards. The statement tells the applicant that by submitting the application he is consenting to his registration with the Selective Service System, if so required by Federal law."

"Transmission of applicants' data to the Selective Service System is accomplished electronically through an existing arrangement each state has with the data sharing system of the American Association of Motor Vehicle Administrators (AAMVAnet) at no extra cost to the state."

"There are two forms of driver's license legislation:

1. **Optional**, where a man, age 18 through age 25, can opt to have his information transferred to Selective Service for registration by checking a box when applying for a state learner's permit, driver's license or renewal, or I.D. card.

2. **Automatic**, where a man, age 18 through age 25, consents to have his information automatically transferred to Selective Service for registration when he applies for a state learner's permit, driver's license or renewal, or I.D. card."

Author's Note: Selective Service is not clear on whether an applicant for a driver's license can turn down optional or automatic Selective Service registration and still get a driver's license, but in many states it is required. In Virginia, for example, their DMV website says "you must authorize DMV to forward your personal information to Selective Service....DMV is prohibited by law from issuing any type of driver's license or ID card to an applicant who is required by federal law to register with Selective Service but who refuses to send his information to the Selective Service."

Current as of July 2015

(Source Selective Service as referenced above; see their site for complete descriptions. See also CC&W
http://www.centeronconscience.org/co/conscientious-objection-and-the-draft/59-state-regulations-on-draft-registration.html)

* Solomon-like restrictions affect eligibility to enter state institutions of higher learning and financial aid, and in some states even veterans dependent financial aid.
**Thurmond-like restrictions affect state employment and/or promotion.

State/D.C./Territory	Optional with driver's license	Automatic with driver's license	Solomon-like restrictions*	Thurmond-like restrictions**
Alabama		√	√	√
Alaska			√	√
Arizona		√	√	√
Arkansas		√	√	√
California	Passed by legislature,	but Gov. Brown vetoed	√	
Colorado		√	√	
Connecticut		√		
Delaware		√	√	√
District of Columbia	√			
Florida		√	√	√
Georgia		√	√	√
Hawaii		√		
Idaho	√		√	√
Illinois		√	√	√
Indiana	√			
Iowa		√		
Kansas		√		
Kentucky	√		√	
Louisiana		√	√	√
Maine	√ Transmission pending		√	√
Maryland	√ Enactment pending			
Massachusetts			√	
Michigan	√			

Minnesota		√		
Mississippi		√	√	√
Missouri	√		√	√
Montana	√		√	√
Nebraska				
Nevada	√			
New Hampshire	√		√	√
New Jersey			√	
New Mexico		√		
New York		√		
North Carolina		√	√	√
North Dakota			√	
Ohio		√	√	
Oklahoma		√	√	
Oregon				
Pennsylvania				
Rhode Island		√		
South Carolina		√		
South Dakota		√	√	√
Tennessee		√	√	√
Texas		√	√	√
Utah		√	√	
Vermont				
Virginia		√	√	√
Washington	√			
West Virginia	√		√	√
Wisconsin		√	√	√
Wyoming				
Subtotals √ or pending	13	28		
U.S. Territories				
Guam	√			
N'n Marianas Islands		√		√
Puerto Rico	√ Transmission pending			
Virgin Islands		√		
Subtotals √ or pending	2	2		
TOTALS √ or pending	15	30		

Worksheet Form 22: Claim for Conscientious Objector
Adapted from Selective Service System Form 22

INSTRUCTIONS TO REGISTRANT: The purpose of this form is to help you provide the information needed by your local board to determine if you qualify for reclassification as a conscientious objector. Your objection may be based on religious, moral or ethical beliefs, or a combination of these beliefs.

PART I
<u>Check the box in this part that pertains to your claim. Note the difference of the two!</u>

☐   1.   I claim **exemption <u>ONLY</u> from training and service as a combatant member** of the Armed Forces **(Class 1-A-O)**. (To quality, you must establish to the satisfaction of the Board that you are conscientiously opposed to participation in combatant military training and service in any war, based on deeply held moral, ethical or religious beliefs.)

(Author's note: person is inducted into the military but does not train with, carry, or use a weapon.)

☐   2.   I claim **exemption <u>FROM ALL</u> training and service as a member of the Armed Forces (Class 1-O)**. (To qualify, you must establish to the satisfaction of the Board that you are conscientiously opposed to participation in combatant and noncombatant military training and service in any war, based on deeply held moral, ethical or religious beliefs.)

(Author's note: this person remains a civilian and does alternative service instead.)

PART II
Prepare and attach written responses to the information requested below. If you wish, you may attach letters from persons who know you and are familiar with your beliefs. You may also attach any other pertinent information you would like the board to consider.

<u>1. Describe your beliefs which are the reasons for your claiming conscientious objection to combatant military training and service or to all military training and service.</u>

_____
_____
_____
_____
_____
_____
_____
_____
_____
_____
_____
_____
_____
_____
_____
_____
_____
_____
_____
_____

2. Describe how and when you acquired these beliefs. Your answer may include such information as the influence of family members or other persons; training, if applicable; your personal experiences; membership in organizations; books and readings which influenced you.

_____
_____
_____
_____
_____
_____
_____
_____
_____
_____
_____
_____
_____
_____
_____
_____
_____
_____

3. Explain what most clearly shows that your beliefs are deeply held. You may wish to include a description of how your beliefs affect the way you live.

_____
_____
_____
_____
_____
_____
_____
_____
_____
_____
_____
_____
_____
_____
_____

PART III

List below the names of individuals and organizations whose letters or documents (papers) you are submitting with this form to insure that all letters or documents have been received.

_____
_____
_____
_____
_____
_____

Visit to Quaker House, Airborne and Special Operations Museum, and Ft. Bragg
Worksheet, Scavenger Hunt, and Focus Questions

Museum:

1. What are some of the first things you notice that indicate this is a war museum? What do they symbolize or portray for the visitor? What impressions do they strike?

2. What inspired the U. S. Army to create paratrooper (or airborne) divisions?

3. Who was the father of the Army Airborne?

4. In what ways does the museum portray casualties, either in numbers or pictures of wounded or dead?

5. Who was Private John Thomas Mackall?

6. Who said: "The principal battleground of this war is not the South Pacific. It is not the Middle East. It is not England, or Norway, or the Russian Steppes. It is American opinion."
   a. President Roosevelt   b. General George C. Marshall   c. Archibald MacLeish
   d. Ronald Reagan   e. George W. Bush   f. Martin L. King, Jr.

7. What was the success rate of the early airborne assaults (paratroop drops)?

8. What one method helped the accuracy of paratrooper drops?

9. Who were the Triple Nickels?

10. Why were the battles at Sainte-Mère-Église and the marshes of the Merderet and Douve so critical?

11. Who said: "The fire was so intense that the men were physically recoiling. We just grabbed our men and walked them out. The physical force of the fire pouring in was such that they just stopped

and started back—not from cowardice at all. We just grabbed them by the shoulders and led them down into this thing and pushed them. We were right there too. This is where your personal presence makes a hell of a lot of difference. I haven't the slightest doubt that if Gavin and I and the battalion commanders had not been there that the crossing of the causeway would not have succeeded. The men would not have gone."

12. Aside from World War II, name six other wars of which the 82nd Airborne was part?

13. What is the image of war and the military from WW II to today that the museum portrays?

14. **EXTRA CREDIT:** Where is the Fayetteville Friends Meeting "slab" commemorating peace hidden among all the other artifacts? What does it say? HINT: Go out the South Entrance and look at the sidewalk.

Focus Questions for General Discussion after Visiting Museum

Quaker House:

15. What do you notice when you arrive at Quaker House? What symbols are used? What impressions strike you? What is the image of war and the military that Quaker House portrays?

16. In what ways is Quaker House a witness to the Friends Peace Testimony?

17. If you were the director of Quaker House, what would you focus on? How would you lead Quaker House in its witness to peace?

18. What would a peace museum look like in Fayetteville or even Chapel Hill? What symbols would it use? Who would it honor? What impressions would it inspire in those who visit it?

Ft. Bragg:

19. What do you observe driving down Bragg Blvd and onto the base of Ft. Bragg? How is the town and this base different from a civilian community or town?

20. What do you notice in this chapel that is different from "civilian" places of worship?

Visit to Quaker House, Airborne and Special Operations Museum, and Ft. Bragg
ANSWER SHEET - Worksheet, Scavenger Hunt, and Focus Questions

Museum:

1. What are some of the first things you notice that indicate this is a war museum? What do they symbolize or portray for the visitor? What impressions do they strike?
   > Tombstones; Flags; Memorials to fallen soldiers; Paratroopers past and present, etc. Symbols of honor, sacrifice of life, bravery, patriotism, etc.

2. What inspired the U. S. Army to create paratrooper (or airborne) divisions?
   > Paratroopers were first used with success to drop soldiers behind enemy lines by the Italians and Soviets, then more extensively by Germany early in the war in Norway and the Netherlands.

3. Who was the father of the Army Airborne?
   > Lt. Colonel William C. Lee

4. In what ways does the museum portray casualties, either in numbers or pictures of wounded or dead?
   > Very little. A few pictures of wounded soldiers in a stretcher. One picture looks like two dead soldiers alongside of road—no blood or guts. One picture of a Chaplain praying over two soldiers. No casualty numbers. Very few bombs and explosions shown.

5. Who was Private John Thomas Mackall?
   > One of the first paratroopers killed in combat during a paratroop assault on Algiers in North Africa in November 1942. By early 1943 an airfield near Ft. Bragg was completed along with 1,750 buildings. The camp was renamed Camp Mackall in his honor.

6. Who said: "The principal battleground of this war is not the South Pacific. It is not the Middle East. It is not England, or Norway, or the Russian Steppes. It is American opinion."
   > a. President Roosevelt   b. General George C. Marshall   c. Archibald MacLeish
   > d. Ronald Reagan   e. George W. Bush   f. Martin L. King, Jr.
   > Answer: Archibald MacLeish, Assistant Director of the Office of War Information, 3/19/1942.

7. What was the success rate of the early airborne assaults (paratroop drops)?
   > Not very good. The first Allied airborne attack, Operation TORCH in Nov. 1942, jumped into Algeria, N. Africa. Many of the transports (planes) ran out of gas due to the 1100-mile trip from England over Spain and into N. Africa. Fog, rain, and clouds hampered accurate drops, many at the wrong locations—only 31 out of 118 "sticks." Sometimes called Night Flight to SNAFU (situation normal, all fouled up). In Operation HUSKY in Sicily, Italy, 23 C-47 transports were shot down by Allied anti-aircraft gunmen ("friendly fire"). For the British only 54 of 144 aircraft made it to their drop spots—most were shot down or landed in the Mediterranean.

8. What one method helped the accuracy of paratrooper drops?
   > Use of "pathfinders." General Matthew B. Ridgway had the idea of dropping pathfinder's (small groups of soldiers) before the main attack group so that they could highlight—through lights, radio equipment, etc.—the approach path of transports carrying paratroopers.

9. Who were the Triple Nickels?
   > The first African American Airborne unit, the 555th Parachute Infantry Battalion, a segregated group of paratroopers. President Truman officially integrated the army in 1947.

10. Why were the battles at Sainte-Mère-Ėglise and the marshes of the Merderet and Douve so critical?

The Merderet River ran parallel to Utah Beach, one of the landings on D-Day, and was a critical river to cross in order to advance from the beachhead. Control of the bridges was vital. Without them, the Allies would have been stuck. The 82nd Airborne was dropped five hours before the amphibious landings. Cloud cover and German fire caused the drops to be dispersed. Despite the confusion and under the command of Lt. Col Krause, the paratroopers took Sainte-Mère-Église, the first town captured by the Allies. The next day, General Ridgway got the order to seize a crossing of the flooded Merderet River at Le Fiere. The river was quite swollen, and the German troops were heavily fortified—panzer divisions mounted a major counter attack. Over the next two days, casualties were very high, but with troop reinforcements they eventually captured the bridges allowing the Allies to advance their massive forces across France.

11. Who said: "The fire was so intense that the men were physically recoiling. We just grabbed our men and walked them out. The physical force of the fire pouring in was such that they just stopped and started back—not from cowardice at all. We just grabbed them by the shoulders and led them down into this thing and pushed them. We were right there too. This is where your personal presence makes a hell of a lot of difference. I haven't the slightest doubt that if Gavin and I and the battalion commanders had not been there that the crossing of the causeway would not have succeeded. The men would not have gone."

    General Matthew B. Ridgway about the battles of Sainte-Mère-Église and the bridge over the Merderet River. This was the inspiration for the climactic battle in the film *Saving Private Ryan*.

12. Aside from World War II, name six other wars of which the 82nd Airborne was part?

    Dominican Republic, Vietnam, Korea, Panama, Dessert Storm, Iraq, and Afghanistan.

13. What is the image of war and the military that the museum portrays from WW II to today?

    Soldiers commingle with civilians and the country's soldiers. Combat is downplayed. Psychological Operations have a greater role. No massive invasion forces. Still no casualties.

14. **EXTRA CREDIT:** Where is the Fayetteville Friends Meeting "slab" commemorating peace hidden among the artifacts? What does it say? HINT: Go out the South Entrance and look at the sidewalk.

    Outside south entrance, 6th row from the entrance; 7th column from the right. "Let us live in that light and power which takes away all reasons for war. – Peace Testimony, Fay Quakers.

Focus Questions for General Discussion after Visiting Museum

<u>Quaker House: (no answers here)</u>

15. What do you notice when you arrive at Quaker House? What symbols are used? What impressions strike you? What is the image of war and the military that Quaker House portrays?

16. In what ways is Quaker House a witness to the Friends Peace Testimony?

17. If you were the director of Quaker House, what would you focus on? How would you lead Quaker House in its witness to peace?

18. What would a peace museum look like in Fayetteville or even Chapel Hill? What symbols would it use? Who would it honor? What impressions would it inspire in those who visit it?

<u>Ft. Bragg:</u>

19. What do you observe driving down Bragg Blvd and onto the base of Ft. Bragg? How are the town and this base different from a civilian community or town?

    Strip joints, pawn shops, Army supply stores, many fast food restaurants, many young men and women in one common dress (or uniform), flags, monuments, memorials.

20. What do you notice in this chapel that is different from "civilian" churches or Friends' Meetings?

    The stained-glass windows include images of soldiers.

A Brief History of COs and Selective Service in America (1656 to Present)

Conscientious objection came to America with the Quakers in 1656 and later with the Mennonites in 1683, the Church of the Brethren (also called Dunkards, Tunkers, and Dunkers) in 1719, the Amish in 1730, the Moravians in 1735, and other lesser-known peace churches (Shakers, Christadelphians, and Rogerenes) following that. These pacifist churches forbade their members from the use of arms in warfare. Hence, this peace testimony started as a religious conviction and practice that eventually influenced legislation, was woven into law, and was refined by judicial rulings. Conscientious objection is not a constitutional right; it is determined at the discretion of Congress and can be suspended by them at any time through new legislation.[1]

Relying heavily on the commentary and documents found in Lillian Schlissel's seminal book, Conscience in America: A Documentary History of Conscientious Objection in America, 1757-1967,[2] as well as other materials, this brief history illustrates how conscientious objection evolved through the 360 years since Quakers and other peace churches first settled in the New World and how conscientious objectors (COs) were treated, sometimes harshly, throughout our country's years of wars and conscription. It will show that conscientious objection is defined by federal legislation which sets its legal framework. In seeking a claim, the CO tacitly acknowledges the state's right to conscript, i.e., Selective Service registration, and is willing to perform alternative noncombatant military or civilian service if drafted. Furthermore, this overview will show how the refusal to bear arms and participate personally in war can be based on many convictions—religious, ethical, moral, secular, philosophical, political, economic, and others—but the criteria for granting a conscientious objection exemption has remained narrow.

Conscientious objection represents a dissonance between moral or religious conscience and one's obligation to the state. It is an individual's inner voice of conscience standing against the nation's drums of war. Schlissel describes this tension as a "collision of convictions—the individual's belief that he must not violate the voice of his conscience or the word of God, and the state's assertion that it must preserve its own viability, by force of arms when need be, and that this heavy burden is for all citizens to share."[3] For the most part, the state has been willing to grant conscientious objection to the quiet pacifist who tacitly acknowledges the government's authority. But both the "absolutist," who refuses both registration and alternate service, and the "political objector," who speaks against the country's war policy, risk prosecution and/or imprisonment.

These dichotomies, and the tensions inherent in them, have not changed in the 360 years of America's history, but a progression has taken place. We have seen a gradual evolution from granting conscientious objection based upon one's membership to a particular peace church to an exemption based upon a person's individual belief. And while that belief originally had to be based solely on a religious training and belief, it now includes moral and ethical considerations. We have also seen the treatment of conscience objectors become more humane, especially when handled through civilian processes and not within the military chain of command. What has not changed is that the conscientious objection must still be against any and all war. Selective or political objection against a particular war, or what an individual deems an unjust war declared by Congress, is not acceptable. Congress was never willing to give up its authority to declare war, raise an army, or defend the nation militarily. That has been consistently affirmed by the judicial system as well. So, let's review some of this history.

The Colonial and Revolutionary Era:

- Conscientious objection came to America in 1656 with the Quakers and later with the Mennonites, the Brethren, the Amish, the Moravians, and other lesser-known peace churches.
- A conscientious objector (CO) exemption was granted according to membership to a peace church, i.e., one's religious denomination.
- Individual colonial or state legislatures that recognized conscientious objection defined it differently while others did not accept it at all.
- No national consensus or federal legislation covered conscientious objection.
- Protection or acknowledgement as a CO often depended upon local community support.
- Noncombatant service, substitutes, or paying fines sometimes fulfilled military service.
- Some COs were abducted into service.

Life in the New World was harsh for everyone, including the pacifists in peace churches. Often, COs were met with persecution and hostility by their neighbors who fought in colonial militias against the indigenous peoples, during the French and Indian Wars, or in the American Revolution. Yet, those who believed in a testimony of peace were steadfast. These pacifists built a reputation in the community as God-fearing, law-abiding, hardworking neighbors, and they fulfilled all civic obligations, except one. Eventually, they won the respect and recognition of the general public, and many state and colonial legislatures exempted them from militia duty.[4]

Unfortunately, early debates and amendments in colonial legislatures and the Continental Congress never fully codified a precise definition or basis for a CO claim. It alternated between an individual's conscience and his membership in a peace church. Church denominations settled in different areas of the New World, where each colony formed its own militia, so laws varied from one colony to another. Massachusetts in 1661, Rhode Island in 1673, and Pennsylvania in 1757 passed laws to allow COs to perform noncombatant service. The Pennsylvania law said: "Quakers, Mennonites, Moravians, and others conscientiously scrupulous of bearing arms were entitled, upon the call to arms, to assist by extinguishing fires, suppressing the insurrection of slaves and other persons, caring for the wounded, and performing other services."[5] (Note: *scrupulous*, though commonly used then but not today, means "extremely careful to do precisely the right, proper, or correct thing in every last detail."[6]) In other colonies, those who refused *to trayne or fight were* required to find substitutes, pay fines, or contribute in other ways that were fitting to their beliefs. Some were forced to help build fortifications. Refusal sometimes led to imprisonment or confiscation of one's property.[7] Others who strayed from the safety of their local community were abducted into military service.

At the outset of the Revolutionary War, George Washington's call to arms went to "all young men of suitable age to be drafted, except those with conscientious scruples against war."[8] However, as the Revolution wore on and financing campaigns became more difficult, a monetary contribution was imposed on noncombatants and, in some cases, goods and supplies were stolen by British and American troops. As can be expected during periods of national crisis, exemption from military service was constrained and publicly chastised.

The Continental Congress debated the issue. In the Constitution and the Bill of Rights, James Madison tried to insert two clauses: in Article 1 he proposed that, "The civil rights of none shall be abridged on account of religious belief or worship…nor shall the full equal rights on conscience be in any manner, or any pretext, infringed…" and into what became the 2nd Amendment, giving people the right to bear arms, he added "but no persons religiously scrupulous of bearing arms shall be compelled to render military service in person."[9]

Several Congressional representatives objected to these insertions for various reasons. Some wanted the exemption tied to membership in a peace church or a *religious sect scrupulous of bearing arms*. Another wanted to add a payment fixed by law as substitute of service, though some felt it was unjust to require payment from people who were acting upon their consciences. Others believed payment was necessary; otherwise the militia concept would not survive. Some wanted the exemption granted by state legislation, not mandated by the federal Constitution. Others doubted whether everyone seeking exemption would be doing so out of religious principles, and they questioned how the government could assess a person's sincerity. Another objected to the exemption saying that everyone receiving protection from the nation's laws also has a moral duty to militia service. During the course of debate, Madison actually changed the basis for exemption from religious affiliation to an emphasis on personal conscience, but when it came up for a vote, he returned to the term, "religiously scrupulous." It was not enough, though, as the majority dropped the language from the 2nd Amendment, and they were inclined to leave the matter up to each state.[10] As conscientious objection has been part of America for 360 years, so have the debates between conscience and obligation to government.

The peace churches held true to their testimony, and conscientious objection was recognized in several state constitutions. In 1776, Pennsylvania's Constitution said, "Nor can any man who is conscientiously scrupulous of bearing arms, be justly compelled thereto, if he will pay such equivalent." Similar language was in Vermont's 1777 Constitution and in New Hampshire's 1784 document. The 1819 Maine Constitution said "Persons of the denominations of Quakers and Shakers…may be exempted from military duty; but no other person…shall be so exempted, unless he shall pay an equivalent, to be fixed by law."[11] Later, new states entering the Union did the same: Illinois (1818), Alabama (1819), Iowa (1846), Kentucky (1850), Indiana (1851), Kansas Territory (1855), and Texas (1859).[12] But CO exemptions came with a price—the payment of a fee or the hiring of substitutes.

The Civil War:
- The War brought the first federal draft, both in the Union North and Confederate South.
- The North imposed a payment of $300 in lieu of service that went to the War Department or later, after Quakers protested, to a Slave Fund.
- Sometimes men were abducted into service; land/property from those not participating in the war was confiscated, especially as resources and personnel became scarce.
- Those who refused to fight were not treated kindly.

Up until this time, the country depended on volunteers from colonial and state militias to do the fighting, so the Civil War brought federal conscription for the first time to the states in both the North and in the South. A national draft started with the Confederate Congress in April 1862 and a year later with the U.S. Congress.

For the North, Lincoln signed the Enrollment Act of March 3, 1863, creating an All-Federal Service where:

> All able-bodied male citizens of the United States, and persons of foreign birth who shall have declared on oath their intention to become citizens under and in pursuance of the laws thereof, between the ages of twenty and forty-five years, except as hereinafter excepted, are hereby declared to constitute the national forces, and shall be liable to perform military duty in the service of the United States when called out by the President for that purpose.[13]

Congress struggled with the inconsistencies between state legislation and their constitutions: which persons were exempt from military service, would it be based upon religious scruples of conscience, and how would those claims be proven? In the end, the bill made no mention of conscientious objection or to people with religious scruples. Instead, Congress legislated that any person drafted could furnish a substitute or pay a $300 commutation fee to the Secretary of War in lieu of their service. The Army reinforced that position: conscientious scruples was not an exemption. The poor viewed conscription as a 'rich man's act.' The $300 fee was beyond their reach, and they could not pay for a substitute. Riots within the Irish community in New York City erupted in July 1863. Not only was this a rich man's draft, but paradoxically Africans were exempted since they were not citizens, yet they competed with the poor for jobs. The riots were anti-rich, anti-black, and anti-Republican. Working-class whites attacked draft headquarters, wealthy homes, and tortured and murdered blacks. About 1,000 people died, and over 2,000 policemen and five army regiments were needed to squash the riots.[14]

At the same time, Quakers particularly, along with other peace churches, objected to a payment that essentially supported war. Lincoln and others were sympathetic to their views. Eventually, a compromise was proposed by William Stanton, Secretary of War, so that the $300 payment would go to a "Slave Fund" which Quakers and others felt amenable. In February 1864, Congress acknowledged the scruples of conscientious objectors and provided that they could perform alternate service instead. Some accepted this; others took the absolutist position that any accommodation to conscription was against their principles. Fortunately in the North, the law, the President, and the Army were sympathetic, and the CO's case was met with understanding. In the South, it was not, especially as the war dragged on. Conscientious objectors who "fell between the cracks"—i.e., those who could not pay the $300 fee, who were conscripted or abducted into the military, who were caught beyond the protection of their local community, or who fell under the authority of the lower ranks of the army— suffered cruel punishment including harsh imprisonment, forced marches and drills, and for some death.[15]

World War I:
- Conscription was universal and with no exemptions, substitutes, or payment in lieu of.
- COs were part of the military system and, if granted, performed noncombatant duty.
- Conscientious objection was granted only to those of traditional peace churches.
- Opposition to war grew from traditional peace churches to other pacifist-minded people including new peace churches, secular pacifists, absolutists, and political objectors.
- COs, especially those who refused military service, were treated harshly and inhumanly.
- Conscientious objection shifted from the quietist stance of individual religious objection to more vocal opposition to war for other reasons—political, philosophical, social, etc.

The lot of COs during World War I did not improve. The Selective Service Law of 1917 made conscription universal for all able-bodied men. Unlike the Civil War, commutation fees and substitutes were no longer permitted. Conscientious objection was recognized but only within the military. Furthermore, if drafted and inducted, the Law provided conscientious objection exemption only to those who were members of a "well-organized religious sect or organization …whose existing creed or principles forbid its members to participate in war in any form," and this referred specifically to Quakers, Mennonites, Amish, and Brethren.[16] Exemptions were decided by a local draft board of three or more civilians, and each board was granted power within its own local jurisdiction. The CO, if exempted, was still "required to serve in a capacity declared by the President to be noncombatant"[17] and to swear a military oath. Hence, while a distinction was made between combatant and noncombatant service, the CO still fell under military jurisdiction. Many COs found this unacceptable.

Those who objected to war and military service were treated harshly. Conscripts who refused to wear a uniform, bear arms, perform basic duties, or submit to military authority were court-martialed. Military tribunals actively sought out and tried men found to be insincere in their conscientious claims. Some objectors, under pressure, accepted noncombatant duties. To the "absolutists" who refused all cooperation with the army, the military courts were most severe. Seventeen were sentenced to death (though never carried out), 142 to life imprisonment (many reduced years later), and 345 to penal labor camps for an average of over 16 years.[18] Some who refused military jurisdiction were sent to federal prisons, sometimes manacled to the bars of their cells, hanged by their thumbs, hosed with water, fed only bread and water, or placed in solitary confinement. It was not until near the end of the war that Congress authorized the Secretary of War to grant "furloughs," like alternative service, without pay to enlisted men for work on farms or in Red Cross units, but by then it was mostly a moot point.[19]

Aside from the military treatment of objectors, the law and public opinion were weighted against COs. The Justice Department, with the assistance of local police and private citizens, carried out "slacker raids" to mete out draft-aged men who were not registered.[20] The Selective Service Act exempted Amish, Mennonites, Quakers, and Brethren but not to other pacifist sects or to immigrants who came to America fleeing conscription from Europe and Russia. They included the Molokans, Dukhobors, Seventh-day Adventists, Jehovah's Witnesses, Russellites, Christadelphians, and the Hutterian, Plymouth, and River branches of the Brethren. Jehovah's Witnesses claimed exemption not as conscientious objectors but as ministers, but since they would fight in their *Biblical Armageddon* or be part of the *Army of Christ Jesus* it disqualified them from the *any and all* wars criteria. 'Absolutists' refused to register. Philosophers and psychologists, such as Henry Thoreau, William James, Randolph Bourne, and Norman Thomas, as well as other secular thinkers, advocated for peace and civil disobedience. Socialists such as Eugene Debs and other members of the I.W.W. (Industrial Workers of the World) were objectors who did not believe in war out of political and humane reasons. This was a shift from the quietist stance of individual religious objection to a more vocal opposition to war for other reasons—political, philosophical, social, and economic. The government had no sympathy for those who felt conscription was against a person's Constitutional right or that conscientious objection was anything other than a religiously justified position of the established peace churches. The government's opinion reflected a prevailing culture of the time which supported a total war effort and nationwide fervor.[21]

The U.S. Supreme Court case of *Arver v. U.S.*[22] on the legality of a draft reflects this pro-war attitude. The defendant challenged Congress' right to pass Selective Service legislation, saying that conscription was a form of involuntary servitude and against the 13th Amendment. The Court, with little legal reference, glibly affirmed the Selective Service law asserting that it was obvious and practical if the Constitution gave the authority to raise a military, that it was based on precedent by previous U.S. wars and the practices of other nations, and that "the very conception of a just government and its duty to the citizen includes the reciprocal obligation of the citizen to render military service."[23] The case briefly addressed noncombatant COs, their 1st Amendment rights (freedom of religious expression), and conscription as involuntary servitude. The Court felt it "to be too frivolous for further notice," "its unsoundness is too apparent to require us to do more," and "we are constrained to the conclusion that the contention to that effect is refuted by its mere statement." They declared itself

> ...unable to conceive upon what theory the exaction by government from the citizen of the performance of his supreme and noble duty of contribution to the defense of the rights and honor of the nation as the result of a war declared by the great representative body of the people can be said to be the imposition of involuntary servitude of the 13th Amendment."[24]

In other words, the Court had no sympathy for the CO who put individual conscience above the patriotic duty of military service, and their argument was woefully empty.

Other court cases pushed objection to war from a quietist, peace church testimony to a more vocal and activist level. Louis Fraina, a political radical, challenged the government's right to recognize only religious objectors. "But since when must a man necessarily belong to a church…before he can have a conscience?"[25] Fraina said that the government "has nothing to fear from the religious conscientious objector…but it has everything to fear from the non-religious… because [he] is not interested in his conscience alone, but…is trying to overthrow a system of things that produces war and produces other evils."[26] In another Supreme Court case, Eugene Debs,[27] a co-founder of the ACLU (American Civil Liberties Union), promoted resistance to the military draft in a speech to Socialists saying, "Let us swear by all that is dear to us and all that is sacred to the cause never to become soldiers and never to go to war."[28] Because of his rhetoric, he was found guilty of sedition under the Espionage Act, sentenced to ten years in federal prison, and served over two-and-a-half years before his sentence was commuted by President Harding.[29] Roger Baldwin, another co-founder of the ACLU, refused to submit to the draft and was sentenced and served a year in federal prison.[30] Pacifism was now linked to social radicalism, atheism, cowardice, national disloyalty, and sedition.

By the end of World War I, Congress, the courts, and the general public held onto a traditional and narrow definition of conscientious objection that was based on established pacifist convictions from members of historic peace churches dating back to pre-colonial times. But objection to war was taken up by a much broader audience, both religious and secular, politically and social intolerant, and vocally dissident. These groups changed the image of a conscientious objector from a pacifist, quietist, individual position of faith to a political, public statement that some considered seditious.

The definitions, limits, and interpretations of conscientious objection continued to be challenged even after World War I. Between World Wars I and II, the courts faced additional challenges but never veered from their traditional stance on conscientious objection. In the *U.S. v. Schwimmer*,[31] a 50-year-old woman and Hungarian pacifist refused to say she would bear arms in her application for U.S. citizenship. The Supreme Court denied her eligibility affirming that "naturalization is a privilege" determined by Congress and that conscientious objection has "no constitutional provision, express or implied." It is granted only by Congressional policy.[32] A case in 1930 representing a Canadian professor at Yale Divinity School who was applying for citizenship ruled similarly.[33] He stated that he would fight only in a war he considered morally just.[34] Despite some dissent, the Court re-affirmed that conscientious objection was at the discretion of Congress. In both *Schwimmer* and *Macintosh*, the Supreme Court reversed lower court decisions which had granted naturalization.

World War II:
- The criteria for conscientious objection shifted from membership in a peace church to individual conscience based upon religious training and belief.
- A Selective Service System, an independent civilian federal agency, decided deferments at a local board level.
- Alternative service programs performing work of national importance and outside of the military were set up for those who refused being part of the military system.
- Non-religious, political, and selective objectors were still not recognized.
- The bias against COs persisted while some noncombatant COs serving in the military were awarded honors.

In preparation for hostilities in Europe, Congress passed and Roosevelt signed the Selective Training and Service Act of 1940 establishing the first peacetime conscription in U.S. history and creating the Selective Service System, an independent federal civilian agency within the Executive Branch. Initially, it required all males between the ages of 18 and 65 to register with Selective Service, conscripting all males aged 21 to 36, and then, a year later when the U.S. entered the war, it increased the age to include males 18 to 45. The Agency's National Headquarters provided directions to local boards about exemptions, but these were general in nature and each board adapted them according to its local conditions and interpretations.

On conscientious objection, Section 5(g) of the new Act diverged significantly from its 1917 World War I statute and officially made provisions for conscientious objectors. The new Act said, (italics by the author):

> Nothing contained in this act shall be construed to require any person to be subject to combatant training and service in the land or naval forces of the United States who, *by reason of religious training and belief*, is conscientiously opposed to participation in war in any form. Any such person claiming such exemption from combatant training and service because of conscientious objections whose *claim is sustained by the local board* shall, if he is inducted into the land or naval forces under this act, be *assigned to noncombatant service* as defined by the President, *or shall*, if he is found to be conscientiously opposed to participation in such noncombatant services, *in lieu of such induction, be assigned to work of national importance under civilian direction*.[35]

The first change was that a CO classification was no longer granted by being part of a group, i.e., membership in a peace church or religious organization. Instead, it was based on individual conscience: *by reason of religious training and belief*. Paradoxically, this change was advocated by peace churches themselves in the early versions of the Senate and House bills. "Raymond Wilson, a Quaker, told the House Military Affairs Committee that the statutory phrase *well-organized religious sect* would benefit Quakers 'but we do not believe that they have any right of preferential treatment. We want the consideration on the basis on conscience rather than on the basis of membership.'"[36] The 1917 statute also had the qualifying phrase *whose creed or principles forbid its members to participate in war in any form*. Dorothy Day, pacifist and editor of the *Catholic Worker* magazine, objected saying it would cover Quakers and Mennonites but excluded Catholics, since it was not part of their creed. Other religious organizations agreed, and Congress changed the requirement to *any person*.[37] Then later in 1948, Congress amended the 1940 Act and added *belief in a Supreme Being*, which was dropped over 20 years later.

Second, in contrast to World War I, a CO claim was determined by a local, civilian draft board, separate from the military. Two classifications were established. The first, known as 1-A-O, drafted COs into the military but assigned them to *noncombatant service* excluding them from combatant training or duties, such as carrying a weapon. These individuals felt a patriotic duty to serve their country but honored their religious convictions by not bearing arms or killing another. Many 1-A-Os became medics. The second group, 1-O, felt any military involvement was against their religious training and beliefs. They were granted exemption outside the military and were *assigned to work of national importance under civilian direction*, or alternative service, administered by a civilian agency or church in conjunction with the government.

Despite these accommodations, two dynamics remained the same. Conscientious objection was still based on a strict adherence to religious training and belief and the bias against COs as unpatriotic, cowardly 'slackers' continued. Alternative service and dissent were not made easy. Of the 13 million Americans who served in the armed forces between 1941 and 1945, nearly 43,000 Americans refused to fight for reasons of conscience, including an estimated 25,000 in the military as noncombatants, 12,000 performing alternative service outside the military, and 6,000 who went to prison.[38]

The alternative service program itself was a glaring example of this bias. Using the New Deal's Civilian Conservation Corps as its model, Congress created Civilian Public Service (CPS) Camps where COs performed alternative service working officially under the supervision of Selective Service, not military authority, but in reality through the auspices of church-appointed administrators, usually representatives of the historic peace churches. But, these COs received no pay and had to be supported by their church or family, even though they usually had been their families' providers. They qualified for none of the benefits given soldiers, such as life insurance or medical care. Many felt their treatment was a penalty imposed because of their pacifist convictions.[39]

The "work of national importance" initially fell under the Forestry Service, National Park Service, or Soil Conservation Service doing reforestation, agricultural experimentation, soil erosion control, and later work on farms that developed labor shortages due to the drain of men into the military. Objectors came to resent what they viewed as "make-work" to keep them out of the public eye. They demanded more useful duties in mental hospitals or in social work agencies. Some volunteered to be guinea pigs in medical experiments on malaria, hookworm, typhus, the control of lice and infectious hepatitis, diet, and endurance. Out of the estimated 12,000 in alternative service, about 500 volunteered for medical experiments and over 2,000 worked in mental hospitals.[40]

Beyond the flaws of the CPS program, non-religious, political, and selective objectors were also still not recognized. Jehovah's Witnesses, who claimed exemption as ministers, were disqualified as COs because they were required to fight at Armageddon, and therefore they were not against all wars. They accounted for an estimated 3,000 to 4,300 of the 5,300 COs put in prison. While many prisoners were paroled by the end of 1946, 455 of the 502 that remained there were Jehovah's Witnesses.[41] Before Christmas 1947, President Truman followed his amnesty board's recommendations and declined both amnesty for political objectors and a pardon for Jehovah's Witnesses. On political prisoners, it wrote:

> These were men who asserted no religious training or belief but founded their objections on intellectual, political, or sociological convictions resulting from the individual's reasoning and personal economic or political philosophy. We have not felt justified in recommending those who thus have set themselves up as wiser and more competent than society to determine their duty to come to the defense of the nation.[42]

On Jehovah's Witnesses, it said:

> While few of these offenders had theretofore been violators of the law, we cannot condone their selective service offenses, nor recommend them for pardons. To do so would be to sanction an assertion by a citizen that he is above the law; that he makes his own law; and that he refuses to yield his opinion to that of organized society on the question of his country's need for service.[43]

Non-religious conscientious objectors, who had no affiliations with recognized religions and who based claims on personal ethics or moral beliefs, petitioned the courts. Lower court decisions were contradictory. In 1943, the Second Circuit Court of Appeals found a defendant's claim for conscientious objection, while not based on church membership or training, was "deep-rooted, based…on a general humanitarian concept essentially religious in character."[44] However, the Ninth Circuit Court in *U.S. v. Berman*[45] made a stricter interpretation saying it believed Congress' intent was plain: a belief in a deity, or the *Supreme Being*, was essential. "While the defendant was opposed to all war, the court said, 'the use of the word 'religious' was not intended to be inclusive of morals or of devotion to human welfare or of policy of government.'"[46] The final decision on the matter would not come from the Supreme Court until the *Seeger* case in 1965.

On political objection, however, the same Second Circuit Court of Appeals in 1943 ruled against the defendant in *U.S. v. Kauten*, saying:

> There is a distinction between a course of reasoning resulting in a conviction that a particular war is inexpedient or disastrous and a conscientious objection to participation in any war under any circumstances. The latter, and not the former, may be the basis of exemption under the [Selective Service] Act. The former is usually a political objection, while the latter, we think, may justly be regarded as a response of the individual to an inward mentor, call it conscience or God, that is for many persons at the present time the equivalent of what has always been thought a religious impulse.[47]

In fact, every court denied the appeals of political objectors who opposed war for social or political, rather than religious, reasons.[48] But beyond its exclusion of political objectors, this case was also significant because it moved away from the narrow confines of religious defined by a belief in a *Supreme Being* and allowed for *a response of the individual to an inward mentor, call it conscience*.

Hence, while the law expanded the exemption of conscientious objection from peace church membership to individual conscience, the nation's bias against COs persisted, revealing deep suspicion that without penalties of some sort "conscience might prove a convenient disguise for cowardice."[49] That CPS men received no pay was not an oversight but an intentional governmental policy. General Lewis E. Hershey, Director of the Selective Service System, asserted that

> It would be argued that conscientious objectors were free of the risks of the GI, therefore they should not be compensated….They get no pay and…they have to be financed. I do not want to impugn the motive of anybody, but it has been a factor in not only keeping them from going [to CPS camps], but once they get there they leave, and take 1-A-O [noncombatant service] in the army when they find out.[50]

Colonel Lewis F. Kosch, speaking before the Senate Military Affairs Committee, reflected the same bias: "The very fact that a man does not get paid is one means of sorting the c.o. from the slacker."[51] Despite cases brought before federal district courts challenging the constitutionality of various aspects of the CPS program, the judiciary would not tamper with Congressional policy.[52]

A case reflecting the same bias in civilian life did reach the Supreme Court (*U.S. v. Summers*). Clyde Summers, a Methodist CO, was denied admission to the Illinois bar by its Committee on Character and Fitness that deemed him "morally unfit." Summers contested that his objection to war conflicted with the oath he would have to take to support the State Constitution which had a militia clause in it. The Supreme Court was divided 5 to 4, with the majority confirming that the bar's actions and Illinois' courts did not limit his free exercise of religion or his due process under the 14th Amendment. Essentially, the Court affirmed state's rights despite federal law that recognized conscientious objection.[53]

On the other side of the spectrum, a noncombant serving as a medic in the military was the first CO to receive the Medal of Honor. Desmond T. Doss, a 7th Day Adventist, wanted to serve both God and country, but he refused to carry a weapon. When he was drafted, he was classified 1-A-O, or noncombatant, and served as Medic Pfc. in the Philippines, Guam, and Okinawa. In the battle for Okinawa in 1945, he cared for and pulled to safety over 75 wounded soldiers from an overhanging embankment while under Japanese fire.[54] Only two other COs received Medals of Honor, both posthumously and both during the Vietnam War: Thomas W. Bennet and Joseph G. LaPointe.[55]

The Korean War - Selective Service Before, During, and After:

- The new Selective Service Act of 1948 added the "Supreme Being" clause.
- With some variation and amendments, the 1948 Act serves as the basis of today's Selective Service System.
- The act included student deferments which laid the groundwork for future deferment categories, which later were considered inequitable and unfair.
- While Congress, the Executive Branch, and the wider public remained biased against conscientious objection, the Federal Judiciary became more accommodating.

The end of World War II led immediately into the Cold War and the threat of communism. The previous Selective Training and Service Act of 1940 was allowed to expire on March 31, 1947, but when manpower fell short it was replaced by a new Selective Service Act of 1948, the second peacetime draft, which created the system that continues as the basis for today's conscription. It was reauthorized in 1951 with the outbreak of the Korean War as the Universal Military Training and Service Act and made the Selective Service System a permanent agency of the U.S. government. For the first time, full-time college students were deferred. On conscientious objection, the new acts buttressed "religious training and belief" by responding to the Ninth Circuit Court's 1946 case, *U.S. v. Berman*, and adding the clause *Supreme Being*:

> Religious training and belief in this connection means an individual's belief in a relation to a Supreme Being involving duties superior to those arising from any human relation, but does not include essentially political, sociological, or philosophical views or a merely personal moral code.[56]

During the Korean War, CO claims continued, but draft boards became more narrow and cautious in granting them. Varied interpretations of the national guidelines resulted in inconsistencies across the country regarding the determination of claims. Also at a time of McCarthyism, the government relied on secretive FBI reports for over 50 prosecutions against COs. The numbers of nonreligious, political, and selective objectors grew, as well as for the absolutist who refused to register with Selective Service, and they often landed in prison.[57] The Supreme Court also reversed its previous position about citizenship and pacifism (the *Schwimmer* and *Macintosh* cases) and held in *Girouard v. United States* that the defendant, a Canadian Seventh-day Adventist, was eligible for citizenship.[58] The Court may have been swayed by the Adventist faith's practice that encouraged draft-aged men into noncombatant service, a position entirely different from refusing noncombatant service or that of the political or selective objector.[59] Hence, the courts were sympathetic to claims based on a "force for good," a tendency that continued into the Vietnam War era, but not to the claimant who made a political judgment about which wars the government could wage.

Following the 1953 Korean War Armistice, the Selective Service apparatus was kept alive by the lobbying of its director, Maj. General Hershey, who cautioned about the looming conflict in Vietnam. He told Congress that "for every man drafted, three or four more were scared into volunteering."[60] Volunteer enlistees got preferential placement and less dangerous assignments. He reasoned that the threat of being drafted increased recruitment numbers because young men were afraid of serving in combat.

The Vietnam War:

- Several Supreme Court liberal interpretations, particularly in 1965 landmark Seeger Case, opened up "religious training and belief" to include morals and ethics.
- The Supreme Court ruled against the "Supreme Being" clause, and Congress later dropped it from the Selective Service Act.

- The courts maintained the exclusion against political and selective objectors.
- The period reflected a huge increase in war dissent, particularly among the youth and with an increase in applications for conscientious objection and "draft dodgers."
- Initially, the draft had many deferments that favored the wealthy and well-connected, making the draft open to considerable bias.
- Eventually, a lottery was established to make the draft more "fair" and equitable.
- Nixon ended the draft on Jan. 27, 1973 and allowed the Selective Service Act to expire.
- Presidential amnesties tried to restore the nation's wounds from the thousands who refused to fight, broke the law, or left the country.

The Vietnam War era was tumultuous for American society. Protest, particularly among college students, grew in intensity, forced a President (Johnson) to abandon his re-election plans, and eventually led to the withdrawal of U.S. troops from Indochina. The draft was unpopular, unfair, and inequitable. The disparity and inconsistencies between and among local boards were widespread. Deferments favored the rich and well-connected; local draft boards across the nation followed no standard policy; and thousands did not register, sought conscientious objector status, or left the country instead of facing induction orders.

But despite all this dissent, these years also saw a liberal shift in the Supreme Court and its interpretations of Congressional law, particularly on conscientious objection. This section will begin with the judiciary and then return to address the dissent.

Though a departure from the traditional or historical roots of religious pacifism, the court became more accommodating to non-religious or secular objectors. This objector stood outside an affiliation with institutional religion and instead based opposition upon his personal moral and ethical principles asserting that these beliefs were just as compelling as those held by religious objectors. At the same time, the court yielded no ground to the political or selective objector who believed some wars and violence were appropriate while other particular wars were not. These selective objectors turned away from an individual conviction of complete pacifism to a personal, sometimes qualified judgement, on society, the use violence, and the government's political decision to partake in war. The Vietnam War era saw a significant increase in both types of these objectors.

As mentioned earlier, two World War II Court of Appeals cases (*U.S. v. Downer* and *U.S. v. Kauten*) conflicted over the interpretation of religious training and belief. This discrepancy did not reach the Supreme Court until 1965 with the *Seeger* case.[61] By this time, the Selective Service Act, as amended in 1948, gave COs recognition only on the grounds of "an individual's belief in relation to a Supreme Being involving duties superior to those arising from any human relation, but [this] does not include essentially political, sociological, or philosophical views or merely a personal moral code."[62] In *Seeger* the Supreme Court struck down the requirement that a CO must affirm a belief in a Supreme Being and derive his claim from that belief. They therefore broadened the legal definition of who would be exempted as a CO. Two years later in 1967, *Supreme Being* was deleted from both the MSSA and the Selective Service CO application.

The Court said Seeger "did not *disavow* any belief 'in a relation to a *Supreme Being*,'" and stated that:

> The cosmic order does, perhaps, suggest a creative intelligence, and, therefore, his application might come under the purview of the Selective Service Act as intended by Congress. It is important Congress sets the law, and therefore the definition of conscientious objection, while the judicial branch assesses what they intended and judges whether it

is Constitutional. Therefore, the courts are generally reluctant to restrict, redefine, or second guess Congressional intent, and they leave it up to Congress to amend or pass a new law if the intent was not clear."[63]

The *Seeger* case went on to clarify and define *religious training and belief*:

(1) [Within] religious training and belief…would come all sincere religious beliefs which are based upon a power or being, or upon faith, to which all else is subordinate or upon which all else is ultimately dependent;
(2) A sincere and meaningful belief which occupies in the life of its possessor a place parallel to that filled by the God of those admittedly qualifying for the exemption comes within the statutory definition; and
(3) Does the claimed belief occupy the same place in the life of the objector as an orthodox belief in God holds in the life of one clearly qualified for exemption? [However, this belief could not be] essentially a political, sociological, or philosophical view or a merely personal code.[64]

In *Welsh v. U.S.*,[65] the Supreme Court went further by saying that the CO's claim did not even need to be religious and that *moral and ethical* was sufficient. On his CO application, Welsh crossed out *religious*; to him it was based on moral and ethical grounds. The Court agreed, including these tests:

(1) If an individual deeply and sincerely holds beliefs which are purely ethical or moral in source and content…and occupy…a place parallel to that filled by…God;
(2) Exempts from military service all those whose consciences, spurred by deeply held moral, ethical, or religious beliefs, would give them no rest or peace if they allowed themselves to become a part of an instrument of war; and
(3) The belief upon which conscientious objection is based must be the primary controlling force in the man's life.[66]

In its ruling, the Court emphasized that *depth and fervency of beliefs* were paramount.

In the following year, the same Court in *Gillette v. U.S.*[67] re-asserted that conscientious objection <u>could not</u> be based on political or selective reasons. It could not be against a particular unjust war. Instead, it "must amount to conscientious opposition to participating personally in any war and all war."[68]

The argument for political or selective objection was pushed further when David Mitchell refused to report for military induction as an opposition to U.S. foreign policy based upon international laws, treaty, and precedent, including the Geneva Convention, the United Nations Charter, and the Nuremberg War Crimes Trials. He asserted that these conventions required of him an individual responsibility to disobey illegal and immoral orders by his government or the military. His action was well beyond a CO's personal stance against <u>his own</u> participation in war but a judgement against the war itself and <u>his government's</u> participation in it. The Second District Court ruled against him, barred his lawyer from presenting evidence showing U.S. aggression or war crimes, and found him guilty of draft evasion. The Supreme Court, in March 1967, refused to hear the case, but Justice William Douglas said in his dissenting opinion that "'there is a considerable body of opinion that our actions in Vietnam constitute the waging of an aggressive war,' that Mitchell should have been allowed to introduce evidence, and that he might have been found guilty as a war criminal if he went to Vietnam as a soldier."[69]

These rulings and Congressional amendments to the Selective Service Act resulted in the following section about conscientious objection; it remains the law today:

Section 6 (j): Nothing contained in this title shall be construed to require any person to be subject to combatant training and service in the armed forces of the United States who, by reason of religious training and belief, is conscientiously opposed to participation in war in any form. As used in this subsection, the term "religious training and belief" does not include essentially political, sociological, or philosophical views, or a merely personal moral code. Any person claiming such exemption from combatant training and service because of such conscientious objections whose claim is sustained by the local board shall, if he is inducted into the armed services under this title (said sections), be assigned to noncombatant service as defined by the President, or shall, if he is found to be conscientiously opposed to participation in such noncombatant services, in lieu of such induction, be ordered by his local board, subject to such regulations as the President may prescribe, to perform for a period equal to the period prescribed in section 4(b) such civilian work contributing to the maintenance of the national health, safety, or interest as the Director may deem appropriate and any such person who knowingly fails or neglects to obey any such order from his local board shall be deemed, for the purposes of section 12 of this title to have knowingly failed or neglected to perform a duty required of him under this title. The Director shall be responsible for finding civilian work for persons exempted from training and service under this subsection and for the placement of such persons in appropriate civilian work contributing to the maintenance of the national health, safety, or interest.[70]

Dissension during the Vietnam War went beyond COs attempts for exemption. Many men burnt their draft cards in symbolic protest. In August 1965, Congress responded by making such action a felony with a maximum $10,000 fine or maximum imprisonment of five years. The courts (*U.S. v. O'Brien*) supported Congress by ruling that burning draft cards was not protected by the 1st Amendment's expression of free speech and that it inhibited the furtherance of an important government objective, the raising of an army. While the Federal government was reluctant to make arrests for such behavior, public opinion remained strong against the "dregs" of young men who burned their draft cards.[71]

Other protests grew in intensity and number. Julian Bond, an African-American elected to the Georgia state legislature, was denied his seat as a result of his public criticism of the government's Vietnam policy. Several U.S. citizens traveled to Vietnam attempting to negotiate a peace and had their passports revoked upon their return. As a protest to the war, Jane Fonda, a popular actress, went to North Vietnam and was photographed there, becoming a lightning rod to the anti-war effort. Army personnel refused to be deployed to Vietnam but were willing to go elsewhere. And Washington D.C. was the focus of large and repeated demonstrations and marches against the war.[72]

Mohammad Ali, the greatest heavyweight boxer of all time, shocked the nation when he received his induction notice, declared that he would not fight in Vietnam, and sought an exemption as a CO based upon of his religious training and belief as a Muslim. The FBI secretly recommended to his local draft board that the exemption be denied because Ali <u>did not meet any</u> of the three criteria for conscientious objection: against any and all wars, based on religious training and belief, and deeply held. When called to his induction hearing, Ali refused to take that "step forward" and become part of the military. The boxing commission revoked his boxing license, and he faced federal imprisonment. Several years later as the case went through appeals, it reached the U.S. Supreme Court. They ruled that his conviction met at least one of the criteria, namely his opposition to war was based on religious training and belief. Hence, they overturned the draft board's denial and granted him his CO status. His license was reinstated, and he continued to box. Many years later, the case was finally declassified and opened to the public.[73]

As the Vietnam War expanded and the draft inducted more men, Selective Service fell under closer scrutiny. Deferments based on family, college enrollment, or other reasons increased, and they were given subjectively and inconsistently by local draft boards. President Lyndon Johnson formed a special commission that recommended revisions to the Military Selective Service Act of 1967 (MSSA), but deferments changed little. The argument made previously by General Hershey, Selective Service Director after World War II, that the draft "forced" many men to enlist voluntarily continued, since it gave them preferential placement or less dangerous assignments. Avoiding combat by selecting one's service and military specialty led an estimated four out of 11 eligible men to enlist.[74] Also, deferments for the nation's so-called "best and brightest," called "channeling," exempted certain occupations, education, and family choices deemed "useful" to the country. Examples included technical and religious training; war industry support such as teaching, research, or skilled labor; and fatherhood, hardship, or other family deferments.[75] Those who were not well-connected or were disadvantaged educationally or economically were either unaware or unable to take advantage of these loopholes.

Pressured by an unpopular war, Johnson chose not to run for re-election in 1968. Then in December 1969 to mollify draft dissent, Richard M. Nixon, his successor, signed an amendment to the 1967 MSSA that implemented the "random" lottery system for Selective Service. His reform called for induction notices to be sent based upon a national lottery system that randomly matched numbers 1 through 365/366 to a corresponding birthdate to indicate a young man's order of selection. Each year a new lottery assigned new numbers. Secondly, a person's eligibility to be called for induction was reduced to the calendar year he turned 20. Both steps eliminated the uncertainty about if and when a person might receive an induction notice.[76] Then, in April 1970, Nixon recommended to Congress that several deferments, including those for students, paternity, and certain occupations, be eliminated.[77] It was Nixon's plan to transition the military to an All-Volunteer Force.

Between 1965 and 1973, an estimated 1.7 million men were inducted through Selective Service while approximately a half million "dodged" the draft through fleeing the country or simply refusing to report for induction. Over 200,000 men were charged with draft evasion and 8,000 convicted. (More statistics in the next section.) Under Nixon, the Department of Defense on Jan. 27, 1973, suspended the draft and the MSSA expired later that June.[78] Nixon adamantly opposed granting amnesty to those who refused to serve in the military, linking both draft evaders and military deserters into one category of law breakers. At a White House News Conference on Jan. 31, 1973, he asserted, "Those who deserted must pay their price, and the price is not a junket in the Peace Corps…the price is a criminal penalty for disobeying the laws of the United States…Now, amnesty means forgiveness. We cannot provide forgiveness for them."[79] Despite ending the draft, Nixon was still disliked for an unpopular war and, with added pressure from the Watergate scandal, was forced to resign from the Presidency on August 9, 1974.

The country was broken. The effect of an unpopular war toppled Presidents, defeated the U.S. military, and had long-range effects on Selective Service, war propaganda, and how the Pentagon would fill the ranks of service members in the future. Since then, Selective Service would become more low-key and efficient in registering young men. At the same time, the Federal government learned more effective ways to conduct war without generating great public dissent. As far as the government was concerned, mistakes, turmoil, and defeat during the Vietnam era would never happen again.

From the End of the Vietnam War to 9/11:
- Large numbers of young men sought deferments, evaded the draft, deserted, or fled to Canada or other nations.
- To heal the nation, amnesty was offered by Ford, then another version by Carter.
- Registration was briefly suspended by Ford then reinstated five years later by Carter.
- Reliance on an All-Volunteer Force met enlistment needs for the few limited or minor military engagements between Vietnam and 9/11.
- CO criteria did not change but, without a draft, Selective Service made it a moot point; they provided no administrative mechanism to document a CO claim at registration time.
- A conscientious objection discharge from the military remained possible for those who had a change of conscience about war, but the process was quite difficult.

The magnitude of dissent and unwillingness to fight in the Vietnam War was monumental. Some young men pursued legal channels to avoid service; others were forced to use illegal means. A demographer determined that "the two groups diverged in social class, with draft resisters being more privileged in terms of social status, wealth, education, etc."[80] Deferments were racially and economically biased, and those who had better connections and resources were more successful in avoiding induction. On the legal side, large numbers of young men sought deferments through conscientious objection or other "favored" exemptions.

Those who pursued illegal means fell into two categories. *Draft evaders* were civilians who refused to report for induction, which kept them out of military jurisdiction and therefore put them in violation of the Selective Service Act as a civil offense. *Deserters* were service members who broke military law by refusing to report for duty or going AWOL (Absent Without Leave) or UA (Unauthorized Absence). Some hid within the United States and changed their identities; others fled the country, mostly to Canada and some to Sweden. In Canada, draft evasion was not a criminal offense, but desertion from the military was. However, according to the extradition treaty between the two countries it was not a crime for which an offender could be extradited back to the U.S. The Canadian government chose to maintain the right to prosecute deserters, but it did not. Under public pressure, border guards did not ask questions.[81]

The reported numbers of draft evaders and deserters are unreliable and vary considerably. For example, in expressing his opposition to amnesty, President Nixon referred to "those few hundreds who went to Canada or Sweden."[82] Non-government sources say the numbers were much higher. A collection of statistics, their sources, and a comparison to World War II numbers appears in the endnotes.[83] As a summary, these include:

> - 1,857,304 men were drafted between 1964 and 1973.
> - 209,517 accused draft offenders were in violation of Selective service.
> - 360,000 men were never charged with a Selective Service violation.
> - 444,000 incidents of military desertion occurred, accounting for 322,000 different service members.
> - 100,000 less-than-honorable military discharges occurred.
> - 20,000 to 50,000 men relocated to Canada, either as draft dodgers or deserters, and another 20,000 fled to other countries or hid in the United States.
> - 4,404 deserters went or attempted to go to foreign countries.
> - 736 draft dodgers and 5,555 military deserters participated in Ford's clemency program.
> - Under Carter's amnesty, 95 men asked for pardons and 85 men returned from exile.
> - 171,000 COs were granted by local draft boards through Selective Service, representing about **9.2 percent of those drafted**.
> - 3,275 service member CO discharges occurred after induction into military. *(See sources in Endnote)*

In comparison, 34 million men were affected by Selective Service during World War II. In that war, about 50,000 service members deserted, of which 20,000 were tried; 72,354 men applied for CO status of which 25,000 accepted noncombatant service. A research group estimated that for World War II, COs "comprised just 0.0029 percent of all men required to register"[84] compared to 9.2 percent who were granted CO status during Vietnam.[85] While comparisons and statistical analysis between the two wars are based on unreliable and varying numbers, it does show that Vietnam represented a much higher incidence of dissention.

Though Nixon ended the draft while in office, his Presidential successors went further to heal the nation's wounds of dissent. In September 1974, President Gerald Ford offered a qualified amnesty to draft evaders and military deserters not yet convicted or prosecuted,[86] but it came with three conditions: (1) they must present themselves to the U.S. Attorney before Jan. 31, 1975; (2) they must acknowledge their allegiance to the United States; and (3) they must complete two years of alternative public service under the auspices of Selective Service. Deserters would be given an 'undesirable discharge' until they completed their alternative service then would receive a 'clemency discharge,' neither of which would entitle them to VA (Veterans Administration) benefits. In lieu of some alternative service, consideration would be given for military service satisfactorily completed. Ford said in his proclamation that "desertion in time of war is a major, serious offense; failure to respond to the country's call for duty is also a serious offense,"[87] but he wanted to give "these young people a chance to earn their return to the mainstream of American society" and that "reconciliation calls for an act of mercy to bind the Nation's wounds and to heal the scars of divisiveness."[88] Many evaders and deserters acted out of their consciences and regarded Ford's conditional amnesty as an admission of wrongdoing and alternative service as a punishment, so they did not take advantage of the President's offer. Then, in March 1975, Ford terminated the Selective Service registration process, "In order to evaluate an annual registration system…and will be replaced by new procedures which will provide for periodic registration."[89]

In January 1977, over two years after Ford's conditional amnesty program and as soon as he was elected, President Jimmy Carter issued a "full, complete, and unconditional" pardon without the requirement of public service for all those who had evaded the draft.[90] Carter, unlike Nixon, interpreted pardon as meaning that what you did, whether right or wrong, was forgiven. However, his amnesty only applied to those who had refused induction, and therefore were still civilians. The amnesty also excluded anyone convicted of a violent offense against Selective Service and any service member who deserted while in the military. Then, in February 1980, two months after the Soviet Union invaded Afghanistan and as a show of military strength and readiness, Carter sought to reinstate Selective Service registration, seeking both funds from Congress and the inclusion of women in registration.[91] In June of that year, Congress approved funding for Selective Service, but only for men. Carter wasted no time, signed his proclamation on July 2, and registration for men started again July 28, 1980.[92]

Carter's attempt to include women set in motion an unintentional and inadvertent precedent. A number of men challenged the new act's constitutionality as a violation of the 5th Amendment's Due Process Clause, and their objection was sustained by a district court. However, in June 1981, the U.S. Supreme Court in *Rostker v. Goldberg*[93] ruled in a 6-3 decision to overturn the lower court. As in previous cases, the Court gave considerable latitude to Congress regarding national defense and reiterated several precedents:

- In no area has the Court accorded Congress greater deference than in the area of national defense and military affairs;
- This Court must be particularly careful not to substitute its judgment of what is desirable for that of Congress;
- Congress carefully considered whether to register only males for potential conscription or whether to register both sexes, [and]…since women are excluded from combat service by statute or military policy, men and women are simply not similarly situated for purposes of a draft or registration for a draft;
- [This is not] the accidental byproduct of a traditional way of thinking about women;
- [Therefore,] Congress acted well within its constitutional authority to raise and regulate armies and navies when it authorized the registration of men and not women.[94]

The Court's ruling was based on military need, not equity *since women are excluded from combat service by statute or military policy.* This is critical in light of the Pentagon's recent change allowing women to fill combat roles. *Rostker v. Goldberg* is no longer valid. Either an amended MSSA by Congress will require women to register or the case will be challenged again in the courts.

The Vietnam War era and the end of the draft set a second, unanticipated precedent that would be used extensively after 9/11: Stop-loss orders. Out of fear that the military would not be able to maintain quotas and retain experienced personnel, Congress, in 1984 and under Title 10, Section 12305,[95] gave "Stop-loss authority" to the President and the Department of Defense. Essentially, Stop-loss prevents service members from separating or retiring once their required term of service is complete. It was first used minimally during the 1990/1991 Gulf War by George H. W. Bush, then again by Bill Clinton in Bosnia and during the Kosovo Air Campaign. Then, after 9/11, George W. Bush used it excessively as a "back-door draft." This policy gave legal justification to retain soldiers during the wars in Iraq and Afghanistan and gave the Bush administration an alternative to reinstating a military draft which would have been both unpopular and political suicide.

During the 1980 Presidential campaign, Ronald Reagan promised to abolish Selective Service, but when elected he did not. In fact, during Reagan's tenure two critical Congressional amendments were passed denying eligibility for certain federal programs to those men who did not register for Selective Service. The Solomon Amendment of 1982 blocked federal student aid, and the Thurmond Amendment of 1985 disqualified a non-registrant from federal training and jobs. Many states passed similar laws, and by 2016 most states also linked Selective Service registration automatically, and often unknowingly, to young men applying for a state driver's license.[96] While these are additional penalties for failing to register, Selective Service does not refer to them in a punitive way. Instead, they say, "Register to be eligible for benefits and programs linked to registration."[97] Yet, prior to Solomon and Thurmond, these programs went to every young person, regardless of compliance with registration. The Center of Conscience & War makes a strong legal argument that these amendments violate the fundamental principle of innocent until proven guilty and that a person should not be punished unless found guilty in a court of law.

> Laws that deny education, employment, or other opportunities amount to an unacceptable burden upon those individuals who cannot in good conscience register…This practice of penalization without prosecution or conviction…penalizes people in ways that are unrelated to their alleged offense (for which they have not been charged) [and] runs counter to our fundamental system of law and our notion of justice.[98]

When Nixon ended the draft in January 1973, his goal was to make the military an All-Volunteer Force (AVF). The AVF was never supposed to replace any future draft, which was left ready in case of a national emergency and call to arms. Therefore, Selective Service remained a fully funded, fully staffed department within the Executive Branch. Its annual FYE' 16 budget, for example, was $22.9 million. In addition, to fill the ranks of an AVF, the Pentagon relied on a recruitment budget of about $6 billion a year to entice enlistees with sign-up bonuses, money for college, health benefits, and job training. For several decades, the AVF worked effectively because of the country's minimal and short-term military engagements, including Lebanon (1982), Grenada (1983), Panama (1989), the Gulf War in Kuwait and Iraq (1991), Somalia (1993), Haiti (1994), Bosnia (1994-95), and Kosovo (1999).

Without a draft and with the reliance on the AVF, conscientious objection for civilians became, in the eyes of Selective Service, a moot point, and unfortunately it did for the public too. Now, conscientious objection is an issue only within the military and only for those men or women who have a transformation of conscience and can no longer participate in war. When confronted with the outbreak of the Gulf War in 1991, for example, over 2,500 service members filed for CO discharges. Since recruits must acknowledge when they sign their military enlistment agreement that they are not conscientious objectors, the procedure for a re-classification must show a change in beliefs after they join. Many CO applications were lost; processing regulations were ignored or delayed; and many were imprisoned. In the end, only an estimated 111 service members were recognized as COs. Others went AWOL—Absent Without Leave.[99]

After 9/11, everything changed. The Bush administration invaded two nations in wars that exceeded estimates of time, resources, blood, and treasure, and they underestimated the resolve and smoldering upheaval in the countries they occupied. But the Bush administration, remembering the political and military debacle of Vietnam, was never going to call for a draft and instead relied on other strategies to maintain a fighting force, pushing the limits of an All-Volunteer Force. The landscape of war became privatized. For those service members unwillingly caught in these wars, conscientious objection remained their only legal option.

The PBS documentary, *Soldiers of Conscience*, reported on the increase of CO applications since 9/11 among service members and the difficulty for them to get a CO discharge.

> During the wars in Afghanistan and Iraq, far fewer soldiers made it through the process to become conscientious objectors. In 2006, the Army reported only 42 applications, of which 33 were approved. Advocates and outside observers argue that these numbers are artificially low because they reflect only those soldiers who complete the lengthy application process. According to the Center on Conscience and War, they received one to two calls per month to their GI Rights Hotline in 2000 and 2001 from someone in the military raising questions of conscience. By 2002 and 2003, they were receiving at least one to two such calls per day.[100]

Quaker House, another major hub of the national Hotline, found similar trends—a spike in CO applications and the difficultly in having them processed. The counselors reported that Command would too often misplace an application, forcing an applicant to start over, or that a chaplain would doubt the CO's conviction and sincerity. As the wars waged on and deployments and combat conditions took their toll on service members, the Hotline saw another shift—increased numbers of desertions and AWOL calls. The PBS special paralleled their experience:

> The conflicts in Afghanistan and Iraq have been the occasion for a growing number of desertions—defined by the military as soldiers absent without leave for more than 30 days. In 2006, the Army reported 3,196 desertions, a sharp increase from two years earlier, which saw 2,357 desertions. At the same time, the number of prosecutions for desertion went up, a move described by military lawyers as an effort to discourage soldiers from leaving their assignments. AWOL calls also peaked during this time period throughout the Hotline.[101]

Summary:

Over the course of 360 years, conscientious objection has been a thorn in the side of the government. Conscientious objection is not a Constitutional right. It is established by Congressional legislation, and a new Congress can eliminate it. While provisions legally accommodated the convictions of pacifists, and especially for the "peace churches," the exemption stayed narrowly confined to religious training and belief, and, during the Vietnam era was expanded to include moral and ethical beliefs. Despite legal recognition, the conscientious objector is still frowned upon and ostracized by the wider public as unpatriotic and/or cowardly, especially in times of war. From the beginning, both the political or selective objector and the absolutist have never been given legal status. The law is consistent. The individual does not have the right to judge whether military intervention by the government is just or even wise. This person is often prosecuted and thrown in jail. The objector's claim must be universally against any and all wars, and the person must submit to the authority and regulations of Selective Service to be granted a CO exemption.

Especially since 9/11, the AVF and the way our government conducts war is very different. Stop-loss orders, outsourcing to contractors, repeated deployments, use of Special Forces, drone warfare, and training that teaches recruits to kill reflexively has created a more professional and privatized "Total Armed Force." Private armed security guards are employed not only by the Department of Defense but also the Department of State, USAID, and other agencies replacing roles traditionally held by and under the authority of the Pentagon. The guards also are not held to the same standard of military conduct yet often have complete immunity.

The Government today is also more careful and astute in framing public opinion about war. Journalists are embedded with the troops so their reports are sanitized. Pictures show precision "smart" bombs but not the aftermath of death and destruction. Embarrassing incidents, including the extent of torture and civilian casualties, are hidden under the realm of "state secrets." Death and injuries to private contractors are not reported along with the numbers of military service member losses. World War II was won with successful propaganda but the Vietnam War was lost because of public dissent. Archibald MacLeish, Assistant Director of the Office of War Information during World War II spoke of the importance of propaganda when he said, "The principal battleground of this war is not the South Pacific. It is not the Middle East. It is not England, or Norway, or the Russian Steppes. It is American opinion."[102]

In a similar way, the Pentagon has learned how to control the media and what to keep out of the public awareness. Selective Service, too, changed as well. It is automatic and hidden. As we have become a "war illiterate" nation, conscientious objection now is fading from our consciousness, and the public, including peace churches, are more fragmented and disinterested in laying its foundation among our young people. A lack of attention and passion may affect legislation where Congress and the political process may no longer find it necessary, as it did through the centuries, to safeguard a CO exemption with Selective Service law.

Hopefully, this brief history will remind readers that conscientious objection is a testimony of hope and peace, declaring that war is not the answer and shining a beacon of light for all of humanity to see.

Endnotes:

[1] Schlissel, Lillian. (1968). Conscience in America: A Documentary History of Conscientious Objection in America, 1757-1967. New York, New York. E.P. Dutton & Co., Inc., pp. 15-18.
[2] *Ibid.*
[3] *Ibid.*, p. 15.
[4] *Ibid.*, pp. 17-18; 28-33.
[5] Fisher, Louis. (2002). Religious Liberty in America: Political Safeguards. Lawrence, Kansas: University Press of Kansas, pp. 82-83.
[6] Webster's New World College Dictionary, Fourth Edition. 2001. Foster City, CA: IDG Books Worldwide, Inc.
[7] Schlissel, pp. 28-30.
[8] PBS Special. 2000. *The Good War and Those Who Refused to Fight It.* Independent Television Service, USA.
[9] Madison, James. 1789. *Proposals to the Congress for a Bill of Rights. Annals of Congress: The Debates and Proceedings in the Congress of the United States*, Vol. I, First Congress, First Session, June, 1789. As quoted in Schlissel, p. 47.
[10] Fisher, pp. 84-87.
[11] *Ibid.* pp. 83-84.
[12] Schlissel, p. 57.
[13] U.S. Congress. 1863. *Thirty-Seventh Congress, Session III, Ch. 74, 75*, March 3, 1863. Retrieved from http://legisworks.org/sal/12/stats/STATUTE-12-Pg731.pdf.
[14] Zinn, Howard. 2005. A People's History of the United States. New York, New York: Harper Collins Publishers, pp. 235-6.
[15] Schlissel refers to several documents from the time. See Document 14a-3, Legislation Providing Noncombatant Service for Conscientious Objectors, pp. 96-101; Document 15, *From Cyrus Pringle, The Record of a Quaker* Conscience, pp. 102-111; Document 19, *From the Diary of Himelius M. Hockett*, pp. 121-124; Document 20, *Quaker Memorial to Jefferson Davis Concerning Draft Laws*, pp. 125-6.

[16] U.S. Congress. 1917. *Selective Service Regulations, 1917.* pp. 55-56. Retrieved from https://ia600200.us.archive.org/14/items/cu31924020164152/cu31924020164152.pdf.

[17] *Ibid.* p. 56.

[18] Schlissel, p. 131; also found in *Conscription in the U.S.*, Wikipedia, ref. #15. Retrieved from https://en.wikipedia.org/wiki/Conscription_in_the_United_States

[19] Schlissel. pp. 130-2.

[20] Schlissel, p. 131; also found in *Conscription in the U.S.*, Wikipedia, ref. #15. Retrieved from https://en.wikipedia.org/wiki/Conscription_in_the_United_States

[21] Fisher. *op. cit,* From Chapter 4, *COs in the History of U.S. Law*, pp. 91-96; also in Schlissel, pp. 128-175.

[22] *Arver v. U.S.*, 245 U.S. 366, 1918. Retrieved from https://supreme.justia.com/cases/federal/us/245/366/case.html.

[23] *Ibid.*

[24] *Ibid.* See also Fisher, pp. 91-96.

[25] *Fraina et al. v. U.S.* (255 Fed. 28, 2nd Cir, 1918). Found in Schlissel, pp. 182-186.

[26] *Ibid.* See also Fisher, pp. 91-96 and Schlissel, pp. 178, 182-186.

[27] *Debs v. U.S.* (249 U.S. 211, 1919). Retrieved from https://supreme.justia.com/cases/federal/us/249/211/case.html.

[28] Debs, Eugene. *Appeal to Reason*, newspaper, Girard, Kansas, August 28, 1915, p.1. Retrieved from https://www.newspapers.com/newspage/67311719/.

[29] Schlissel, p. 129-30.

[30] Schlissel, p. 132, 142-149. See also The Individual and the State: The Problem as Presented by the Sentencing of Roger N. Baldwin, New York, 1918.

[31] Schlissel, p. 179.

[32] *U.S. v. Schwimmer* (No. 484, 279 U.S. 644, 1929). Retrieved from http://caselaw.findlaw.com/us-supreme-court/279/644.html and https://supreme.justia.com/cases/federal/us/279/644/case.html.

[33] Schlissel, p. 179.

[34] *U.S. v. MacIntosh* (283, U.S. 605, 1931). Retrieved from https://supreme.justia.com/cases/federal/us/283/605/case.html

[35] U.S. Congress. *The Selective Training and Service Act of 1940.* 76th Congress, Chs. 719, 720, September 13, 16, 1940. Retrieved from http://lawandthemultiverse.com/wp-content/uploads/2011/07/selective-training-and-service-act-of-1940.pdf.

[36] Fisher, p. 97.

[37] *Ibid.*

[38] PBS Special. 2000. *The Good War and Those Who Refused to Fight It.* Independent Television Service, USA. *Also in Schlissel, p. 214.*

[39] Schlissel, p. 20 & 215.

[40] Schlissel, p. 215; see also in Schlissel, Doc. 36, *Reports of Superintendents of State Mental Hospitals on the Work on Conscientious Objectors, 1943-45*, pp. 234-241.

[41] Schlissel, p. 180, pp. 216-217.

[42] Sibley, Mulford Q. and Phillip E. Jacob, *Conscription of Conscience: The American State and the Conscientious Objector 1940-1947*, p.505, as quoted in Schlissel, p. 217.

[43] Sibley and Jacob, p.507, as quoted in Schlissel, p. 217.

[44] *U.S. v. Downer* (135 F.2d 521, 1943).

[45] *U.S. v Berman* (156 F.9d 377, 1946).

[46] *U.S. v Berman* (156 F.9d 377, 1946), as quoted in Schlissel, p. 255.

[47] *U.S. v. Kauten* (133 F. 2d 703, 1943). Quoted in Schlissel, pp. 254-255 and Retrieved from http://www.leagle.com/decision/1943836133F2d703_1612/UNITED%20STATES%20v.%20KAUTEN

[48] Schlissel, p. 181.

[49] Schlissel, p. 20.

[50] Schlissel, p. 216; Doc 35, Testimony before Congressional Subcommittees on Conscientious Objectors, 1941, 1942, pp. 225-233.

[51] *Ibid*, p. 216.

[52] *Ibid.* p. 216.

[53] Schlissel, p. 180; referencing Doc 32, p. 204-209. Also *U.S. v. Summers*, 325, 561, 1944. Retrieved from https://supreme.justia.com/cases/federal/us/325/561/case.html.

[54] See video at www.desmonddoss.com; See also newspaper article, *Desmond T. Doss, 87, Heroic War Objector, Dies*, NY Times, 3/25/2006, Richard Goldstein.

[55] Selective Service. Retrieved from https://www.sss.gov/Alternative-Service/CO-Story-1.

[56] Selective Service Act of 1948, Public Law 759-80th Congress, Title I, Section 6 (2) j, Retrieved from http://www.loc.gov/rr/frd/Military_Law/Morgan-Papers/Vol-I_PL-759.pdf.

[57] Schlissel, p. 217.

[58] *Girouard v. United States* (328 U.S. 61, 1946).

[59] Schlissel, p. 180.

[60] House Committee on Appropriations Hearings. (1958). Retrieved from https://en.wikipedia.org/wiki/Conscription_in_the_United_States.

[61] *U.S. v. Seeger* (380, 163, 1965). Retrieved from https://supreme.justia.com/cases/federal/us/380/163/case.html.

[62] U.S. Congress. (1948). *Military Selective Service Act of 1948.* Public Law 759 – 80th Congress, Chapter 625 – 2nd Session, S. 2655. https://www.loc.gov/rr/frd/Military_Law/Morgan-Papers/Vol-I_PL-759.pdf.

[63] Schlissel, p. 255; See also *U.S. v. Seeger* (380, 163, 1965).

[64] *U.S. v. Seeger* (380, 163, 1965). Retrieved from https://supreme.justia.com/cases/federal/us/380/163/case.html.

[65] *Welsh v. U.S.* (398, U.S. 333, 1970).

[66] *Ibid.*

[67] *Gillette v. U.S.* (401, 437, 1971).

[68] *Ibid.*

[69] Schlissel, p. 258; See also Schlissel, pp.257-8 and 283-295 citing *U.S. v. Mitchell* (354, F. 2d 767, 1966); and *Mitchell v. U.S.* (Memorandum Case No. 1012); and *U.S. Supreme Court Reports* (18 L ed. 2d, April 14, 1967, pp. 132-33).

[70] The Military Selective Service Act, 1950, Section 6(j), as amended by Public Law 112-166, Aug. 10, 2012, printed February 5, 2016. Retrieved from http://legcounsel.house.gov/Comps/Military%20Selective%20Service%20Act.pdf):

[71] Schlissel, p. 256.

[72] Schlissel, p. 258-259.

[73] *Clay, aka Ali v. United States* (403 U.S. 698, 1971).

[74] Useem, M. (1973). Conscription, Protest and Social Conflict: The Life and Death of a Draft Resistance Movement. New York: Wiley; and Oi, W. 1982. *The Economic Cost of the Draft*, in M. Anderson (ed.), The Military Draft: Selected Readings on Conscription. Stanford, CA: Hoover Institution Press, pp. 317–346). Cited in https://en.wikipedia.org/wiki/Conscription_in_the_United_States

[75] https://en.wikipedia.org/wiki/Conscription_in_the_United_States.

[76] Selective Service System. https://www.sss.gov/About/History-And-Records/How-The-Draft-Has-Changed-Since-Vietnam. See also Richard Nixon, Executive Order 11497, *Amending the Selective Service Regulations to Prescribe Random Selection*, November 26, 1969, retrieved from http://www.presidency.ucsb.edu/ws/?pid=106002.

[77] Nixon, Richard. 132- Special Message to the Congress on Draft Reform. April 23, 1970. Retrieved from http://www.presidency.ucsb.edu/ws/?pid=2483.

[78] http://www.britannica.com/topic/Selective-Service-Acts.

[79] Ripley, Anthony. (Feb. 1, 1973). *Nixon, Restating Opposition to Amnesty, Stresses Punishment*, New York Times.

[80] Jones, John. (2005). Contending Statistics: The numbers for U.S. Vietnam War Resisters in Canada. Vancover: Quarter Sheaf, p. 74. Retrieved from http://www.vcn.bc.ca/~jjones/vwrcencyc.html.

[81] Keung, Nicholas. *Iraq war resisters meet cool reception in Canada*, Toronto Star, Aug. 20, 2010; and see also *Iraq Draft Evasion*, https://en.wikipedia.org/wiki/Draft_evasion.

[82] Ripley, Anthony. *Nixon, Restating Opposition to Amnesty, Stresses Punishment*, New York Times, Feb. 1, 1973).

[83] Jones. *op. cit.* and also Jones, John. *Historical Notes on Vietnam War Resister in* Canada, Vancouver Community Network, created February 2006, http://www.vcn.bc.ca/~jjones/hstrnt.html. In his in-depth analysis, Joseph Jones, from the Vancouver Community Network, composed these numbers from various sources:

- "Canada's *Immigration Statistics* show that about 16,000 American males aged 19-25 formally immigrated to Canada in the period 1966-1972."
- "An official U.S. review of the data cites 209,517 cases of accused draft offenders and 100,000 less-than-honorable military discharges for absence offenses – a total that exceeds 300,000. By the 1977 Carter pardon, the same source estimates a total of 11,000 American offenders at large, the 'overwhelming majority' in exile."
- Many draft evaders were not in violation of the law: some left the U.S. in opposition to the War, others anticipated a draft offense that never occurred, and still others mistakenly assumed they committed a draft offense.
- "For the Ford clemency program, an official U.S. review of the data cites participation by 736 draft offenders and 5,555 deserters. (These figures include some 2,000 exiles.) In the first six months after the Carter pardon, 95 individuals asked the Justice Dept. for pardon certificates, and 85 exiles made a permanent return to the United States. On June 1, 1978 the U.S. Immigration and Naturalization Service stopped keeping records, having tallied the return of 381 men, of whom 114 intended to remain in the United States."
- Jones concluded that combined evidence pointed to "an estimated a range of 20,000 to 40,000 relocated to Canada."

Other sources post these figures:
- Baskir and Strauss projected that 30,000 of the 210,000 Americans accused of dodging the draft left the country (Baskir, Lawrence and Strauss, William. (1987). Chance and Circumstance: The Draft, the War, and the Vietnam Generation. New York: Alfred A. Knopf.

- "Of the 1,857,304 people drafted between 1964 and 1973, about 210,000 were believed to have violated the Selective Service Act—though only 4 percent of those were actually convicted. At least 30,000 were believed to have fled the country, many to Canada" (Pusey, Allen. *Jan. 21, 1977: Carter pardons Vietnam-era draft* dodgers. Posted Jan. 1, 2014, http://www.abajournal.com/magazine/article/jan._21_1977_carter_pardons_vietnam-era_draft_dodgers)
- "All in all, about 100,000 Americans went abroad in the late 1960s and early 70s to avoid being called up… For its part, the U.S. government continued to prosecute draft evaders after the Vietnam War ended. A total of 209,517 men were accused of violating draft laws, while another 360,000 were never formally charged… In the end, an estimated 50,000 draft dodgers settled permanently in Canada" (Glass, Andrew. *Carter pardons draft dodgers Jan. 21, 1977*, 1/21/08 Posted on Politico, http://www.politico.com/story/2008/01/carter-pardons-draft-dodgers-jan-21-1977-007974).
- John Hagan, a sociologist, estimated that approximately half of the evaders returned to the U.S. from Canada after the 1977 pardon (Hagan, John. 2001. <u>Northern Passage: American Vietnam Resisters in Canada</u>. Cambridge, MA: Harvard University Press).
- "In total, some 100,000 young Americans went abroad in the late 1960s and early 70s to avoid serving in the war. Ninety percent went to Canada… In addition to those who avoided the draft, a relatively small number—about 1,000—of deserters from the U.S. armed forces also headed to Canada… For its part, the U.S. government continued to prosecute draft evaders after the Vietnam War ended. A total of 209,517 men were formally accused of violating draft laws, while government officials estimate another 360,000 were never formally accused…. Though many transplanted Americans returned home, an estimated 50,000 settled permanently in Canada." An "estimated 500,000 to 1 million active-duty personnel went AWOL (absent without leave) or deserted during the war" (History.com staff writers. *January 21, 1977: Carter Pardons Draft Dodgers*. http://www.history.com/this-day-in-history/president-carter-pardons-draft-dodgers
- "A total of 170,000 men received C.O. deferments; as many as 300,000 other applicants were denied deferment. Nearly 600,000 illegally evaded the draft; about 200,000 were formally accused of draft offenses. Between 30,000 and 50,000 fled to Canada; another 20,000 fled to other countries or lived underground in America" (Swarthmore College Peace Collection. *Conscientious Objection in America*. Retrieved from https://www.swarthmore.edu/library/peace/conscientiousobjection/co%20website/pages/HistoryNew.htm).
- "A total of 170,000 men received CO deferments; as many as 300,000 other applicants were denied deferment. Nearly 600,000 illegally evaded the draft; about 200,000 were formally accused of draft offenses. Between 30,000 and 50,000 fled to Canada; another 20,000 fled to other countries or lived underground in America" (*Recruits: Conscientious Objectors*. Retrieved 6/25/16 from http://www.nebraskastudies.org/0800/frameset_reset.html?http://www.nebraskastudies.org/0800/stories/0801_0107.html).
- Citing a DoD report *Incidents of Desertion: Fiscal Years 1959 through 1975, dated 8 October 1975*, Bruce Bell claimed, "Between 4 August 1964 (Tonkin Gulf Resolution) and 28 March 1973 (withdrawal of U.S. forces from Vietnam), there were more than 507,000 incidents of desertion within the Department of Defense (DOD). When this figure is adjusted for multiple incidents by the same individual, there were about 444,000 individual deserters. The comparable figures for the Army alone are 367,000 incidents and 322,000 individuals… Between June 1966 and March 1973, DOD found that 4,404 individuals (2,374 from the Army) had gone or attempted to go to foreign countries. At the end of the period (1973), 2,705 were still at large overseas. Most (71%) were in Canada; the remainder were in some 58 countries" (Bell, Bruce. October 1979. Research Report 1229, *Characteristics Of Army Deserters In The DoD Special Discharge Review Program*. Personnel and Training Research Laboratory U.S. Army Research Institute for The Behavioral And Social Sciences; 5001 Eisenhower Avenue, Alexandria, Virginia 22333, Office, Deputy Chief of Staff for Personnel, Department of the Army. Retrieved 6/25/2016 from http://www.dtic.mil/dtic/tr/fulltext/u2/a078601.pdf).

Compared to World War II, these numbers show a much higher incidence of dissention, "with conscientious objectors comprising just **.0029 percent of all men required to register** (The Gale Group, Inc. *Conscientious Objections*. Dictionary of American History, 2003. http://www.encyclopedia.com/topic/conscientious_objector.aspx). In WWII, "the Selective Training and Service Act of 1940 dictated the terms by which more than 34 million American men, ages 18 to 44, participated in the war effort. Of the men who registered for the draft, there were 72,354 who applied for conscientious objector status. Of those, 25,000 accepted noncombatant service in the army, agreeing to work for the medical Corps or in anything that did not involve actual combat. Another 27,000 failed the basic physical examination. In the end, 6,086 C.O.s (4,441 of them Jehovah's Witnesses) went to prison for refusing to cooperate with Selective Service. Another 12,000 men entered Civilian Public Service (CPS)" (Swarthmore College Peace Collection. *Conscientious Objection in America*. Retrieved from https://www.swarthmore.edu/library/peace/conscientiousobjection/co%20website/pages/HistoryNew.htm). Reports claim that 50,000 American soldiers deserted of which 20,000 and were tried and sentenced. Forty-nine were sentenced to death, though 48 of these death sentences were subsequently commuted. Only one was executed for it, Eddie Slovik (Glass, Charles. The Deserters: A Hidden History of World War II. https://en.wikipedia.org/wiki/Desertion).

[84] The Gale Group, Inc. (2003). *Conscientious Objections.* Dictionary of American History. Retrieved from http://www.encyclopedia.com/topic/conscientious_objector.aspx.

[85] Baskir, Lawrence, and Strauss, William. Chance and Circumstance: The Draft, the War, and the Vietnam Generation. New York: Alfred A. Knopf. 1987.

[86] Ford, Gerald. 78 - Proclamation 4313, *Announcing a Program for the Return of Vietnam Era Draft Evaders and Military Deserters,* Sept. 16, 1974. Retrieved from http://www.presidency.ucsb.edu/ws/?pid=4714

[87] *Ibid.*

[88] Ford, Gerald. *Remarks on Clemency for Vietnam Era Draft Evaders.* Sept. 16, 1974. Retrieved from http://millercenter.org/president/ford/speeches/speech-3522.

[89] Ford, Gerald. Proclamation 4360, *Terminating Registration Procedures Under Military Selective.* March 29, 1975. Retrieved from http://www.presidency.ucsb.edu/ws/?pid=23818.

[90] Carter, Jimmy. Executive Order 11967: Proclamation 4483, *Granting Pardon for Violations of the Selective Service Act,* January 21, 1977). Retrieved from https://www.justice.gov/pardon/proclamation-4483-granting-pardon-violations-selective-service-act.

[91] Carter, Jimmy. *Selective Service Revitalization Statement on the Registration of Americans for the Draft.* February 8, 1980. Retrieved from http://www.presidency.ucsb.edu/ws/?pid=32906.

[92] Carter, Jimmy. Proclamation 4771 *Registration Under the Military Selective Service Act.* July 2, 1980. Retrieved from http://www.presidency.ucsb.edu/ws/?pid=44697.

[93] *Rostker v. Goldberg*, 453 U.S. 57, (1981). Retrieved from https://www.law.cornell.edu/supremecourt/text/453/57.

[94] *Ibid.*

[95] Henning, Charles, Specialist in Military Manpower Policy. *U.S. Military Stop Loss Program: Key Questions and Answers.* CRS Report Prepared for Members and Committees of Congress. July 10, 2009. https://www.fas.org/sgp/crs/natsec/R40121.pdf.

[96] Selective Service. *Other Legislations by States, Territories, and the District of Columbia.* Retrieved from https://www.sss.gov/Registration/State-Commonwealth-Legislation/Other-Legislations.

[97] Selective Service System. *Benefits and Penalties.* https://www.sss.gov/Registration/Why-Register/Benefits-and-Penalties.

[98] Center on Conscience and War. *Selective Service Registration: Coercion of Conscience.* 2015. Retrieved from http://www.centeronconscience.org/co/conscientious-objection-and-the-draft/320-selective-service-registration-coercion-of-conscience.html. See the entire article for their detailed argument.

[99] Marsh, Michael. (1992). *Breaking Ranks with the Gulf War.* Viet Nam Generation Journal and Newsletter, V3, N4, January 1992. Retrieved from http://www2.iath.virginia.edu/sixties/HTML_docs/Texts/Scholarly/Marsh_Ranks_Gulf_War.html; and PBS. *Soldiers of Conscience,* Premiere: Oct. 16, 2008. http://www.pbs.org/pov/soldiersofconscience/background.

[100] PBS. (2008). *Soldiers of Conscience,* Public Broadcasting Station. Premiere: Oct. 16, 2008, http://www.pbs.org/pov/soldiersofconscience/background/

[101] *Ibid.*

[102] MacLeish, Archibald, Assistant Director of the Office of War Information, 3/19/1942, speaking of the importance of propaganda during World War II. A display from the 82nd Airborne and Special Forces Museum in Fayetteville, NC, home of Ft. Bragg

CO Letters Documenting a Claim

Letters written by young men and woman during the past 14 years are verbatim,
while omitting some identifying information.
See also the DVD *Excerpts from Our CO Letters*

Letter #1:

I am writing this letter to document my declaration as a conscientious objector and to ask for your support in doing so. Becoming a conscientious objector has been a pressing issue for me because I recently turned eighteen and had to register with Selective Service.

I have been attending the ANYTOWN Friends Meeting since birth and was raised with Quaker values of non-violence. I am opposed to war in all forms. I do not support any war for any reason. I believe that there is the light of God in every human being. Therefore, all humans share a spiritual connection no matter what race, gender, or any other classification they happen to be. Harming another human being not only hurts the victim, it harms the perpetrator as well. Since all people are spiritually connected, it is unnatural and emotionally traumatic to the perpetrator to hurt someone else. I know personally that when I get really angry and mentally wish harm to someone else, very quickly afterwards I reassess the situation and feel sick for ever wishing harm to someone else. To be put into a position where I was ordered to kill another human being would be a violation to my soul and everything I believe in.

I do not feel that I could serve the military in either a combatant or noncombatant role because even if I wasn't directly killing people, I would be helping other people kill people. These are my own personal beliefs and I respect other individual's right to choose whether or not to participate in a war effort. However, I myself do not wish to ever aid any war and will not participate in a war in any supportive role.

Letter #2:

On DATE, of this past year I turned 18 years old and am, therefore, required to register for the selective service. Due to my beliefs as a Quaker, I will be writing that I am a conscientious objector on the selective service form. Unfortunately, the registration form does not ask for this information specifically, and I am in need of a record of my convictions. I ask that two representatives of this Meeting serve as witnesses to my testimony, and that Meeting keep a copy for permanent records.

Although I firmly believe that the truth will continue to reveal itself to me, I can state now and with clarity my current beliefs. I disdain and refuse to personally participate in war of any form. This conviction was founded on the religious instruction and training I have received during my short life. The community of the Meeting Houses in ANYCITY and here in ANYTOWN, along with LOCAL Friends School, have taught me to appreciate and foster peace in every act I perform. I learned a respect for all human life, and that we were all connected through the bond of God in each and every one of us. I sincerely feel that I do not have the right, God given or otherwise, to take the life of another human being.

Please accept this letter as a declaration of my convictions. I hope in the future this country and the world will actualize the potential of peace, and that military action will finally be seen as a problem, not a solution. I thank you for your willingness to stand with me in witness of my convictions.

Letter #3:

In early 20XX, I registered to vote. At the same time, I registered with the Selective Services. Because it is not possible to make a statement of beliefs when registering for the draft, I feel the need to express mine now, for the record.

I am opposed to war in all forms, and I do not believe that it is ever acceptable or justifiable to take the life of another human being. This ethical and religious belief is deeply seated in my upbringing in the Religious Society of Friends, or Quakers. I attended a Quaker school from pre-school until middle school, and have been attending the meeting for more than a decade; because of this, the Quaker community has heavily influenced my personal beliefs. Quakerism is founded upon the firm belief that there is that of God in every person. This sentiment is in direct opposition to the practice of war. Also finding its roots in Quakerism is my belief that war is never the answer, and that there is a nonviolent solution to any conflict.

War, as a phenomenon, is never innocuous and is inherently an ineffective means of problem solving. To quote Martin Luther King Jr., "Violence ends up defeating itself. It creates bitterness in the survivors and brutality in the destroyers." Defeat doesn't end in a sudden epiphany on the part of the subdued.

In addition, there is a great deal of hypocrisy in our legal system. Killing, when the victim is another American, is punishable by death. Killing when ordered by the Pentagon, is cause for a medal. This superficial distinction is only caused by completely subjective point of view, and does not constitute an adequate reason for taking another's life.

In conclusion, I am firmly opposed to the participation in war. I could never reconcile the taking of another life with my own religious beliefs or morals. Because of this, I consider myself a conscientious objector.

Letter #4:

My beliefs at this time are still crystallizing. I don't know at this time in my life if I would register as a CO, but I do know that I could not kill a person while participating in war. I am against the present war in Iraq, not because of a political stance, but because it is the only war I am presently witnessing. Therefore, it is the war in Iraq that has made me think about my own views about personal participation in war.

I am a Quaker and was raised under certain beliefs that are common to our meeting. One of the most important for me is that killing another person is unacceptable. This does not mean that I would refuse to join the military. Innocent people get injured in war, and I feel an obligation to help and to serve my country. However, this obligation falls short when it comes to taking someone's life. My dad was in the Air Force. I respect his views but sometimes they stand against typical Quaker views. So, at this point in my life, if I were drafted, I would seek 1-A-O status, in which I would participate in the military but would refuse to be a combatant. I could serve as a medic or a similar role which would be consistent with my current beliefs. I would like to thank the meeting for support and to ask the meeting to please keep this letter for documentation.

Letter #5:

On DATE, I turned 18 years old and am required to register for the draft under the Selective Service code. On the registration form, I will indicate my status as a conscientious objector. Although the form does not ask for this information specifically, I need a record of my convictions. In this regard, I ask that two representatives of the meeting serve as witnesses to my testimony. I also request that the meeting keep a copy of this letter and my witnessed registration form as a permanent, secure record.

While my beliefs continue to crystallize, I can state the following as a basis of my current position:

- I have a deep, firm, and fixed belief against personal participation to war in any form. I believe that there is that of God in everyone and therefore killing another human being is considered murdering something divine. Any institution that supports war and the violation of this principle, or is involved in it directly or indirectly in any way is against my beliefs.
- This conviction is based upon my moral, ethical and religious training and beliefs. From the age of three to the age of fifteen I attended LOCAL Friends School, the Quaker school in my community. I was raised a pacifist and taught Quaker principles in this environment, as well as others. My father is a Quaker, and I have attended Friends Meeting in ANYTOWN, NC, my

entire life. Through many experiences and teachings I have come to consider myself a quaker and a member of the meeting.

- I sincerely feel that I was not raised to harm others and that no person has the right to take another person's life. I am not a violent person and try to surround myself with people who are open minded and tolerant, and whom seek solutions that respect the rights of all others. I want to lead my life answering that of god in everyone.

Please accept this letter and a copy of my Selective Service registration form as record of my convictions. I sincerely hope our country will pursue peaceful means to resolve conflict and that a military draft and war will not be necessary. In the meantime, I thank you for your willingness to stand with me in witness of my beliefs.

Letter #6:

Tomorrow, DATE I will turn 18 years old and will be required to register with the selective service. It feels unnerving and disturbing to me that young men my age can be called by the draft to fight in war, to risk their own life and to take the lives of others.

For much of my life the US has been at war, but as a child war seemed distant and imaginary. Now, I have peers who will join the military. I would be considered eligible for the draft. I can [hardly] imagine what it would be like to fight in a war. What would it be like to be ordered to shoot at another person? How helpless would it feel to know that I was responsible for someone's death? How could I fight in war?

I value human life. I'm amazed by the compassion humans can show. I'm fascinated by the curiosity and wonder with which we explore the world. I'm proud of what humans can create, invent and imagine. My moral framework is centered around my value for human life. I believe that by being nurturing towards others I can create a mutually beneficial future. How could I destroy the lives of humans when they give me meaning? How could I fight in a war?

I try to maintain a generosity of spirit. When I meet someone I make a certain set of assumptions; I assume that they are unique, they are interesting, they have value and they have made mistakes. I believe that if I listen to the needs of others then I can resolve conflict. How could I view other people as enemies if I recognize the uniqueness and humanness of individual people? How could I fight in a war?

I could not participate in a war of any kind. I love life too much. Not just my life, but human life in general. My conscience will not allow me to participate in War. I recognize that sometimes people need to use protective force in matters of self-defense. I know that there is violence in this world, but I also know that there are empowering peaceful alternatives.

I was fortunate to grow up in a nurturing and peaceful environment; everyone deserves to feel safe, to feel loved. Growing up with friends meeting helped build my moral framework. I give my thanks to friends like Curt and John were there to listen to my thoughts.

My parents and the environment I grew up in played a large role in forming my views. Many of the folk songs we sang when I was a child had messages about peace. I remember the day before my seventh birthday was also the day before the US went to war in Iraq. My mom and I went to a peace vigil and sang, "Every man neath his vine and fig tree, shall live in peace and unafraid."

Music has always been important to me. When I was 13 I discovered a topical singer song-writer named Phil Ochs. His music and convictions influenced mine. Songs like "I ain't a marching anymore." and "What are you fighting for?" gave a melody to my beliefs about violence and war.

I gained perspectives by reading about conflict and nonviolence. One book I read, "Beyond War", described from an anthropological perspective how humans are capable of resolving conflicts without war. Books like that expanded and impacted my thinking.

While I learned my beliefs and moral frameworks from my parents and my community, I want to be independently consistent and critical. I want to be able to discern for myself what is a productive way of looking at the world. To some extent I have been freely able to introspect on my own thoughts and values and decide how they fit together with the world. I try to test my moral frameworks and values against other philosophies and systems of thinking.

One perspective I find useful as a test of moral decision making is to ask whether an action is Universalizable. What would the outcome be if everyone took a certain action or if everyone used a certain decision making strategy? Fighting in a war is not universalizable: at the extreme, in a war in which everyone fought, everyone would die. In contrast if everyone refused to fight in a war, there would be no war.

There are many sides to human nature. I focus on the nurturing and caring side of human nature, because I believe it is possible to amplify and encourage those characteristics. It is true that humans are capable of both wonder and of atrocity. By being nurturing towards other people, by providing people with positive ways to fulfill their needs, and by providing the resources and infrastructure for nonviolent conflict resolution it is possible to lessen the likelihood of violence among individuals and among nations.

Central to my being is that I value life and I am optimistic of other humans. I could not fight in a war. Both economically and socially I will avoid contributing to war. I wish to help humans have a better chance. I want to build, create and imagine because there is so much more that is possible.

Letter #7:

I turned 18 years of age on DATE. This is a time when young men are required to register with Selective Service. I registered as required, but feel it is necessary for me to put forth my beliefs so that they can be known to all.

I am opposed to war. I do not see how in this modern world when we can communicate with others so easily how conflict is needed. Added to the fact that we now have the ability to destroy our own world, how can sensible beings be willing to take such a risk by indulging in conflict.

I believe that everyone should have the right to make his or her own choices in life.
I think that war puts people in inhuman situations. Placing young men and woman in situations where they must do things that go against what they would consider common decency in any other situation.

Presently, as presented in this country, war is conducted in a manner in such a fashion that people don't really understand all the horrible results of war. People do not realize how war forces people from their homes, causes great harm to people living near it and participating in it.

The violence that takes place in a war is rooted in anger, and this anger is spread by war becoming a poison to our greater community. I've seen this anger while living in Africa and how it can spread from person to person, as each new person in the chain is hurt. And the anger does not die over time. After a war it is rare that people confront this poison in the population with reason, understanding and compassion and thus it never goes away. It grows in a community until something happens and the community releases the anger back into the world through more violence beginning a cycle of war, Diaspora, and hate.

I would like to request that the meeting keep a copy of this letter to document my beliefs.

Letter #8:

On DATE, it became my legal obligation, as a male and United States citizen, to register with the selective service. During this process, it was brought to my attention that the registration form does not take into account the participant's moral, ethical, or religious position on war. Therefore, this letter should be read as an addendum to my registration form and documentation of my opposition to war and violence.

It is my firm understanding that I could never kill, or be involved in the killing of, another human being. This feeling is rooted in my moral belief that all people should be treated equally and the idea that there is that of god in everyone. William Penn famously once said, "True godliness does not turn men out of the world, but enables them to live better in it and excites their endeavors to mend it." This quote resonates strongly with me and speaks for the Quaker value of equality. Similarly, Jesus Christ once said, "thou shalt treat thy neighbor as thyself." Both of these quotes advocate nonviolent conflict resolution and compassion for all people.

During my time at The NAME OF INSTITUTE, a small Quaker school focused on peace, justice, and sustainability, my views on the United States military became much clearer. One project that made a significant impact was a documentary about military recruitment in public high schools. Every day soldiers across seas are subjected to horrible atrocities that will scar them for the rest of their lives. According to a study by the RAND Corporation, twenty percent of Iraq and Afghanistan veterans have reported symptoms of Posttraumatic Stress Disorder or serious depression. While I would never claim that this experience made me an expert on the subject, the interviews I filmed, that included seven high school students, a conscientious objector, an army recruiter, a teacher, and the director of Quaker House, certainly broadened my understanding and helped strengthen my opposition to war.

If I am allowed to stay true to my moral, ethical, and/or religious values, then it is obvious to me that I cannot in good conscience serve in the United States army or any instrument of war. While I hope that the Department of Defense never decides to reinstate the draft, I hope that, if they do, my personal values are not overlooked and that I am given conscientious objector status.

Letter #9:

I am writing now to make known my opposition to war and my decision to declare myself a conscientious objector.

While I only started attending this Friends Meeting last year, I was raised at the LOCAL Friends School from the time I was three years old until last school year, and Quaker values and practices have always made up a huge part of who I am. I do not know what God is, except that a piece of this being exists inside me, and it will not allow me to kill another human being, or to condone killing done by another man or woman.

One of my central tenets is that every human being has a Light within them; that all of these Lights are connected, and that by its very nature war disrespects this unity. My belief is not pacifism in the sense of non-action: I believe that evil must be resisted, but only with nonviolent means. Ends do not justify means. I also hold that achieving peace is impossible through violence: so much that is called peace is simply the exhausted rest of enemies, instead of the problem actually solved.

As I cannot support war, I cannot allow myself to take a noncombatant role in the military. That would be hypocritical and cowardly. It would allow me to keep the blood off my hands while in actuality supporting the war. When soulless aliens made in the image of machines invade earth, I will fight them with all the cruel means our modern military has discovered, but until then I must stand aside.

I cannot deny that some of my ethical and spiritual beliefs have changed during my life, at least cosmetically, nor can I deny that they will continue to change. This is called growing. If anything, they are getting only even more contra to war and more rooted in Quakerism and other nonviolent beliefs. I still cannot answer to what I would have done had I been alive during history's many conflicts in order to solve them, and it will surely take time before I can. All I can say now is what I believe at this time, and that my current beliefs have deep roots in my life as a whole.

In conclusion, I recognize that I am taking a stance that is considered pure silliness by the larger segment of the population. However my moral duty is not to follow what anyone else believes is right, but it is instead to do to the best of my ability what I believe is right. My belief in the Inner Light of every human testifies that peace is possible; that it is possible to the exact extent that we believe it so and are willing to act on it with love and humility. I ask for you to stand by me just as I will stand by my beliefs should a military draft be reinstated. I also ask that this letter and a copy of my Selective Service change of information form be kept in the Meeting records.

Thank you very much for your time and support,

Letter #10:

On DATE of this year, I turned 18 years old. I knew this age was a special age for many reasons; one being the age that one must begin thinking of registering for the selective service, for the males at least. As of turning 18, I knew I wanted to set an example for other women. So, I ask that this meeting keep this letter as documentation of my beliefs.

Whenever the idea of war would come up, I always knew where I stood. I've been raised a pacifist through the ideas and morals I was taught since birth. I attended LOCAL Friends School, the local Quaker school, from the age of 3 to 13. In school, we were taught such things as words before violence and other peaceful ways. As well as LOCAL Friends School, I've attended the Religious Society of Friends Meeting since birth. Both my mother and father were Quakers and taught me the pacifist morals I have today. I sincerely consider myself a Quaker, and in that, will not take the life of any human being.

This moral belief comes from my belief that there is that of God in everyone. In believing in God, I believe that He/She has put Himself/Herself in everyone because every person is of divine presence. Therefore killing any other human being is murdering a beautiful creation of God. God gave men and women life and only His/Her hands can take it away without the help from any violent act.

Although I am not required to produce this letter, I feel strongly about stating my views. I believe that everyone has a voice to be heard and everyone's opinion is of great importance. One never knows what may happen, and it is always good to prepare for anything that may occur. Many women do not think about this right as they turn 18, or after. I want to be an example for other women to know that it is important for them to state their views. All people have a voice and all should be heard.

If a draft occurs and women were included, I would be morally against any physical connection with war. I am aware of noncombatant rolls that people are put in, and I will state now that I would not be involved with that either. I am strongly against any personal participation in a war or in aiding a war. I believe that I can support my country without participating in a war simply supporting those I am around in my community and my family. I can be patriotic without being involved in a war.

I promise to love and support my country forever. I am extremely proud of my country, but I believe I can show that and not be involved with or supportive of a war. I want to make it clear that although I do not support the idea of war, it does not mean that I do not respect those who are fighting for my country. I do respect that they are risking their life for my country and me, and just as I respect them, I expect them to respect my choices.

As largely praised and respected Albert Einstein once said; "I am not only a pacifist but a militant pacifist. I am willing to fight for peace. Nothing will end war unless the people themselves refuse to go to war."

Letter #11:

I am a seventeen-year-old Quaker who is rapidly approaching eighteen, when I am required by law to register for Selective Service. Because the form has no place to indicated CO status, I am asking the meeting to help support my claim for such a classification.

I am opposed to war based on my faith as a Quaker. I attend ANYTOWN Monthly Meeting, and I belong to several meeting associations--REGIONAL Young Friends and, via them, REGIONAL Yearly Meeting and Association. Quaker meetings through history have opposed war based on spiritual beliefs. Consistent with these well-accepted Quaker beliefs, I believe every human being has an Inner Light or piece of the divine in them. This is what creates goodness in every human. Some choose to display this goodness openly in their person and some choose to hide it. I feel that killing someone is a horrible act, because in doing so you are killing both part of yourself and part of the divine in the other person.

Before becoming a Quaker at the age of nine, I felt that bullying and fighting were how people got ahead, because at my elementary school bullies ruled like princes. They had gangs to keep order and

PTA parents to control the teachers. The more I saw of this the more I realized that fighting and violence were wrong. I feel it is important to state my strong objections to war and lethal violence against other human beings. In my opinion, war and lethal violence against others only begets more war and more killings. From studying world history I realize that all wars between rival civilizations only make more wars until one side kills the other side in an act of total genocide. In the words of former president James Earl Carter, "Though it may be the lesser of two evils no matter how you look at it war is evil." War and killing are evil, and there is no greater evil than to deprive someone of their life or to forcefully take a loved one from their family forever through violence. Even when it was unpopular in the flag-waving fervor of the lead-up to the Afghan war, I marched on Washington to oppose it. I was also near the front of a peace march in my hometown of ANYTOWN against the Iraq war, and I frequently discuss with my classmates my anti-war opinion.

I was inspired by the work of Gandhi from a young age and did several projects on him in elementary school. I realized war, lethal violence, and bullying were not the answer. After moving to North Carolina at the age of twelve, I became more involved in the Quaker community. I became more antiwar, and it has really changed my life.

Letter #12:

In light of our approaching 18th birthday, my male peers have been required by law to fill out a selective service form, and many have considered conscientious objection. Although I am female, and am not required to do either, I am interested in doing so to take a stand for males and females alike. I write this letter to show through my faith and personal mind that I have no wish to see myself, or others of my generation engaging in any conflict simply because my country calls it my "patriotic duty." Though I am only 17, I have lived long enough to see the violence and destruction, and I do not wish to take part in it. I am stating now, to the Friends meeting that I am personally opposed to any participation in a war and would seek claim as a conscientious objector.

Saying this I would like to explain why. Since my father met my stepmother NAME, my sister, my father and I attended her place of worship. I was six. This was The Society of Friends-Quakers-or the "oatmeal people" as my friends sometimes joke. Since then I have grown into their beliefs, finding pieces of myself along the way. We are people of peace and simplicity, and a society that does not believe in violence. Yes, it is true that I have not held these beliefs my entire life, and though I may still be searching for myself, I do know that I agree with what Quakers stand for. It was not until I found this faith that I was able to put a name to my beliefs. But even before I found my place in this faith, I have been a non-confrontational person-except maybe to my sister, but that is a different story. I was never someone to fight or get in an argument; in fact I find I try to avoid it. My nature was never one of destruction or violence. This is one reason I found the Society of Friends [to be so] receiving.

I find that I am very thankful to live in a land of the freedom and home of the brave. But as such, I do not understand why we must kill in the name of that? Why gain things by fear and brute strength, rather than by words of wisdom and empathy. Why must we pretend to be "God" to these reduced oil countries, when at home we cannot even agree on a bill to help our sick and elderly? We may have fought for our freedoms not so long ago, but why must we continue to fight when our freedom is not even at stake? When I hear on the news that these men and women give up their lives to protect our freedoms, I am confused. Our freedom is not at stake, our dignity is.

I do hope that our country never returns to the draft and that we realize there are other ways then asking for our sons and daughters to fight. I live for the day that this country is able to look down on war and violence just as we looked down on prejudice, apathy and inequality. So let this be letter and this committee be my witness, that if the day were to come when the names are drawn and the weapons are ready, I will fight to open the eyes of America, not to take another life in the name of America.

Letter #13:

As I prepare to claim myself an adult, I must face the question of how I will handle signing up for Selective Service. As a forward to this letter on my beliefs, however, I would like to mention that, when I got my driver's license, soon after my birthday on September the twenty-ninth, my personal information was sent to Selective Service through the DMV. I was told that, in order to obtain my driver's license, I was required to allow the officer at the DMV to send my information and, since the officer was just hearing the phrase "conscientious objector" for the first time, she was not able to make any kind of notation on my beliefs regarding the draft.

I hope that this letter can prove witness to my convictions against war. Primarily, I do not feel that any person has the right to take the life of another under any circumstances. All life is precious and in all people there is an inner beauty. I do not feel that I could take the life of another with the knowledge that I would be depriving the world of that person's potential for good.

To "assassinate," according to the American Heritage Dictionary, is "to murder by surprise attack, as for political reasons." This act is one I am sure most Americans would not admit to favoring. However, while one could justify participation in the killing of enemies as being for the benefit of society, I can't help but wonder if others had the same justifications for killing in the past. For instance, one can be certain that President Lincoln, having emancipated the slaves, may not have been popular with southerners of the time. My only question is, "who decides if a cause to kill is just or not?" In my mind and in my heart, I know that there is no time that the sacrifice of another's life has an acceptable justification.

In writing this letter, I am taking the time to look over criteria for conscientious objector ship, insuring [ensuring] that I truly believe myself a conscientious objector. Though my objections to war are based on morality, they are also based on respect. I trust others to treat me in the manner I want to be treated: with respect and tolerance. In return, I strive to treat others in an equally respectful manner. Included in ways to respectfully treat others, I endeavor not to use violence against other people under any circumstances. Though I may attempt to defend my kin and myself from attack, I refuse to be trained in the tactics of combat.

While I am opposed to the killing of human beings, I am not opposed to killers. This is a true statement in the sense that I continue to see killers as fellow humans. I am willing to help my proverbial brothers and sisters in any way that it is needed of me; I will gladly give their tired bodies nourishment and I would gladly tend to their ailments, if it were asked of me. I wholly disagree with war and I realize that soldiers must endure and witness powerful and grotesque hardships in carrying out their duties. My heart would be broken if I were to discover that not one person would tend to their basic physical and psychological needs. I feel proud in stating that was I to be asked to aid my brothers in having their basic needs met, I would gladly accept.

Among material I have been encouraged to consider while composing this very statement is a list of procedural items for how I should handle proving that I have some right to profess myself a conscientious objector. First on the list includes starting a record of my attendance and participation in meeting for worship, my upbringing as a Quaker, nonviolent activities that I have participated in, et cetera. Firstly, no, I do not attend Friends Meeting with the frequency of some of my fellow Friends. However, my beliefs are my own and I do not harbor them in my heart because they were put there by any religious organization. Friends Meeting has been a place for me to feel at home and to worship in the presence of those I trust. My involvement with Quaker Meeting has helped to shape me as a person, but my views on the world are entirely my own and come from within myself, not my surroundings. The fact that I was brought up in a Quaker household only provides testimony to the truth that I have been taught respect for others and the beliefs of others. Again, I am against war due to a personal truth, not because I was told that war is wrong. As for documenting my participation in nonviolent activities: I strive for all my actions to be caring actions, without violence. I have done nothing with the intention of being nonviolent, but I do everything with the intention of being loving.

So, I don't suppose I have any concrete proof that I am against all violence, including war. It is my hope, though, that this letter acts as the closest thing to proof that I can offer: my truth.

Letter #14:

I am not required at this point to re-register with selective service. Nor do I ever expect to ever be called up in a draft if it were reinstated due to a war that the U.S. was involved in or chose to become involved in or started on its own volition. Nonetheless, one never knows what future legal requirements might be instated in the future. Thus, I desire that my present thoughts are documented so that they might serve as a record of my beliefs.

I want it known that I would not engage in or fight in any war for any country, nor for that matter for any entity, group, or so called noble idea. My experiences as a full-time volunteer in Belfast and Croatia during times of civil unrest only served to solidify my belief that contributing to a cycle of violence is counterproductive. I saw whole societies torn apart by conflict and generations that only knew retaliation and bitterness that would not easily dissipate. One side's violence in a conflict is consistently justified by the violence inflicted on it by the other. Very few sides in a conflict (whether it's an individual, group, ethnic group or country) ever analyze what they have done beyond blanket statements of justification. No country or group has been above this. None.

Would I perhaps be willing to serve in a non-combat role in the military if that was an option? In short: No, I would not. Doing so, in my belief, legitimizes the military action that a country is engaging in and I am not willing to do that. Whether I was working in a position that supplied materials or arms to those on the front line or had some job that appeared non-militaristic in nature, it would still represent the first step that reinforces the soldier firing the weapon. My working in such a position would free up someone else to go fight and potentially kill in the place of me. Thus, although I may not be the one who committed the act, the result would be the same.

One can argue the concept of a "Just War" to me to no avail, because even if one feels he/she can pinpoint a "Just War" in history through well-constructed arguments, it does not follow that any individual need be compelled to fight in that war. I was not put on this earth to take another person's life. Taking another person's life, even if deemed an enemy by the country that I am a citizen of, would be something that I could not morally live with. It is as simple as that.

NOTE: The 1970 Welsh vs. U.S. Supreme Court decision, which defined objectors as "all those whose consciences, spurred by deeply held moral, ethical or religious beliefs, would give them no rest or peace if they allowed themselves to become part of an instrument of war" does a great job of encapsulating my thoughts.

Letter #15:

About a month ago, I became eighteen years of age. This means that I am required to turn in a selective service registration form within 30 days. On the form, I am going to indicate that I would like to apply for conscientious objector status even though there is no such place to indicate it on the form. I plan to fill this request in the margins. Along with several other requirements, I am supposed to prove that my beliefs are deeply held and thus need to have documentation of my intentions prior to being drafted. Because of this, I ask that two representatives of the meeting act as witnesses to my testimony of non-violence. I also request that the meeting keep a record of this letter in its lockbox for further proof of my convictions.

I understand that I am still developing my beliefs and ideas about life, and I recently met before a Clearness Committee of this meeting to further help me explore my thoughts. This meeting helped me affirm my convictions about a co- status in three areas:

- I have a deep, firm, and fixed belief against personal participation to war in any form. War and any violence should only be used as a last resort. Self-defense is the only form of violence I condone in any way, and war has virtually never been in this fashion. No war has been fought on US soil for purely self-defensive purposes since the Revolutionary War. There is always another option to violence, no matter how small a situation and I personally try to find that alternative. This is why I feel that I could not personally participate in a war. I cannot however, forcefully stop others from controlling their own lives because that would also be a form of war.

- This conviction is based upon my moral and ethical training. During my raising, I was taught never to use violence. My parents helped to show me the alternatives by never hitting me or using any violence. There are many times that I did something that another one of my friends would have been hit for, but I was never struck. This only reinforced my morals and ethics involving non-violence.
- I sincerely feel that everyone has the right to enjoy his own life without the forceful interference from others. To kill another individual, in any situation, would be to take away her chance to make her own decisions and take away any chances at future happiness and fulfillment. War kills people. While other things both good and bad arise from the outcome and the process of war, the simple fact that people die cannot be escaped. While many of these individuals decided to willfully join the fight and thus accepted that their may be a fate of death and killing, I personally could never fight without violating severely my deeply bound ethics.

Please accept this letter and a copy of my Selective Service registration form as a record of my convictions. I sincerely hope that this documentation is never going to be needed and our country will begin to look for more peaceful ways of resolving conflict. I also hope that if our country believes that war is needed that those that go off to fight, on both sides, truly believe that it is what they want. In the meantime, I thank you for your support and willingness to stand by me and my beliefs.

Letter #16:

On DATE I will turn 18. As a male in the United States of America I am required to register for the Selective Service. Because there is not a draft in effect it is not possible for me to declare myself as a conscientious objector, but I am writing this letter now as a symbol that I have and will be opposed to warfare in any form. I am asking the ANYTOWN Friends Meeting to safe a copy of this letter and support me in my stance against war.

I was born into and have grown up in a Quaker family, and because of the Quaker values have become the basis of my moral code. Among these religious beliefs are Peace, not opposite of violence, and Community, something that war tends to tear apart. These moral codes are so embedded in my everyday life that when I was given the opportunity to shoot a gun, at a target, it sent shivers down my back, and I refused to shoot it, even though the target was just a bandana. In fact I would take a shoot [shot] before I would shoot another person, even just to injure. On the same note, I find it very disturbing that people could bring themselves to shoot anyone, this is just not natural for humans. Even just wishing for someone to die is morally wrong.

In general war is not the way to solve our conflicts, violence only escalates the problem, peaceful ways will always be the best. I have grown up in a time when we live in fear of others, if we would just confront that by asking questions like why? Violence only increases fear and thus we find ourselves in a vicious circle. Not only that but our wars seem to be centered around greed, this is not a cause that I will support in any way or form. Even just being in a nonviolent position that supports the armed forces is something that I could and will not take a part in. I grew up not being willing to kill cockroaches, and to this day to see any living creature in pain is distressing to me. And one last time I will reiterate that war, and other forms of violence, is not the answer and will only increase our problems.

Letter #17:

I celebrated my eighteenth birthday in DATE of this year, and I was hoping that as I filled out my registration form for the Selective Service System that you would stand by me as I claim my status as a conscientious objector.

I am personally opposed to any and all war, however I do not look down on those who do approve of and desire to serve in times of war. For example, one of my good friends, who lives in my neighborhood, wishes that he can one day enter the military and serve. I have known this individual for a long time, and even though I feel that he should not enter the military, I will support him no matter what he chooses to do.

I believe that my objection is based on not only my religious beliefs as a Quaker, but also on my moral beliefs as well. Growing up in a Quaker family, but having friends from many different backgrounds and religions has allowed me to realize that my beliefs would not fit in with any religion other than Quakerism. I feel that while there may not be a single being above us all who is titled as God, that there is a special entity within all of us that links us together and that that link may be called God. Thus if we are all linked together by a common thing then we are destroying a part of ourselves whenever we decide to harm another human being.

I hold these beliefs so deeply that if I was denied my conscientious objector status then I would rather go to jail and serve the time as one who dodged the draft and have my name soiled rather than take part in a situation that aids the potential harming of others.

Please support me in my decision to object to any form of participation in the military as I file for status as a class 1-O objector. I feel that while I wish to help all those who are in need, I feel like I could better achieve that goal by working in the community that I live in rather than aid a war in a foreign country.

Letter #18:

On DATE, I will turn 18 years old and am required to register for the draft under the selective service code. On this form, I will indicate that I am a conscientious objector. Phil Edmund [Esmonde] from Quaker House has advised having two witnesses also sign this form. I request that you keep a copy of this as permanent record with this Meeting.

While my beliefs continue to crystallize in my conscience, I can state the following as a basis of my current position.

I have a deep, firm, and fixed belief against personal participation to war in any form.

This conviction is based upon a religious training and belief. In particular, I was raised in a Quaker household and taught the values of a pacifist life-style. My parents never used physical violence to punish and abhor violence on others. Therefore, I was raised believing violence is wrong. It is inherently against the fundamental Quaker principle of "answering that of God in everyone."

I sincerely feel no person has the right to take another's life. I do not act violently towards others and am known among my friends for acting in this manner. I seek solutions that respect the rights of all others.

Please accept this letter and a copy of the draft registration form as record of my convictions. I sincerely hope that this country will not engage in war in the future and that this information will not be necessary to substantiate my beliefs. In the meantime, I thank you for your willingness to stand with me in this regard.

Letter #19:

I'm writing this letter to let the meeting become aware of my personal decision regarding the Selective Services. I hope this letter to be documentation of my faith, beliefs and reasons for coming to the conclusion of recognizing myself as a consciences objector.

Throughout my life as a Quaker, and a member of the ANYTOWN Friends Meeting I have become aware of my personal faith, guided by teachings of Quakerism, that have helped shape my beliefs regarding my objection to warfare, and killing of other people. I strongly believe that violence is not the answer, and there are many other ways of conflict resolution that don't entail bloodshed. The idea that killing another human being will solve a problem or justify another wrong seems unmoral, and against the teachings of God. I believe all people have that of God in them, and are to be treated with that respect, and viewed as equal under the eyes of God. And with that being the case, I don't feel I could justify killing against my faith as a mechanism of resolution.

Another option that I know many pacifists take when dealing with this situation is to declare themselves incapable of fighting in the Army, but to accept another non-combat position in the military. This is something I have considered, but realized it still undermines my faith and beliefs. To accept a noncombatant position would still be supporting the military in the greater scheme of things, and participating in the killing of others. I also feel that to accept a noncombatant position instead of fighting would be very hypocritical, and weak. I feel that my belief is strong enough that I must follow it the entire way, and not take the easy way out, by supporting the military in a noncombatant role.

This decision has come from a long process of deep thought, and inner seeking to find my true faith respecting this complicated and possibly life changing choice. I do truly believe though that this decision reflects my personal beliefs and faith towards an issue I strongly believe in. I will stand strong by my decision and endure all possible consequences that may come from it, but I will know I'm doing what I believe is right under my faith.

Letter #20:

Today, the DATE, I become eighteen years of age and as such am required to register to the selective services within 30 days. I feel that it best for me to obey this law though I am against the way I am being used to brag to other countries of the number of able-bodied men available for warfare. I am an able-bodied man but am definitely not available for war. On the registration form there is no place for my declaration of my status of conscientious objector. The military, in drafts of the past, has favored COs who provide records of their objection before the draft was instated. It makes perfect sense then that if the military wishes you to fight why then would they aid those who wish to claim CO status by making a box on the registration form. It is up to me to organize my own portfolio and I am doing that here and now by requesting that two representatives of this Quaker meeting sign as witnesses to the miracle of pacifism of a young man in today's violent world. I would also like to request that the meeting keep this letter as further record to attest to my beliefs.

With my beliefs ever-evolving it would be a most dramatic change of a magnitude I have never experienced that would sway me to believe that war was the answer. I have been raised in a nonviolent household while attending Quaker Friends meeting regularly from my role as baby Jesus in the Christmas pageant to being a Quaker teen for other Quaker youth to look to for guidance in today's war-hungry atmosphere. I became involved in anti-war protests and young friends retreats. I could not ever allow myself to participate in warfare of any form. I personally believe that there is literally the good of God in every man, woman and child and to extinguish that part of another human being would be killing my own God and therefore a piece of myself. I have asked myself what I would do with that amount of blood on my hands and guilt on my conscience and I have come to believe that I could not live with myself.

I plead with the meeting to accept this letter and a copy of my selective service registration form as a small token of my convictions concerning warfare. I only hope that more young men find themselves with similar feelings of pacifism and that our country finds more peaceful solutions to its conflicts than it has in the past. Until we find that peaceful utopia, thank you for standing behind my pacifism as a witness to its sincerity.

Letter #21:

I believe that every person, no matter what they have thought or done in their life, has a purpose in this world. By ending a life, one is taking away someone's humanity that I can and should learn from. I am not saying that everything we learn will be nice, or fun. I'm definitely not saying that the person has to be free of fault. What I am saying is that, whether or not a person is fighting for the "enemy", has committed a terrible crime, or holds a belief that we cannot condone, that person exists on this earth for a reason and should not be taken from it. These beliefs cause me to request status as a conscientious objector from all war.

I came to these beliefs throughout my life. I have always been peaceful. When I was small, I could not stand to kill anything, even bugs. I became vegetarian at the age of 9 because I could not stand to eat an animal I had seen grazing in a field. I never fought in school, or verbally abused other children. Once when I accidentally hurt my brother, I spent the next hour crying because I felt so badly about it. I learned a foundation for my beliefs within my community at the ANYTOWN Friends Meeting, where I attended with my family throughout my childhood. Quakerism is one of the traditional peace churches, and growing up in Meeting I gained a deep connection to the peace testimony. I also learned much of my nonviolence from the Quaker testimonies "equality." If I view all others as equal, how can one person deserve to live and another not? On that basis, how can killing another human being ever be okay?

I have been actively supporting groups that support nonviolence for most of my life. In middle school I supported People of Faith Against the Death Penalty during the fundraiser that takes place at my Meeting every Christmas. I had the sad opportunity to confirm how I felt about the death penalty when a close friend was killed in an accident with a drunk driver during high school. While her family initially tried to get the harshest penalties against the driver who killed their daughter, I forgave him and hoped that the court would help him redeem himself and become a fruitful part of society.

I had the opportunity to work directly with people with similar stories to the man who killed my friend the year after I graduated from college, when I spent a year working at the ANYCITY Economic Resource Center. [A]ERC is a non-profit organization in ANYCITY, North Carolina that does job training and placement for people with criminal records, substance abuse history, and mental illness. One of the biggest things I learned from my year there was that a person can do unequivocally terrible things in his/her life and still have worth as a human being. I worked with people who redeemed themselves.

I am unwilling to participate in a system that does not give the "enemy" an opportunity for redemption, assuming they need to be redeemed at all. I have experienced loss and anger in my life. I know what it is like to desire retribution. However, I do not feel that I have the right to determine whether someone lives or dies. Human beings are so complex. I cannot possibly know all the reasons for why a soldier is participating in war. Even if I did know, I do not believe any human is capable of single-minded killing. There are too many underlying reasons for every action. I do not believe that anyone is truly unforgivable, and therefore no one is worthy of death. Please accept this letter as my written statement of this belief.

Letter #22:

Although I am already eighteen years old (my eighteenth birthday was DATE) and have registered for the Selective Service, I have recently come to the decision, guided by my conscience, that I should assert my desire to become a conscientious objector, should the situation ever arise. Although there is no current legal procedure to become a conscientious objector, I need to have documentation of my convictions. In this regard, I ask that two representatives of the meeting serve as witnesses to my testimony. I also request that the meeting keep a copy of this letter and my witnessed registration form as a permanent, secure record.

Although my beliefs are constantly maturing, I can unequivocally state the following:

Ever since childhood, I have been taught, by my family and by religious instructors both Catholic and Quaker, that to harm or kill others is fundamentally wrong. I am of the belief that every human life is precious, unique, and irreplaceable, both intrinsically so and because each one of us contains something of God and reflects Him. That should never be willfully destroyed by another human being. I sincerely believe that this inherent worth of all humans extends to all people, even ones who hate my country and hate the very beliefs which I am now professing. I am guided in this by the teachings of Jesus, who said, "Love your enemies, do good to them which hate you," and "And as ye would that men should do to you, do ye also to them likewise." I deeply believe that Jesus teaches us to be opposed to any and all wars.

I do not want to go to war not so much out of fear of losing my life, but because I know I may be ordered to kill another. Jesus taught that it is hypocritical for a Christian to serve both God and human masters. "No man can serve two masters: for either he will hate the one, and love the other; or else he will hold to the one, and despise the other." It would mean betraying all my beliefs to ignore what I feel is right and follow the orders of some military officer. All these sincerely held beliefs of mine are based on my personal moral principles and on what I have absorbed throughout a lifetime of religious teaching.

Please accept this letter and a copy of my Selective Service registration form as record of my convictions. I hope and pray that the current military conflict does not escalate to the point that a draft is necessary, rather, that we try to resolve the conflict using peaceful means. In any case, I would like to express my heartfelt thanks to you for supporting me and witnessing to what I believe.

Letter #23:

Being of Quaker upbringing, I have always leaned steeply towards the side of nonviolence. Since late middle school I have never doubted that each life is beautiful and highly precious. My moral and ethical beliefs do not permit me to involve myself in the killing carried out by any organization. Therefore, I ask the ANYTOWN Meeting of the Religious Society of Friends recognize my position as a conscientious objector.

In my journeys, I have determined that so far nearly every war and act of violence has had two sides, each claiming a sacred or noble goal. One of these goals triumphs and brings happiness to its supporters while the other fails and demoralizes its followers. Regardless of the winner, shattered dreams, ruined families, and angry, violent friends of the fallen lie in the aftermath. The angry and violent friends will start another war which will shatter more dreams and ruin more families and create more angry friends that continue the process indefinitely, each time claiming another sacred or noble goal and insisting that once this goal is achieved, no more battles need happen.

I will admit that some wars saved the lives of some innocent people. For example, I respect the soldiers who were willing to give their and other people's lives to end the Holocaust. They were truly brave men and women doing what they thought was best with no regard to their personal safety. However, most of the Germans participating in the Holocaust were not so inherently evil themselves. Incredible propaganda and lethal danger to those who refused coerced many normal, everyday Germans into doing horrible acts that safe, secure Americans and Englishmen could not, and still cannot imagine. Thus, if I were to participate in the war, I would be killing, among the few real evil Nazis (assuming that anyone can be truly evil), many poor, scared Germans whose only defining difference from me was their place of birth. I respect those who, for a cause as noble as saving the Jews, ventured out onto the battlefield, but I personally would have sought to help my country elsewhere and strove to prevent future wars before they happened.

No mortal cause can be sacred enough and sure enough for me to take even one human life. I am not semi-omniscient, not godlike, not able to see into the future, and not led by anyone who is. The only things I can be absolutely certain of when I take a life is that I am shattering a dream, punching a hole in a family, and snapping a link in a circle of friends. Therefore, I, NAME cannot trust any human's cause, even an end to war and human suffering, enough to take a life or personally participate in war.

This person then updated his letter 7 years later to say:

War begets itself. In the history of violent conflict, the decision of who is right and who is wrong is always contested but the bloodshed and permanent disablement of healthy young men and women, and the violence and orphaned children is a constant. These constants become the justification for more war which brings more destruction and chaos and nourishes the seeds of hatred and animosity. It is not for me to say whether any single given war's horrors are a necessary evil in a given set of circumstances but I stand against war because the horror will continue until someone chooses forgiveness, peace, and fair treatment for all nations. It is for this reason that I conscientiously object to participation in war. Thank you.

Letter #24:

I turned 18 on DATE and through the process of seeking financial aid for college was required to register with Selective Service. I am actively opposed to warfare in any form, as well as my personal participation it, and I would rather let myself die then feel I have been directly responsible for the death of another, even if the other was deemed an enemy of the state. I am not opposed to the United States Government; I sincerely love this country, and I am proud to live here. However; I am opposed to the United States' involvements in war. I do not believe that killing is justified for any reason. Regardless of whether my family or I were in any form of a worst-case scenario, I would still choose to resolve conflicts nonviolently.

I have been regularly attending Quaker Meeting my entire life, first in ANOTHERTOWN Friends Meeting when I lived in Connecticut and now for the last eight years in ANYCITY and ANYTOWN Friends meeting in North Carolina. At first it was my parents' choice to bring me to Quaker Meeting but I have come to respect and understand the Meeting, and it is my choice to now call myself a Quaker.

I choose to call myself a Quaker primarily because I strongly agree with the Quaker belief that there exists the presence of God in <u>every</u> human being. To kill another human being is to kill part of that most sacred existence.

Outside of being active through Quaker Meeting, I have been a Peace activist for the last 5 years of my life. Having been raised a Quaker, I always found the idea of taking the life of another horrifying, but it wasn't until I was thirteen and I met several American soldiers who had recently returned from the Middle East that I fully realized my position on warfare and violence in general. These men gave me a diverse image of what warfare meant, confirmed my worst fears, and gave me new fears about war that I did not know I had. Since then, I have been regularly attending peace marches and rallies throughout North Carolina and several in Washington DC.

I have given much thought to the concept of war, and I know that I could not work in a noncombatant role knowing that I was directly supporting a cause that I did not stand for. As said before, I would rather die than feel responsible for the death of another, and if I have to go to jail to not support the spread of violence, then that is a small price to pay. This is not a judgment on others; this is simply where I stand. I believe everyone has to do what he or she believes is right, and this is what I know to be right for me.

Letter #25:

I am writing this letter to document my beliefs and feelings about selective service. I hope that this letter adequately explains my reasons for declaring myself a conscientious objector.

My entire life, I have been around nonviolent people, a nonviolent family, and most importantly, a nonviolent community. I have been a familial member of the ANYTOWN Friends Meeting of the Religious Society of Friends since 19XX, and for the last 16 years of my life, the members of the meeting have been my family. Certain people in the meeting I have labeled even as surrogate grandparents. Gerry Gourley was one of these. In fact it was at Gerry Gourley's apartment in LOCATION where I saw my first violent movie that depicted a human killing others. That movie was Bambi. Starting with Bambi, movies began to leave an indelible mark me. As I have gotten older, movies such as 'The Longest Day,' 'Saving Private Ryan,' 'Black Hawk Down,' and other 'war' movies have left their mark as well. Coming out of movies like that, with adrenaline surging through my body, I feel almost sick to my stomach. Not because of the movie theatre popcorn, but because I have just seen two hours of people senselessly killing other people in an attempt to solve problems. Ever since Bambi,

I have been drawn to war movies for the adrenaline, but repulsed by the wars and killing that they depict.

I also remember when I was a kid arguing with my little brother when we got in a fight. We would say, "I'm allowed to hit you, it's the golden rule, you hit me first." This is, of course, flawed logic and a misuse of what we had learned in First Day School that Jesus had said. 'Do unto others as you would have them do unto you.' We interpreted this as, if he hit me, I would have the right to hit him. I no longer use this childish logic, largely because of my exposure to other religions during First Day School at the ANYTOWN Friends Meeting. Not only did I learn about Quakerism, but I also learned about other cultures and religions. This teaching has helped me develop my moral sense as well as taught me tolerance of other religions. It is not only Christianity whose greatest prophet promoted the golden rule. Moses, Confucius, Muhammad, Hillel, the Hindu Mahabharata, and Buddhist texts, to name a few, all say that one shouldn't inflict on anyone else what you wouldn't want inflicted on yourself.

What my brother and I practiced was a typical version of the cycle of violence that has been happening in our world since the beginning of human history. Feelings are built up until one side or the other strikes, justified in their own minds. The other side feels it is an unjustified act, and so takes it upon themselves to right the wrong. Their retaliation feels justified, but the victims and original aggressors see only revenge. This whole process then repeats itself because it engenders more feelings of hate, and the cycle spirals out of control.

I have never been in a situation where I have had to take part in a war, but because of my upbringing I have become aware of my capacity – and the capacity of others – for compassion, and I am convinced that the only way to break the cycle of violence is by not participating in it. I believe wars take place because of the cycle of revenge that permeates almost every culture. Because of my desire to break the cycle of violence, I could not, in good conscience, take part in fighting to perpetuate this cycle, and so could not take part in any war for any country or entity at any time in my life. This includes noncombatant roles because I believe they also support the cycle of revenge.

I appreciate this Meeting's support and nurture over the past 17 years, and ask your continued support as I use the selective service registration to declare my position as a conscientious objector.

Letter #26:

I am writing this letter to document my beliefs and feelings about selective service. I hope that this letter adequately explains my reasons for declaring myself a conscientious objector.

Ever since I was a week old, and passed around my meeting as a baby, I have been a part of the ANYTOWN Monthly Meeting of the Religious Society of Friends (Quakers). This Quaker community has taught me many valuable lessons and shaped the person that I am today. One of the core beliefs of the Quaker community is that of non-violence and I have continuously learned about this belief throughout my upbringing. I practiced non-violence when I was a child by not playing with toy weapons or violent video games. As I grew older I learned more and understood more about the Quaker core belief of non-violence and practiced it in more sophisticated ways. I started to attend anti-war rallies in Fayetteville, and helped support Quaker House with service trips there. Now my religious belief has become a deep core moral belief that I believe I will hold onto forever.

I have attempted to involve myself with communities that share my belief in non-violence and I am now taking up leadership positions in these communities. I attend REGIONAL Yearly Meeting retreats and I am on the nurturing committee for that youth group. This past year I was on the nurturing committee for the Friends General Conference High School Program, and this coming summer I am going to be co-presiding Clerk for the high school program.

I also attend LOCAL Friends School, a private Quaker school, and am part of the Staff Student Discipline Committee. The Staff Student Discipline Committee is an integral part of the SCHOOL'S community and it is valued because it is the community's alternative to punishment as retribution. The Discipline Committee's purpose is to look at any given situation and make sure the entire truth is uncovered from any and all perspectives. It is the role of the committee to listen, obtain the entire truth, and then think of a consequence for the perpetrator that restores all the relationship within the community that have been broken. This consequence is what differentiates this discipline system from most because every case is looked at individually and the consequence is created to make sure the perpetrator understands what he or she did wrong. It is made so the perpetrator does not feel like he or she is being punished for what was done, but is supposed to make the perpetrator understand why what they did was wrong, and to perform restitution for any damage caused and restore relationships. When one is just punished for a something bad it is not productive at all, if someone does something bad, one should try to understand why the action was done and then try to have the perpetrator understand why his action was wrong.

My core belief in non-violence is so strong that I have begun to nurture younger members of the nonviolent communities I am in. I believe I have started to become a role model for other young Friends who are going through the same process I did of forming there [their] identities and figuring out exactly what they believe. My belief in non-violence is such a part of me, and so strong, that I could not, in good conscience, take part in any war, for any entity, at any point in my life. This would be going against who I am as a person, contradicting my moral and religious beliefs that I have built up my whole life. I could not even participate in a noncombatant role in a war because this would abet those participating in war. I appreciate this Meeting's support and nurture over the past 18 years, and ask your continued support as I use the selective service registration to declare my position as a conscientious objector.

Letter #27:

I am writing this letter to state my moral objection to violence and to declare myself a conscientious objector. I do not support war in any form, nor do I condone the use of violence. In addition to wanting to personal avoid violence, I also do not wish to support any form of violence either directly or indirectly. I believe that everyone has an equal right to life and that no one has a right to take someone's life or hurt them in any way.

I have been attending the ANYTOWN Friends Meeting since I was born. I have attended many Quaker youth retreats such as SAYF. I am currently going to FRIENDS College which is a Quaker school. My belief in nonviolence has shaped my life and is present in my daily life. I do not see violence as a just or effective solution to problems so I solve any problems that may arise in my life in a nonviolent manner. When confronted by people with aggressive tendencies, one can either respond in kind, thus escalating the situation or seek peace through a mutual understanding.

When I turned 18 over two years ago, I filled out the selective services form that is required by law to fill out. Since there was no official place to designate conscientious objector status, I wrote "I am a conscientious objector in between the lines and kept a record of it for myself. I am writing this letter now because I want to let the wider Quaker community know that these are my beliefs and I would like them to support me in them. I believe that the Quaker community has done a great deal to shape my beliefs regarding equality and non-violence through understanding people's personal experiences and meaningful discussion that allow for expression of opinions and leave room for dissent.

Letter #28:

I would like to write to you all expressing my belief in nonviolence and against war. As I am soon to turn 18 years old, I will be required to register with Selective Service. I do not believe that there is any justification for one human being to harm another. Thus, to show my opposition towards violence, I would appreciate it if the meeting would hold a copy of this letter for future reference.

I strongly object to violence on a moral and ethical basis and therefore believe that violence should never be perpetrated towards another human being. Both my parents are pacifists as well, and I have been attending either the ANYTOWN or OTHER Friends Meeting for all of my life, and both my family and the Quaker meeting have had a large impact on me. Ultimately, however, the belief comes down to a personal decision I have made. I have seen the images of war that are so readily made available by the media these days, and I have been sickened by the hate I have seen on people's faces and the horrifying result of their actions.

I fervently believe that all conflicts can be resolved nonviolently through dialogue and mediation, and that there is never an excuse to use war as a diplomatic tool. There is historical precedent for my belief as well; after the devastation of World War 1, the Kellogg-Briand Pact, signed by 62 nations including the United States, was a treaty that "provid[ed] for the renunciation of war as an instrument of national policy." This remains an internationally binding treaty; however, almost every war since the signing of the pact that the United States has been involved in has been a direct violation of this. So not only are my moral and ethical beliefs preventing me from engaging in any kind of war, there is a legal justification for my opposition to war as well.

I would like to reiterate that I do not feel as if I could ever directly be involved in any war, including any noncombatant role in the military. However, I would be glad to serve in some sort of civil service position in the United States if it was required of me. I am certainly patriotic and feel pride in my country, but I believe that there is never any reason to commit violence towards another human being.

Letter #29:

I am writing this letter to inform the Meeting of my decision concerning the Selective Service. It is among my core beliefs that violence in any form is wrong, and because of that I am going to file for conscientious objector status in the Selective Service. I ask that the Meeting support me in my decision.

I have believed in peace and nonviolence my whole life. Growing up in the Quaker Community, I was taught never to physically harm another person. Everyone has an inner light, and I have no right to hurt or take away that light.

As I have continued to grow, I have become aware of my own true beliefs. Taking into account both the ideas I have been taught and those that I have learned on my own have helped me to understand what I truly believe in. I hold true to the notion that there exists an inner light inside of everyone. It is this light that binds us together. Rather than separate individuals, we are small parts of a single entity. To harm another would be to harm myself. To kill another would be to kill a part of myself. I cannot bear to hurt the force that holds us all together, so there is no way I could participate in war of any kind.

As a conscientious objector, there is the option of participating in the military service as a noncombatant unit, such as a medic or mechanic. Although such duties are less violent than that of a soldier, they are still participating with the act of war. I cannot bring myself to be part of a war in any way, so I cannot be a noncombatant either.

It has taken me a full eighteen years to know myself well enough to truly understand my core values. I have put deep thought into my decision, and I know that I am making the correct one. As I try to picture myself in the possible future of the world, I cannot see myself taking the life of another in any situation. The act of violence goes against everything I believe in. If I am to go against my beliefs, then I am to go against myself. No matter how many people may disagree with it, I cannot go against myself. I request that the Meeting support me with my decision and that they aid me in filing to be a conscientious objector.

Letter #30:

I am writing this letter to make known to the meeting my personal decision to recognize and declare myself as a conscientious objector. As the Selective Service does not provide any official process for gaining recognition as a conscientious objector, it is up to me to organize a portfolio to document both my decision and my personal beliefs, reasons, and values that have led me to this decision. I request that two representatives of the meeting sign this letter as witnesses and also ask that the meeting keep a second signed copy of this letter as a record of my current beliefs.

Throughout my life - or at least for as long as I can remember - I have been morally and ethically opposed to violence. I believe all violence - including that framed as conflict resolution, self-defense, or fighting for the greater good - is evil, as all violence increases the pain, anger, and distrust in the world. I refuse to support such a corrosive degradation of human society and general well-being. I am especially opposed to warfare - again no matter the circumstances or justifications. I value each and every human being. It makes no difference to me what they believe, what they own, where they live, how they think, what they think of my country, or what they think about me. It makes no difference if they are freely participating in war against my country, or if they would willingly kill me. I see something - a light - that universal spark of humanity - in everybody, and I cannot, could not, and will never under any circumstances be able to bring myself to snuff out another human being and deny them the opportunity for life. Although I have always been of this mindset, my beliefs have been strengthened, bolstered, and supported by my Quaker upbringing both at home and at the ANYTOWN Friends Meeting, which I have attended since early infancy. The only thing I will agree to do to another human being is to show them compassion. Only in such a way can any improvement be made in the world. War is an evil chain - with each death, a family is ruined and friends are torn by anguish. Anger boils and the survivors seek revenge and compensation through more war and violence. The cycle continues. Some would say this is an endless circle. However, I disagree - the chain of war can be broken - but only through conscientious efforts at compassion and understanding.

I know that many other pacifists choose to accept non-combat positions in the military. I am not willing to accept such a position as I would still be supporting the activities of the military. In other words, although I, in theory, would be able to keep my own hands clean, I would still be supporting and, in a larger sense, participating in the killing of my fellow human beings. Therefore, I am claiming 1-O conscientious objector classification for exemption from all training and service in the military. In place of military service I will be happy to serve our country, and humanity as a whole, by volunteering to help change the world for the better.

Letter #31:

Let this letter document my feelings as a conscientious objector to war. I am unable to participate in any military service, or occupation that supports a military organization.
This fact is based on both my deeply held moral and religious beliefs.

My studies of the Quaker faith have shown me that violence is not a viable technique for conflict resolution, and should be avoided at all costs. Compromise, compassion, and seeking understanding are the skills used to peacefully solve problems, and are not present in the making or waging of war. Furthermore, the practices used to wage modern war are morally bankrupt. Until the 20th century, wars were waged on the battlefield with honor and adherence to the laws of war. Our modern conflicts are not regulated by the rules of yore. The consequence of this is that the common citizen is put into harm's way every day of conflict. Civilian casualties are unacceptable, and I could not bring myself to participate in any organization that brings them about.

If my country still felt that it required more service of me than my positive role in my community, I would not be objectionable to partaking in some other civil duty, such as a firefighter or foreign aid worker.

Letter #32:

On DATE, I will turn eighteen years old and am required to register for the draft under the Selective Service code. On the registration form I will indicate my status as a conscientious objector. As the form does not ask for the information specifically, I need to provide a record of my convictions. In this regard, I ask that two representatives of the meeting serve as witnesses to my testimony. I also request that the meeting keep a copy of this letter as a permanent and secure record.

While my beliefs continue to crystallize in my conscience, I can state the following as a basis of my current conviction:

I have a deep, firm and fixed belief against personal participation in war. Throughout my childhood and adolescence I have been raised to reject violence in any form. I have been taught to find a peaceful solution to any conflicts that may arise. I refuse to believe that violence, except in cases of self-defense, is ever necessary, and I believe that any situation can be resolved through peaceful means.

This conviction is based on both religious and moral training and beliefs. As a Quaker, I believe in pacifism and non-violence. I also believe that there is that of God in everyone, and therefore that if one was to attack another person, one would also be attacking God. Through my experiences with Quakerism, both at my Meeting and at school, I have often heard speakers telling of their experiences both in war and as a CO, and through those teachings I have come to fully realize that I am unable to participate in war in any form.

I sincerely believe that violence, under any circumstances, is wrong. I live nonviolently, trying to never act out of anger or aggression. I, as a human being, have no right, nor am I able, to participate in war or take another person's life. That is not how I have been raised, and that is not how I choose to live my life.

Please accept this letter and a copy of my Selective Service registration form as record of my convictions. I sincerely hope that our country will pursue peaceful means to resolve conflict and that a military draft will not be necessary. In the meantime, I thank you for your willingness to stand with me in witness of my beliefs.

Letter #33:

On DATE, I will turn 18 years old, and be required to register for the draft under the Selective Service code. On the registration form I will indicate my status as a conscientious objector, and because the form does not ask for this information specifically, I need a record of my convictions. In this regard, I ask that two representatives of the Meeting serve as witnesses to my testimony. I also request that the Meeting keep a copy of this as a permanent, secure record.

While my beliefs continue to crystallize in my conscience, I can state the following as a basis of my current position. I have a deep, firm, and fixed belief against personal participation to war in any form. This conviction is based upon a religious training and belief that I received from my parents and the Meeting. As I grew up, I attended the Meeting regularly learning about my duties to God and about my personal beliefs as a Quaker. Even though it has been hard for me to attend Meeting in the last few years, I have dedicated time each day to find a little bit of God in everything around me. From this I strongly feel that violence is not the answer. In my household, I grew up with a strict moral code, which has continued on with me to this day. I am opposed to violence and harm to others. I sincerely feel that it is not in God's wishes for a person to fight with another or even help someone harm another.

Please accept this letter and a copy of my selective service registration form as record of my convictions. I sincerely hope our country will pursue peaceful means to resolve conflict and that a military draft and war will not be necessary. In the meantime, I thank you for your willingness to stand with me in witness of my beliefs.

Letter #34:

Currently, I am not required to register for the draft because I am female. However, if society continues to progress in the direction of true gender equality, as I hope it will, I will be required at some point to register as well. Therefore, I am writing this letter to reflect upon my beliefs and express my objection to serving in the military if I was ever called upon to do so.

Growing up in a Quaker school and in the Quaker meeting, I experienced daily the power of consensus and peaceful decision making to resolve conflict and was taught that violence and retaliation are never appropriate responses to hostility. Over the years, these lessons have continued to shape my conscience and interactions. I believe war is a cornerstone in the endless cycle of brutality and conflict which has plagued the world since the invention of weapons. I cannot morally participate in and facilitate this cycle by being part of the military.

During meeting I often reflect on the welcoming nature of the Society of Friends and the importance of the prison outreach program to our community. From the meeting and the visitors from

SOME County Correctional I have learned that there is no black and white, there is no good and evil. There are only groups of people brought together by different circumstances and from different backgrounds. This central belief is what would not allow me to see our nation's declared enemies as legitimate targets of deadly force. There is nothing within me that would allow me to believe that the people I would be asked to kill, directly or indirectly, are not deserving to live.

For some people, the ability to determine whether another person lives or dies would be empowering; to me, it is repulsive. I would not be able to separate myself from my belief that there is inherent goodness within each human. I would not be able to live with myself, no matter how heroic my actions would be deemed or what victory I would help to achieve. My thoughts would immediately go toward the families who have lost a loved one and the light that I extinguished; this would pain me forever.

In this world in which we are further and further removed from the consequences of our military actions, it is growing harder to protest against serving. We are no longer asked to look the person we are attacking in the eye. This separation from our targets makes no difference to me; whether fighting on a battlefield or ordering a drone attack, I would not be able to participate in the taking of lives.

Nor do I feel I could work to support an organization that endorses killing in warfare or otherwise, even in a non-combat position. Everything I have learned as a Quaker leads me to reject the notion that killing in the name of my country is justified and as a part of the military establishment I would be endorsing that notion.

In short, my own humanity is bound with that of others and taking the life of another would take a part of me.

Letter #35:
My name is NAME, and I recently turned 18. Like most men my age in the United States, I registered with the Selective Service, as required by law. However, I am opposed to war in all forms, and I believe that it is never right to take the life of another human being. I believe that all wars are fundamentally caused by human greed and hatred, and I refuse to be used as a pawn of the United States government to further an immoral conquest of innocent lands and people.

In the television show M*A*S*H, Hawkeye Pierce states his beliefs on war: "War isn't Hell. War is war, and Hell is Hell. And of the two, war is a lot worse." When asked for his reasoning behind that statement, Hawkeye responds: "There are no innocent bystanders in Hell. War is chock full of them - little kids, cripples, old ladies. In fact, except for some of the brass, almost everybody involved is an innocent bystander." This quote perfectly encapsulates my beliefs about war. War is wrong because innocent people are hurt and killed, and for the most part, only innocent people are hurt and killed. The brass are safe in their command bunkers, while they send innocent young men out to kill other innocent young men, and "little kids, cripples, and old ladies" die in the process.

Wars simply perpetuate the cycle of violence and do not make things better for anyone. More people are still being added to the World War I casualty figures every year, 100 years later, because of the unexploded ordinance and toxic chemicals that still litter its battlefields. WWI led directly to World War II, which some use as an example of a "just war". However, ending the Holocaust was merely an afterthought as far as the causes of World War II are concerned. While America tries to claim the moral high ground, in 1939 we forced the SS St. Louis, a ship full of Jewish refugees, to return to Europe into the waiting arms of the Nazis. Another example of our failure is that whenever we criticized the Soviet Union on human rights abuses, they responded with "And you are lynching Negroes." The only reason we could claim the moral high ground during World War II was because our enemies committed the most brutal crimes against humanity in history.

I love and support the United States, my country, and its citizens. However, I could never serve in a combat role in any military organization. A noncombatant humanitarian role would be the only way I could serve in good conscience. Because of these beliefs, I consider myself a Conscientious Objector.

Excerpts from Our CO Letters (written 0-14 years ago)
Transcript of 14½-minute video (CO Letter number from group of 35)

CO Letter Writer #1—0:07

I am writing this letter to document my declaration as a Conscientious Objector and to ask for your support in doing so. Becoming a Conscientious Objector has been a pressing issue for me because I recently turned eighteen and had to register with Selective Service.

I have been attending the ANYTOWN Friends Meeting since birth and was raised with Quaker values of non-violence. I am opposed to war in all forms. I do not support any war for any reason. I believe that there is the light of God in every human being. Therefore, all humans share a spiritual connection no matter what race, gender, or any other classification they happen to be. Harming another human being not only hurts the victim, it harms the perpetrator as well. Since all people are spiritually connected, it is unnatural and emotionally traumatic to the perpetrator to hurt someone else. I know personally that when I get really angry and mentally to wish harm to someone else, very quickly afterwards I reassess the situation and feel sick forever wishing harm to someone else. To be put into a position where I was ordered to kill another human being would be a violation to my soul and everything I believe in.

I do not feel that I could serve the military in either a combatant or noncombatant role because even if I wasn't directly killing people, I would be helping other people kill people. These are my own personal beliefs and I respect other individuals' rights to choose whether or not to participate in a war effort. However, I myself do not wish to ever aid any war and will not participate in a war in any supportive role.

CO Letter Writer #2—1:45

Although I firmly believe that the truth will continue to reveal itself to me, I can state now and with clarity my current beliefs.

- I disdain and refuse to personally participate in war of any form.
- This conviction was founded on the religious instruction and training I have received during my short life. The community of the Meetinghouses in ANYCITY and here in ANYTOWN, along with LOCAL Friends School, have taught me to appreciate and foster peace in every act I perform. I learned a respect for all human life, and that we were all connected through the bond of God in each and every one of us.
- I sincerely feel that I do not have the right, God given or otherwise, to take the life of another human being.

CO Letter Writer #5—2:26

- I have a deep, firm, and fixed belief against the personal participation to war in any form. I do believe that there is that of God in everyone and therefore killing another human being is considered murdering something divine. Any institution that supports war and the violation of this principle, or is involved in it directly or indirectly in any way, is against my beliefs.
- This conviction is based upon my moral, ethical and religious training and beliefs. From the age of three to the age of fifteen I attended LOCAL Friends School, a Quaker school in my community. I was raised pacifist and taught Quaker principles in this environment, as well as others. My father is a Quaker, and I have attended the Religious Society of Friends Quaker Meeting in ANYTOWN, NC, my entire life. Through many experiences and teachings I have come to consider myself a Quaker and an integral part of the meeting.

136

- I sincerely feel that I was not raised to harm others and that no person has the right to take another person's life. I am not a violent person and try to surround myself with people who are open minded and tolerant, and I seek solutions that respect the rights of all others. I want to lead my life answering that of God in everyone.

CO Letter Writer #6—3:45

I can [hardly] imagine what it would be like to fight in a war. What would it be like to be ordered to shoot at another person? How helpless would it feel to know that I was responsible for someone's death? How could I fight in war?

I value human life. I'm amazed by the compassion humans can show. I'm fascinated by the curiosity and wonder with which we explore the world. I'm proud of what humans can create, invent, and imagine. My moral framework is centered around my value for human life. I believe that by being nurturing towards others one can create a mutually beneficial future. How could I destroy the lives of humans when they give me meaning? How could I fight in a war?

I could not participate in a war of any kind. I love life too much. Not just my life, but human life in general. My conscience will not allow me to participate in a war.

My parents and the environment I grew up in played a large role in forming my views. Many of the folk songs we sang when I was a child had messages of peace. I remember the day before my seventh birthday was also the day the U.S. went to war in Iraq. My mom and I went to a peace vigil and sang, "Every man 'neath his vine and fig tree, shall live in peace and unafraid."

CO Letter Writer #10—5:25

Whenever the idea of war would come up, I always knew where I stood. I've been raised a pacifist through the ideas and morals I was taught since birth.

This moral belief comes from my belief that there is that of God in everyone. In believing in God, I believe that He/She has put Himself/Herself in everyone because every person is of divine presence. Therefore, killing any other human being is murdering a beautiful creation of God. God gave men and women life and only His/Her hands can take it away without the help from any violent act.

CO Letter Writer #11—6:00

I am opposed to war based on my faith as a Quaker. I attend ANYTOWN Monthly Meeting, and I belong to several meeting associations—including REGIONAL Young Friends and, through them, REGIONAL Yearly Meeting and Association. Quaker meetings throughout history have opposed war based on spiritual beliefs. Consistent with these well-accepted Quaker beliefs, I believe every human being has an Inner Light or piece of the divine in them. This is what creates goodness in every human being. Some choose to display this goodness openly in their person and some choose to hide it. I feel that killing somebody is a horrible act, because in doing so you are killing both part of yourself and part of the divine in the other person.

In the words of former president James Earl Carter, "Though it may be the lesser of two evils no matter how you look at it war is evil." War and killing are evil, and there is no greater evil than to deprive somebody of their life or to forcefully take a loved one from their family forever through violence.

CO Letter Writer #12—7:08

In light of our approaching 18th birthday, my male peers have been required by law to fill out a Selective Service form, and many have considered conscientious objection. Although I am female, and am not required to do either, I am interested in doing so to take a stand for males and females alike. I write this letter to show through my faith and personal mind that I have no wish to see myself or others of my generation engaging in any conflict simply because my country calls it my "patriotic duty."

Saying this I would like to explain why. Since my father met my stepmother NAME, my sister, my father and I attended her place of worship. I was about six. This was The Society of Friends-Quakers-or the "oatmeal people" as my friends sometimes joked. Since then I have grown into their beliefs, finding pieces of myself along the way. We are people of peace and simplicity, and a society that does not believe in violence. Yes, it is true that I have not always held these beliefs my entire life, and though I may still be searching for myself, I do know that I agree with what Quakers stand for. It was not until I found this faith that I was able to put a name to my beliefs.

CO Letter Writer #13—8:17

I hope that this letter can prove witness to my convictions against war. Primarily, I do not feel that any person has the right to take the life of another under any circumstances. All life is precious and in all people there is an inner beauty. I do not feel that I could take the life of another with the knowledge that I would be depriving the world of that person's potential for good.

Though my objections to war are based on morality, they are also based on respect. I trust others to treat me in the manner I want to be treated: with respect and tolerance. I strive to treat others in an equally respectful manner, if it were asked of me.

No, I do not attend a Friends Meeting with the frequency of some of my fellow Friends. However, my beliefs are my own and I do not harbor them in my heart because they were put there by any religious organization.

CO Letter Writer #15—9:25

I understand that I am still developing my beliefs and ideas about life, and I recently met before a Clearness Committee of this meeting to further help me explore my thoughts. This meeting helped me affirm my convictions:

- This conviction is based upon my moral and ethical training. During my raising, I was taught never to use violence. My parents helped to show me the alternatives by never hitting me or using any violence. There are many times that I did something that another one of my friends would have been hit for, but I was never struck. This only reinforced my morals and ethics involving non-violence.
- I sincerely feel that everyone has the right to enjoy his own life without the forceful interference from others. To kill another individual, in any situation, would be to take away her chance to make her own decisions and take away any chances at future happiness and fulfillment. War kills people. I personally could never fight without violating severely my deeply bound ethics.

CO Letter Writer #23—10:17

I have determined that so far nearly every war and act of violence has had two sides, each claiming a sacred or noble goal. One of these goals triumphs and brings happiness to its supporters while the other fails and demoralizes its followers. Regardless of the winner, shattered dreams, ruined families, and angry, violent friends of the fallen lay in the aftermath. The angry and violent friends will start another war which will shatter more dreams and ruin more families and create more angry friends that continue the process indefinitely, each time claiming another sacred or noble goal and insisting that once this goal is achieved, no more battles need happen.

No mortal cause can be sacred enough and sure enough for me to take even one human life. I am not semi-omniscient, not godlike, not able to see into the future, and not led by anyone who is. The only thing I can be absolutely certain of when I take a life is that I am shattering a dream, punching a hole in a family, and snapping a link in a circle of friends. Therefore, I, NAME, cannot trust any human's cause, even an end to war and human suffering, enough to take a life or personally participate in war.

CO Letter Writer #19—11:22

I strongly believe that violence is not the answer, and there are many other ways of conflict resolution that doesn't entail bloodshed. The idea that killing another human being will solve a problem or justify another wrong seems unmoral, and against the teachings of God. I believe that all people have that of God in them, and are to be treated with that respect, and viewed as equal under the eyes of God.

This decision has come from a long process of deep thought, and inner seeking to find my true faith respecting this complicated and possibly life changing choice. I do truly believe though that this decision reflects my personal beliefs and faith towards an issue I strongly believe in. I will stand strong by my decision and endure all possible consequences that may come from it, but I will know I'm doing what I believe is right under my faith.

CO Letter Writer #21—12:07

I believe that every person, no matter what they have thought or done in their life, has a purpose in this world. By ending a life, one is taking away someone's humanity can and should learn from.

I came to these beliefs throughout my life. I have always been peaceful. When I was small, I could not stand to kill anything, even bugs. I became vegetarian at the age of 9 because I could not stand to eat an animal I had seen grazing in a field. I never fought in school or verbally abused other children. Once when I accidentally hurt my brother, I spent the next hour crying because I felt so badly about it

I have been actively supporting groups that support nonviolence for most of my life. In middle school I supported People of Faith Against the Death Penalty during the fundraiser that takes place at my Meeting every Christmas. I had the sad opportunity to confirm how I felt about the death penalty when a close friend was killed in an accident with a drunk driver during high school. While her family initially tried to get the harshest penalties against the driver who killed their daughter, I forgave him and hoped that the court would help him redeem himself and become a fruitful part of society.

CO Letter Writer #26—13:16

Ever since I was a week old, and passed around my meeting as a baby, I have been a part of the ANYTOWN Monthly Meeting of the Religious Society of Friends. This Quaker community has taught me many valuable lessons and shaped the person that I am today. One of the core beliefs of the Quaker community is that of non-violence and I have continuously learned about this belief throughout my upbringing. I practiced non-violence when I was a child by not playing with toy weapons or violent video games. As I grew older I learned more and understood more about the Quaker core belief of non-violence and practiced it in more sophisticated ways. I started to attend anti-war rallies in Fayetteville and helped support Quaker House with service trips there. Now my religious belief has become a deep core moral belief that I believe I will hold onto forever.

My core belief in non-violence is so strong that I have begun to nurture younger members of the nonviolent communities I am in. I believe I have started to become a role model for other young Friends who are going through the same process I did of forming their identities and figuring out exactly what they believe. My belief in non-violence is such a part of me, and so strong, that I could not, in good conscience, take part in any war, for any entity, at any point in my life.

Ends—14:43

Reflections on Writing Our CO Letters (written 0-14 years ago)
Transcripts on 18-minute tape (CO Letter number from group of 35)

Question #1: What was it like to write this letter and present it to your faith community?
CO Letter Writer #13: 0:14

Writing my conscientious objector letter was an experience of self-exploration. It prompted me to explore parts of my psyche, parts of my spirituality, that I had not before considered. It helped me a lot in reflecting on what my convictions are, what my feelings about of violence and war are. And putting my beliefs into words and giving my beliefs a voice helped me to better understand my conviction in being a conscientious objector. I read the conscientious objector letter in 2006 during Meeting for Business, and the reception that I received was one of respect one of acceptance and one of love. And, I felt heard. I felt understood.

CO Letter Writer #2: 1:28

It was sort of very cementing for me. I think I felt like it was a culmination of everything I had been doing as a young Friend up to that point and since I was graduating and heading off to college, it was like I was graduating from the Friends meeting in a way. Now that I've been supported and bolstered by the community now I was going out and standing out on my own with my own conviction.

CO Letter Writer #5: 1:57

Writing this letter was really a great experience for me. I had a chance to really look into myself and reflect on how I felt about these questions that were primarily focused at the 18-year-old guys who were in my youth group at that time. So, I think it was a really great opportunity for me to look inside myself and think about my own beliefs, and not necessarily just for the sake of stating my conscientious objector status. And from what I remember is other members of the meeting signing this letter. I think that as a young adult having the support of a group of people and of your peers, and that experience of having my seniors sign this letter and commend me for it and recognize it as something important and real was really special.

CO Letter Writer #15: 3:03

I remember there was a lot of support from the meeting and from my friends and family to help me gather my thoughts and help me put them down on paper. And I also remember that it was a little nerve-wracking to go in front of a large group of people and speak and read this letter but again everyone was very supportive throughout the whole process.

Question #2: In what ways did this process help crystallize your views about conscientious objection and the Peace Testimony? 3:22
CO Letter Writer #1: 3:28

I think before writing this letter that I agreed with the Quaker Peace Testimony, and I agreed with the values of nonviolence, but I think I hadn't really reflected on why we had those values in meeting or why those were important values to have, or how those really connected with the Quaker concept of that of God in everyone and how that was really the central tenet holding everything together of everyone has this value to them.

CO Letter Writer #10: 4:01

Through writing this letter, I was able to crystallize my ideas about conscientious objection by figuring out myself. Like I had to sit down and think, "Well, why do I want to be a conscientious objector?" And by doing that I thought, "Well, because I'm a pacifist." Because I have a moral belief against participating in war. Ah, so... I knew I was a pacifist, since I could define the word, but I don't think before I wrote my conscientious objector letter, I don't think I necessarily thought about why.

CO Letter Writer #19: 4:35

It helped crystallize my beliefs in that beforehand I knew what my beliefs were but this process really kind of brought it all together and was an avenue to let me talk about it with my family, with people in the meeting, and others. And really was just able to help me kind of establish a firm grasp of all these different parts bringing it together.

Question #3: Did the process of writing this letter change you in any way? 5:02

CO Letter Writer #2: 5:09

I'm not so sure if it changed me as much as it revealed to me what was true for myself. I think that conviction to nonviolence was sort of always present, but it just sort of became less amorphous. And, it was sorted of cemented there as "yes, this is where I stand." So, maybe more of a revealing and less of a change.

CO Letter Writer #5: 5:36

Absolutely! It really impacted in a way that it helped me to understand like as I go through life what my true feelings are about war and violence and about conscientious objection, and I think that it meant a lot to me later in my life to have this letter and to be able to go back and look on it.

CO Letter Writer #6: 5:57

It didn't so much change my ideas in terms of their substance, but it did change the way that I see certain ideas as connected. Because in the process of writing the letter, I was pushed to really understand why do I believe that nonviolence is possible; why do I believe that peace is both the most beneficial way for resolving conflict and that challenged me not just to hold beliefs but explain why I hold those beliefs.

CO Letter Writer #23: 6:36

Well, I think that I grew. I feel that I probably grew a lot because I had to think about things that I would just normally not think about and took for granted. And I understand a little bit more of the greater complexity of this issue.

CO Letter Writer #19: 6:54

I don't think it changed me but it did help me both, as I said before, to crystallize what my beliefs are and bring them into one document. And it did give me a sense of this is a path that I wanted to take, and I felt more reassured when talking to with other people outside the meeting who might not be familiar with this process and what a conscientious objector is.

Question #4: Women are not required to register for Selective Service. Why did you choose to write this letter and come before your faith community? 7:19

CO Letter Writer #5: 7:26

I think that it was something we were all coming together and doing together, and I was the only girl so I wanted to participate and I was encouraged by my youth group leader to participate if I wanted to. So, I wrote my own letter, and I think there was an opportunity for me to reflect on a lot of the same things that my peers were going through, even if it wasn't like socially or technically something that I would have to face in the near future.

CO Letter Writer #10: 7:56

I wanted to make a statement. And I thought it was important to me personally not participating in war; I am a pacifist; I have these moral beliefs and because of that I am a conscientious objector. I think everybody should stand for something in life. By stating I am a conscientious objector, I was able to take control of that life and be a powerful female.

CO Letter Writer #12: 8:24

I think it's important for women to realize that you don't have to be a man to have an opinion about war and peace.

Question #5: In what ways has this letter framed your thoughts about peace in general and the testimony of peace in particular? 8:31

CO Letter Writer #1: 8:38

Today I'm going to medical school. I think it wasn't a direct relationship to it necessarily but it did kind of put me on a path thinking about how can I best do something that, or what I really wanted in my life was something that I felt gave back to everyone, and not something like violence that takes away from your community or just the world.

CO Letter Writer #11: 9:01

It's been a while but the main tenets still stand up. I still believe that war doesn't really accomplish anything except start more wars. I also believe that killing people is wrong. There's something special about each individual person. And those basic ideas are the core beliefs, or my core beliefs on how I view the Peace Testimony.

CO Letter Writer #12: 9:33

I wasn't born into a Quaker family, I kind of came into it, because of my dad's remarrying, and so I kind of came to Quaker testimonies later as opposed to kind of like growing up with them, like the Ten Commandments, like some people do. So that was my first time really exploring the Peace Testimony specifically. It's important to embody and to constantly think about in your day-to-day life; not just about a war, but in your interaction with people.

CO Letter Writer #21: 10:05

It's helped me realize how complicated the issue is and how many aspects of my life and the world I feel like peace affects, especially thinking of it like I did in my letter from the view of equality. And then there are all the connections…, you can also make connections between what we do to nature. But I feel like the peace testimony covers so much of our world.

Question #6: Since you wrote this letter, have your beliefs and convictions changed about conscientious objection? 10:36

CO Letter Writer #19: 10:43

My beliefs have definitely not changed since this letter. I still strongly believe what I wrote. Over the past 10 years in what has happened in the world, though, I would want to see more information about what a conscientious objector is and the process and how other people can seek that process if they want.

CO Letter Writer #26: 11:09

I think my beliefs about conscientious objection have stayed fairly the same but I think one thing that this letter had help start to help with the process was, when I looked at those situations and about the Selective Service and what they market as a way of being be able to serve your country and that type of thing, that is something that I don't want to shy away from. I definitely am for service and in my whole upbringing doing service trips is that type of kind of thing is something that I've found great joy in doing and I continually want to do. So that kind of solidified that if I was going to move forward and have service as part of my life then I needed to figure out other ways to do that.

Question #7: Now that you went through this process, what would you say to others turning 18 and to men who have to register for Selective Service? 12:00

CO Letter Writer #2: 12:08

Sort of in the same way like how sometimes people think Quakers are extinct; sometimes I think people think that conscientious objectors were something that just happened in the Vietnam War. And I think it's an important question in that way for everyone to consider. So spend the time learning about what the Selective Service is, what it means to be a conscientious objector, whether you agree or disagree with it, and figure out or at least starting the process of where you stand with regards to violence.

CO Letter Writer #6: 12:32
It's very important that we think about war and we think about nonviolence. All too often it is easy for us to distance ourselves from violence because much of the war we have occurs in distant places. It occurs in other countries. I think the process of working on a CO letter can make someone a lot more mindful of that.

CO Letter Writer #1: 13:02
Well, first of all, I would say that whether you are a man or a woman, whatever your gender identity is, that this is something worth thinking about. Certainly for Selective Service but just because whether or not there ever is a draft or you have to register, it's a good thing to think about. It should really come from what you want to do. If you look within yourself and decide that you want to be a CO, this is a very helpful process, because you're not told what to think, you are not told how to do this, it's really a chance to think about what your values are and really explore them.

CO Letter Writer #11: 13:38
It's good to think about when you have that in front of you, what you believe. And I guess I'm not saying to make one decision either way. But just to really think deeply about what you believe, and meditate on it and have introspection, then decide based upon that what or how you'd like to approach it.

CO Letter Writer #23: 14:00
There is no space to write conscientious objector on the draft card, or at least there isn't a check box to check so you have to write it in. And if you are watching this video, you are probably getting all the useful advice that I could give you.

CO Letter Writer #21: 14:17
Take registering for Selective Service very seriously. We have not had a draft for years, so I know even for me the only way I even think about a draft is because I grew up in a Quaker meeting where writing a conscientious objector letter was often just suggested to our teens. But I think a lot of people don't realize what they are doing… what they are doing when signing up for Selective Service and just to recognize that not only is it possible that at any time we could have a draft again.

CO Letter Writer #26: 15:02
Going through this process really makes you go through and really dig down and see what your beliefs are and solidify those beliefs so that if you are faced with that situation or faced with that decision then you have thought about it and it's not something that you have to come up with what your beliefs are at a moment's notice. It's something that you've thought about for a longer time.

Question #8: What would you say to faith communities considering this process? 15:25
CO Letter Writer #13: 15:32
I would suggest that monthly meetings who have attendees or members who are turning 18, especially young men, provide their attendees and members with information about what options are available to young people.

CO Letter Writer #15: 15:53
I think this process is very useful for people especially to those who are around the age of 18 when they are not necessarily very good at expressing their thoughts; very good at understanding what their convictions are and whether they come out wanting to be a conscientious objector or whether they decide that violence is sometimes justifiable, they need to be able to have that opportunity to think about it. I think this process helped me, and I also think it would help people and it's a very good age to start

thinking deeply about what those beliefs are. And I think, it's very helpful to have a large group of supportive people behind you.

CO Letter Writer #19: 16:36

That it's a very important process and I think all men turning 18 should be, or should go through, or at least be aware of this process, and learn what the steps are if they choose to take this. Because at 18, if I hadn't had the meeting giving me this information, I don't know if I would have done the same thing, or if I'd have even have known that this is an available option.

CO Letter Writer #21: 17:09

I wouldn't have known that conscientious objection letters existed if my Meeting hadn't mentioned it to me. My parents didn't bring it up very often. My brother wrote one. But it was because the Meeting was so persistent in reminding us of verbally and through writing a way of expressing your beliefs about the peace testimony and expressing your beliefs in nonviolence and I mean writing something this personal and speaking in from of the entire meeting and giving your permission to have them hold on to it for however many years is a big deal.

17:45 End of CO Letter Writers; Beginning of Adult Responses

Parent (17:47):

I would recommend the process of writing conscientious objector letters to any faith community. I have really appreciated the letters that our young people have written. When those letters are read in meeting that is one of my very favorite Meeting for Worship with Attention to Business activities. And the reason for that is it's an opportunity for young people to really think about what they believe in a very structured process, and then to present what they believe to the entire community, which is really meaningful not just for the young person but for also for the whole community to hear a young person's thoughts and them articulate what it is they believe. It's almost a rite of passage for them.

Parent (18:40):

When the CO letters are read at our meeting for worship with attention to business, it is always moving to the entire room. You can just see it. We spend so much time talking about budgets, committees, you know very mundane kind of things, and there is an energy that these young people bring just by being young people. But when it is in the form of a CO letter, it is an intensely positive energy. It just brings us that hope for the future where we can have a world of peace.

One thing is clear. Jesus was a pacifist. And so many, many faith communities have a testimony on pacifism. And it's just a very practical, real world way to apply Christian principles. And we found that doing it with our young people really helps them to very seriously think about what they really believe and what it means in the world.

Parent (19:48):

I was Clerk when SON read his letter, and FATHER was Clerk when DAUGHTER read her letter. And I know for a fact that both my children gave a lot of thought and they took it very seriously and the integrity testimony was important to them that they be writing from a place of what they truly believed and not just stating what Quakers believe but they what they believe. And they were very distinct letters, and they were letters that were really them, that really represented them and their beliefs.

Adult/Elder #3 (20:24):

I am first of all impressed with the maturity of their thinking and I realize that this is a real issue facing our young people today as much as it was in my time during the Second World War. I am also impressed with the freeness that they express their deep thoughts. They have written a beautiful statement that I almost couldn't believe could come out of such young and thoughtful people.

I think people at 18 are incredibly experienced in the world. I don't think it's too soon at all to think about these issues. We see the evening news and young people need to be involved with shaping the world that they are going to live in. I like the truth seeking courage which they showed. I realized that I was on their side to make a difference and they were there and doing it.

Parent (21:37):
I don't think he would have done this by himself. I think it meant that he had to think very seriously what he believed in areas of faith, or beliefs, and values that he hadn't really explored in depth before. Not just thinking about this particular issue but in seeing himself as an adult with responsibilities to his country and to his faith community. And I think that it was a good exercise for him because he realized that it was really integrated with not just what he learned in his faith community but his experience within our family in what his grandfathers and grandmothers went through and how those faiths and beliefs are shaped not just by your family and your culture and your faith community but by the period of time in which you live.
Going through this process with my son helped me to think about it personally also, even though I'm not in that point of having to make a decision about it, it really made me reflect on my own personal faith and practices in terms of the death penalty or war or community service or patriotism. So it was helpful to me personally as well.

Parent/Elder (23:02):
We give place in this life for the development of our child. But the spirit of the child needs to be stretched, grown, and for that having that child be asked to discern what he feels about taking another's life, what he feels about conscientious objection, what he feels about these matters is a piece in the child's life. If we don't ask that question, we don't grow the child. We don't ask ourselves the most crucial questions. So for my sense, my kid was asked <u>the</u> most important question. And that's why I am profoundly grateful.

Teen Advisor (23:54)
I think that it's invaluable and that if you are a meeting that finds that the peace testimony is one of your major focuses, I would say that this is a great way of following through with that. You are allowing your youth a way to have some sort of rite of passage in a way, and not just for males but also for females as well that was important. So no matter what your gender, being able to really wrestle with or explore the peace testimony in a real way I think is valuable.
It is a great process for taking time to stop, think, reflect, make a statement, have others to hear your statement and for them to also stop, think, and reflect on what you said. And maybe plant a seed in other people's minds as well.

Parent/Author (24:55):
What has pleased me very much is that originally we did this so that young people would have documentation in case there was a draft and they wanted to make a claim to be a conscientious objector. And we thought it was really important for them to write letters before there was a draft. Should there be a draft then they could say to the draft board, "Well, three years ago when we didn't have to do this, I wrote a letter." That really shows they were pretty sincere. What I have found since is that what it has done is helped nurture the sense of nonviolence and respect for all life with our young people. And that has had a meaningful impact on them since. Doing these post-interview tapes has just been so heartwarming to me to realize that this process was valuable to them and their beliefs and their approach the world.

End (25:50)

Hebrew, Christian, and Islamic Scripture on Peace and God's Law

Bible passages from *New Revised Standard Version*; Qur'ān from *The Meaning of The Holy Qur'ān* by 'Abdullah Yūsuf 'Ali

Hebrew Bible

THE CREATION STORY: GOD CREATED ALL AND ALL OF CREATION IS GOOD
(Genesis 1:1 - 2:3). God created humankind in his image, in the image of God he created them; male and female he created them. (1:27)
God saw everything that he had made, and indeed, it was very good…(1:31)

THREE OF THE TEN COMMANDMENTS Exodus 20:1-3, 13, & 17 (also Deuteronomy 5:8-21) .
> Then God spoke all these words: I am the LORD your God, who brought you out of the land of Egypt, out of the house of slavery; you shall have no other gods before me….
> You shall not kill…
> You shall not covet your neighbor's house; you shall not covet your neighbor's wife, or male or female slave, or ox, or donkey, or anything that belongs to your neighbor.

…you shall not profit by the blood of your neighbor….but you shall love your neighbor as yourself. (Leviticus 19:16 & 18)

You shall love the Lord your God with all your heart, and with all your soul, and with all your might. (Deuteronomy 6:5)

Depart from evil, and do good; seek peace, and pursue it. (Psalms 34:14)

The LORD is good to all, and his compassion is over all that he has made. (Psalms 145:9)

Wash yourselves; make yourselves clean; remove the evil of your doings from before my eyes; cease to do evil, learn to do good; seek justice, rescue the oppressed, defend the orphan, plead for the widow. (Isaiah 1:16-17)

He shall judge between the nations, and shall arbitrate for many peoples; they shall beat their swords into plowshares, and their spears into pruning hooks; nation shall not lift up sword against nation, neither shall they learn war any more. (Isaiah 2:4)

For a child has been born for us, a son given to us; authority rests upon his shoulders; and he is named Wonderful Counselor, Mighty God, Everlasting Father, Prince of Peace. His authority shall grow continually, And there shall be endless peace for the throne of David and his kingdom. He will establish and uphold it with justice and with righteousness from this time onward and forevermore. The zeal of the Lord of hosts will do this. (Isaiah 9:6-7)

He shall judge between many peoples, and shall arbitrate between strong nations far away; they shall beat their swords into plowshares, and their spears into pruning hooks; nation shall not lift up sword against nation, neither shall they learn war any more; but they shall all sit under their own vines and under their own fig trees, and no one shall make them afraid; for the mouth of the Lord of hosts has spoken. (Micah 4:3-4)

…and what does the LORD require of you but to do justice, and to love kindness, and to walk humbly with your God? (Micah 6:6-8)

146

Christian or New Testament
THE SERMON ON THE MOUNT (Matthew 5:1 – 7:29. Also, Lk 6:17-49)

Blessed are the peacemakers, for they will be called children of God. (Matthew 5:9)

You have heard that it was said, 'An eye for an eye and a tooth for a tooth.' But I say to you, Do not resist an evildoer. But if anyone strikes you on the right cheek, turn the other also…You have heard it was said, 'You shall love your neighbor and hate your enemy.' But I say to you, Love your enemies and pray for those who persecute you, so that you may be children of your Father in heaven; for he makes his sun rise on the evil and on the good, and sends rain on the righteous and on the unrighteous. (Matthew 5:38-39; 43-45. Also Lk 6:27-36 below)

No one can serve two masters; for a slave will either hate the one and love the other, or be devoted to the one and despise the other. You cannot serve God and wealth. (Matthew 6:24. Also Lk 16:13 below)

Do not judge, so that you may not be judged. For with the judgment you make you will be judged, and the measure you give will be the measure you get. Why do you see the speck in your neighbor's eye, but do not notice the log in your own eye? Or how can you say to your neighbor, 'Let me take the speck out of your eye,' while the log is in your own eye? You hypocrite, first take the log out of your own eye, and then you will see clearly to take the speck out of your neighbor's eye. (Matthew 7:1-5, Lk 6:37-38)

In everything do to others as you would have them do to you; for this is the law and the prophets. (Matthew 7:12)

…Give therefore to the emperor the things that are the emperor's, and to God the things that are God's…(Matthew 22:21. Full story Mt 22:15-22, Also Mk 12:13-17 & Lk 20:20-26)

Teacher, which commandment in the law is the greatest? He said to him, You shall love the Lord your God with all your heart, and with all your soul, and with all your mind. This is the greatest and first commandment. And a second is like it: You shall love your neighbor as yourself. On these two commandments hang all the law and the prophets. (Matthew 22:36-40. Also, Mt 19:19, Mk 12: 28-34, Lk 10:27)

Jesus said to him, Put your sword back into its place; for all who take the sword will perish by the sword. (Matthew 26:52. Full story Mt 26:36-56)

Then the devil led him up and showed him in an instant all the kingdoms of the world. And the devil said to him, "To you I will give their glory and all this authority; for it has been given over to me, and I give it to anyone I please. If you, then, will worship me, it will all be yours." Jesus answered him, "It is written, 'Worship the Lord your God, and serve only him.' (Luke 4:5-8. Full story Lk 4:1-13)

But I say to you that listen, Love your enemies, do good to those who hate you, bless those who curse you, pray for those who abuse you. If anyone strikes you on the cheek, offer the other also; and from anyone who takes away your coat do not withhold even your shirt. Give to everyone who begs from you; and if anyone takes away your goods, do not ask for them again. Do to others as you would have them do to you. If you love those who love you, what credit is that to you? For even sinners love those who love them. If you do good to those who do good to you, what credit is that to you? For even sinners do the same. If you lend to those from whom you hope to receive, what credit is that to you? Even sinners lend to sinners, to receive as much again. But love your enemies, do good, and lend, expecting nothing in return. Your reward will be great, and you will be children of the Most High; for he is kind to the ungrateful and the wicked. Be merciful, just as your Father is merciful. (Luke 6:27-36)

Do not judge, and you will not be judged; do not condemn, and you will not be condemned. Forgive, and you will be forgiven; give, and it will be given to you. A good measure, pressed down, shaken together, running over, will be put into your lap; for the measure you give will be the measure you get back. (Luke 6:37-38)

Just then a lawyer stood up to test Jesus. "Teacher," he said, "what must I do to inherit eternal life?" He said to him, "What is written in the law? What do you read there?" He answered, "You shall love the Lord your God with all your heart, and with all your soul, and with all your strength, and with all your mind; and your neighbor as yourself." And he said to him, "You have given the right answer; do this, and you will live." But wanting to justify himself, he asked Jesus, "And who is my neighbor?... (Story of Good Samaritan v. 30-35)…Which of these three, do you think, was a neighbor to the man who fell into the hands of the robbers?" He said, "The one who showed him mercy." Jesus said to him, "Go and do likewise." (Luke 10:25-29, 36-37)

(*Woman caught in adultery to be stoned*). When they kept on questioning him, he straightened up and said to them, "Let anyone among you who is without sin be the first to throw a stone at her." (John 8:7)

And now I give you a new commandment: love one another. As I have loved you, so you must love one another. (John 13:34)

If you love me, you will keep my commandments. (John 14:15)

…We must obey God rather than any human authority. (Acts 5:29)

Then Peter began to speak to them: "I truly understand that God shows no partiality, but in every nation anyone who fears him and does what is right is acceptable to him. (Acts 10:34-35)

Therefore you have no excuse, whoever you are, when you judge others; for in passing judgment on another you condemn yourself, because you, the judge, are doing the very same things. (Romans 2:1)

Do not be conformed to this world, but be transformed by the renewing of your minds, so that you may discern what is the will of God—what is good and acceptable and perfect. (Romans 12:2)

Let love be genuine; hate what is evil, hold fast to what is good; love one another with mutual affection; outdo one another in showing honor. Do not lag in zeal, be ardent in spirit, serve the Lord. Rejoice in hope, be patient in suffering, persevere in prayer. Contribute to the needs of the saints; extend hospitality to strangers. Bless those who persecute you; bless and do not curse them. Rejoice with those who rejoice, weep with those who weep. Live in harmony with one another; do not be haughty, but associate with the lowly; do not claim to be wiser than you are. Do not repay anyone evil for evil, but take thought for what is noble in the sight of all. If it is possible, so far as it depends on you, live peaceably with all. Beloved, never avenge yourselves, but leave room for the wrath of God; for it is written, "Vengeance is mine, I will repay, says the Lord." No, "if your enemies are hungry, feed them; if they are thirsty, give them something to drink; for by doing this you will heap burning coals on their heads." Do not be overcome by evil, but overcome evil with good. (Romans 12:9-21)

Let us therefore no longer pass judgment on one another, but resolve instead never to put a stumbling block or hindrance in the way of another. I know and am persuaded in the Lord Jesus that nothing is unclean in itself; but it is unclean for anyone who thinks it unclean. If your brother or sister is being injured by what you eat, you are no longer walking in love. Do not let what you eat cause the ruin of one for whom Christ died. So do not let your good be spoken of as evil. For the kingdom of God is not food and drink but righteousness and peace and joy in the Holy Spirit. The one who thus serves Christ is acceptable to God and has human approval. Let us then pursue what makes for peace and for mutual upbuilding. (Romans 14:13-19)

Finally, be strong in the Lord and in the strength of his power. Put on the whole armor of God, so that you may be able to stand against the wiles of the devil. For our struggle is not against enemies of blood and flesh, but against the rulers, against the authorities, against the cosmic powers of this present darkness, against the spiritual forces of evil in the heavenly places. Therefore take up the whole armor of God, so that you may be able to withstand on that evil day, and having done everything, to stand firm. Stand therefore, and fasten the belt of truth around your waist, and put on the breastplate of righteousness. As shoes for your feet put on whatever will make you ready to proclaim the gospel of peace. (Ephesians 6:10-15)

Those conflicts and disputes among you, where do they come from? Do they not come from your cravings that are at war within you? You want something and do not have it; so you commit murder. And you covet something and cannot obtain it: so you engage in disputes and conflicts. You do not have because you do not ask. You ask and do not receive, because you ask wrongly, in order to spend what you get on your pleasures. (James 4:1-3)

Those who say, "I love God," and hate their brothers or sisters, are liars; for those who do not love a brother or sister whom they have seen, cannot love God whom they have not seen. The commandment we have from him is this: those who love God must love their brothers and sisters also. (1 John 4:20-21)

Islam, the Qur'ān, and Sayings by Muhammad (PBUH) and Ali Ibn Abi Taleb
From *The Islamic View of War*, Professor Maqsood Jafri

The Qur'ān severely condemns injustice, cruelty and bloodshed. It sets strict rules on the conduct of warfare and grants complete amnesty and acceptance upon victory.

Qur'ānic Verses (*all translations by Abdullah Yusaf Ali*):
♦ Islam emphasizes peace and abhors war. Fourteen hundred years ago, the Qur'ān invited the people of the Book to come to full peace through dialogue. Allah Almighty says: *But if the enemy incline towards peace, do thou (also) incline towards peace, and trust in Allah: for He is the One that hearth and knowth (all things).* (8:61)
♦ The Qur'ān teaches religious tolerance and no compulsion in religion. In Sura "The Heifer" it says: *O ye who believe! Enter into Islam wholeheartedly; and follow not the footsteps of the Evil One; for he is to you an avowed enemy.* (2:208). Likewise, no one is permitted to kill anyone on religious differences. The Qur'ān in Sura "The Woman" declares: *If a man kills a*

Believer intentionally, his recompense is Hell, to abide therein (forever): and the wrath and the curse of Allah are upon him, and a dreadful penalty is prepared for him. (4:93)

♦ But when war is thrust upon Muslims, then they are asked to defend themselves. However, Islam does not permit transgression or aggression in any case. The Qur'ān says: *"Fight in the cause of Allah those who fight you, but do not transgress limits; for Allah loveth not transgressors."* (2:190) In Sura Mumtahana (The Woman to be Examined) the Qur'ān says: *Allah forbids you not, with regard to those who fight you not for (your) Faith nor drive you out of your homes, from dealing kindly and justly with them: for Allah loveth those who are just. Allah only forbids you, with regard to those who fight you for (your) Faith, and drive you out, of your homes, and support (others) in driving you out, from turning to them (for friendship and protection). It is such as turn to them (in these circumstances), that do wrong. (60:8-9)*

Muhammad's Sayings:

♦ The saying of the Prophet of Islam (PBUH) that: *the first thing that Allah will look at on the Day of Resurrection will be blood* suggests that all bloodshed is cursed.

♦ The Holy Prophet (PBUH) has said: *He who aids and abets in the killing of a believer has taken himself out of Islam.*

♦ About the non-believers the Prophet of Islam (PBUH) time and again said that their blood, life, property, and honor is as sacred as of the Muslims. The Holy Prophet (PBUH) said: *He who kills a man from the people of the Dhimma (non-Muslims under the protection of Islamic state) will be forbidden paradise.* The motto, message, mission, and mantra of Islam is universal peace.

♦ On different occasions the Prophet also said about war: *The emissary is not to be killed. Trees are not to be felled. The animals are not to be slaughtered. The houses are not to be razed and the supply of water is not to be cut off.* Islamic views on war teach us that Islam promotes peace and discourages war and bloodshed.

Hazrat Ali Ibn-e-Abi Talib says in *Nehj Al Balagha*:

♦ *People are of two types: either your brother in religion or your equal in creation.*

Additional Passages from the Qur'ān
(English translations by Abdullah Yusuf Ali from *The Meaning of the Holy Qur'ān*)

Let there be no compulsion in religion: Truth stands out clear from Error: whoever rejects Evil and believes in Allah hath grasped the most trustworthy handhold, that never breaks. And Allah heareth and knoweth all things. Allah is the Protector of those who have faith: from the depths of darkness he will lead them forth into light…(2:256 &7)

Whoever recommends and helps a good cause becomes a partner therein: And whoever recommends and helps an evil cause, shares in its burden: Allah hath power over all things. (4:85)

O ye who believe! Stand out firmly for Allah, as witnesses to fair dealing, and let not the hatred of others to make you swerve to wrong and depart from Justice. Be just: that is next to Piety: and fear Allah. For Allah is well-acquainted with all that ye do. (5:8)

For those who believe and do deeds of righteousness hath Allah promised forgiveness and a great reward. (5:9)

On that account: We ordained for the Children of Israel that if anyone slew a person—unless it be for murder or for spreading mischief in the land—it would be as if he slew the whole people: and if anyone saved a life, it would be as if he saved the life of the whole people. Then although there came to them Our Messengers with Clear Signs, yet, even after that, many of them continued to commit excesses in the land. (5:32)

We ordained therein for them: "Life for life, eye for eye, nose for nose, ear for ear, tooth for tooth, and wounds equal for equal." But if anyone remits the retaliation by way of charity, it is an act of atonement for himself. And if any fail to judge by the light of what Allah hath revealed, they are not better than wrongdoers. (5:45)

…Take not life, which Allah hath made sacred, except by way of justice and law…(6:151)

…No burden do We place on any soul, but that which it can bear—whenever ye speak, speak justly, even if a near relative is concerned; and fulfill the Covenant of Allah….(6:152)

He that doeth good shall have ten times as much to his credit: he that doeth evil shall only be recompensed according to his evil: no wrong shall be done unto any of them. (6:160)

Nor can Goodness and Evil be equal. Repel Evil with what is better; then will he, between whom and thee was hatred, become as it were thy friend and intimate! And no one will be granted such goodness except those who exercise patience and self-restraint—none but persons of the greatest fortune. (41:34-35)

The recompense for an injury is an injury equal thereto in degree: but if a person forgives and makes reconciliation, his reward is due from Allah: for Allah loveth not those who do wrong. But indeed if any do help and defend themselves after a wrong done to them, against such there is no cause of blame. The blame is only against those who oppress men with wrongdoing and insolently transgress beyond bounds through the land, defying right and justice: for such there will be a Penalty grievous. But indeed if any show patience and forgive, that would truly be an exercise of courageous will and resolution in the conduct of affairs. (42:40-43)

Those who patiently persevere seeking the countenance of their Lord; establish regular prayers; spend, out of the gifts We have bestowed for their sustenance, secretly and openly; and turn off Evil with good: for such there is the final attainment of the Eternal Home. (13:22)

Allah commands justice, the doing of good, and liberality to kith and kin, and He forbids all shameful deeds, and injustice and rebellion: He instructs you, that ye may receive admonition. (16:90)

Not take life—which Allah has made sacred—except for just cause. And if anyone is slain wrongfully we have given his heir authority to demand Qisas or to forgive: but let him not exceed bounds in the matter of taking life: for he is helped by the Law. (17:33)

Repel evil with that which is best: We are well-acquainted with the things they say. (23:96)

Those who involve not, with Allah, any other god, nor slay such life as Allah has made sacred, except for just cause…(25:68)

O mankind! We created you from a single pair of a male and a female, and made you into nations and tribes, that ye may know each other, not that ye may despise each other. Verify, the most honored of you in the sight of Allah is he who is the most righteous of you…(49:13)

Contacts and Resources
Websites, addresses, and phone numbers subject to change, 9/1/16

Some Not-for-Profit Organizations Long Established in the Support of COs:
Quaker House, Lynn and Steve Newsom, Directors
     223 Hillside Avenue, Fayetteville, NC 28301 910-323-3912
     www.quakerhouse.org

GI Rights Hotline, Steve Woolford and Lenore Yarger, (QH) 919-663-4334 OR 1-877-447-4487
     www.girightshotline.org

Center on Conscience and War, Maria Santelli, Executive Director (military counseling)
     1830 Connecticut Avenue, N.W., Washington D.C. 20009 202-483-2220; 800-379-2679
     www.centeronconscience.org. Go to their site for Registration Packet for repository.

Courage to Resist (provides legal aid and support, most notably stood by Chelsea Manning)
     http://couragetoresist.org/

Friends Committee on National Legislation (FCNL), Quaker Lobbying and Resource Group
     245 Second St. NE, Washington, DC 20002 202-549-6000; 800-630-1330.
     http://fcnl.org/

Committee Opposed to Militarism and the Draft (COMD)
     PO B7ox 15195, San Diego, CA (619) 265-1369
     www.comdsd.org

Project YANO, Rick Jahnkow, Program Coordinator, 760-634-3604
     PO Box 230157, Encinitas, CA 92023
     www.projectyano.org. (For *What You Should Know before Joining the Military* go to:
     http://projectyano.org/index.php/literature-and-resources/military-enlistment/28-the-military-s-not-just-a-job)

Resisters Information. Edward Hasbrouck. Website re: Selective Service and war issues.
     http://www.resisters.info. Or, on the medical draft http://www.medicaldraft.info.

American Friends Service Committee (issues of global and regional peace building)
     http://www.afsc.org/key-issues/issue/community-peace-buiding
     Truth in Recruitment activities and resources: http://afsc.org/resource/counter-recruitment
     See their site for their *Alternatives to Military Service Guide* (pdf)

The Peace Abbey Foundation (see downloadable form for national CO Registry or repository)
     PO BOX 216, Sherborn, MA 01770-0216
     http://www.peaceabbey.org/programs-projects/conscientious-objectors/ or download at
     http://www.peaceabbey.org/wp-content/uploads/2015/04/nationalregistry.jpg.

The Selective Service System. (One of the largest and most polished of all the sites.)
     www.sss.gov. See Appendix: *More on Selective Service* for outlined list of topics sites.

Other Religious and Secular Organizations
Church of the Brethren—On Earth Peace Assembly
     http://onearthpeace.org/ (The Brethren et al. merged with Every Church a Peace Church)
Mennonite Central Committee (militarism and conscientious objection)

https://mcc.org/learn/what/categories/militarism

Episcopal Peace Fellowship	www.epfnational.org
Presbyterian Peace Fellowship	http://www.presbypeacefellowship.org/
On Conscientious Objection	https://www.pcusa.org/resource/conscientious-objection-q/
Other Statements by Religious Faiths at CC&W	
	http://www.centeronconscience.org/words-of-conscience.html
War Resisters League	www.warresisters.org
War Resisters Support Campaign (Canada)	www.resisters.ca/index_en/html
Iraq Veterans Against the War	www.ivaw.org
Veterans for Peace	www.veteransforpeace.org
Military Families Speak Out	mfso.org
Student Peace Action Network	studentpeaceaction.org
ASVAB out of schools, Pat Elder	http://www.studentprivacy.org/
Student Peace Action Network	www.studentpeaceaction.org
Fellowship of Reconciliation	www.forusa.org
Nonviolent Peaceforce (Peacemaking teams)	http://www.nonviolentpeaceforce.org/
Alternatives to Violence Project	http://avpusa.org/

Useful Articles from the Internet:

Supreme Court Rulings, Conscientious Objection and the Draft (search conscientious objection)
    http://straylight.law.cornell.edu/supct/index.html, Or go to https://www.law.cornell.edu.

Who Is a Conscientious Objector?
    http://www.scn.org/ip/sdmcc/co.htm

What's New in Conscientious Objector Law (2014)
    http://nlgmltf.org/military-law/2014/whats-new-in-conscientious-objector-law/

Frequently Asked (Legal and Related) Questions about Conscientious Objection
    https://www.libertyinstitute.org/conscientious-objector-faq

Chronology of Conscription in the U.S.
    http://www.teachervision.com/lesson-plans/lesson-5669.html

Conscientious Objection and Alternative Service (from Selective Service System)
    https://www.sss.gov/About/Alternative-Service

History of Conscientious Objection in the US and Elsewhere
    https://www.swarthmore.edu/library/peace/conscientiousobjection/co%20website/pages/Primary
    ResourcesNew.htm. AND www.nationalpeacemuseum.org/history.html;

Videos and DVDs

Witnessing the Power of Conscience, Maria Santelli, working with COs in the military:
http://www.bupipedream.com/news/51179/tedxbu-2015-witnessing-the-power-of-conscience/
    https://www.youtube.com/watch?v=d7GSzqjUq50

Recovering from the Darkness of PTDS and Moral Injury. Matthew Hoh, A Quaker House presentation,
    July 28, 2015. https://www.youtube.com/watch?v=p_VkLfm1lnI.

The Conscientious Objector: A True Story of an American Soldier. Desmond T. Doss. For DVD go to
    www.desmonddoss.com.

Good Kill (Moral Injury suffered by remote drone pilots). Directed by Andrew Niccol. 2014.

The Good War and Those who Refused to Fight It – the Story of World War II COs. Paradigm
    Productions/Lobitos Creek Ranch. Film by Judith Ehrlich and Rick Tejada-Flores. 2000.

The Good Soldier. Out of the Blue Productions. www.thegoodsoldier.com. 2009.

Soldiers of Conscience – featuring COs from Iraq and Afghanistan. Luna Productions. As seen on PBS.
    Home copy from www.lunaproductions.com. 2007.

Selected Bibliography on War and Peace, Conscientious Objection, and Peace Building

Andreas: *Addicted to War: Why the U.S. Can't Kick Militarism.* Joel Andreas. Joel Andreas, Publisher. Canada. 2002, 2003.

Associated Press: *Robert Bales, convicted of killing 16 Afghans, wanted life sentence reduced.* Posted 6/7/2015 @ http://www.cbc.ca/news/world/robert-bales-convicted-of-killing-16-afghans-wanted-life-sentence-reduced-1.3104126.

Bainton: *Christian Attitudes Toward War & Peace: A Historical Survey and Critical Evaluation.* Roland H. Bainton. Abingdon Press, Nashville, TN. 1960 & 1990.

Baskir: *Chance and Circumstance: The Draft, the War, and the Vietnam Generation.* Lawrence Baskir and William Strauss. Alfred A. Knopf, New York, New York. 1987.

Bible: *The Harper Collins Study Bible, New Revised Standard Version.* HarperCollins Publishers, Inc. New York, NY. 1993.

Bonhoeffer: *Discipleship.* Dietrich Bonhoeffer. From Bonhoeffer Works, Vol. 4. Fortress Press, Minneapolis. 2003.

Boston Research Center: *Abolishing War: Dialogue with Peace Scholars Elise Boulding and Randal Forsberg.* Boston Research Center, Boston, Massachusetts. 1998.

Boulding: *Elise Boulding: A Life in the Cause of Peace.* Mary Catherine Bateson (forward) and Mary Lee Morrison. McFarland and Company. 2005.

Boulding: *Cultures of Peace: The Hidden Side of History* (Syracuse Studies on Peace and Conflict Resolution). Elise Boulding et al. Syracuse University Press: Syracuse, New York. 2000.

Brennan Center for Justice: *Automatic Registration in the U.S.: The Selective Service Example.* Laura Seago. Brennan Center for Justice: New York University School of Law. 2009. https://www.brennancenter.org/sites/default/files/legacy/publications/selective%20service.color.FINAL.pdf

Brown: *Biblical Pacifism.* Dale Brown. Co-published by Herald Press and Evangel Publishing House: Nappanee, Indiana. 1986, 2003.

Broderbund: Several graphics came from *ClickArt*.

CC&W (Center on Conscience & War), Cole: *Bibliography on Conscientious Objection.* Dan Cole. Center on Conscience and War (formerly NISBCO). Can be downloaded from www.centeronconscience.org.

CC&W (Center on Conscience & War), Cole: *Bibliography on Conscientious Objection.* Dan Cole. Center on Conscience and War (formerly NISBCO). Can be downloaded from www.centeronconscience.org.

CC&W (Center on Conscience & War), Zuses. *Words of Conscience, 11th ed.* Rachel S. Zuses. Center on Conscience & War. 2001.

CC&W (Center on Conscience & War). See their other publications on line at www.centeronconscience.org.

CCCO (Central Committee for Conscientious Objectors), Seeley: *Advice for Conscientious Objectors in the Armed Forces, 5th edition.* Robert A. Seeley. Central Committee for Conscientious Objectors: Philadelphia, PA. 1998.

CCCO (Central Committee for Conscientious Objectors), Tatum: *Guide to the Draft, 3rd Edition, Revised*, Arlo Tatum and Joseph S. Tuchinsky. Beacon Press: Boston. 1969, 1970.

CCCO (Central Committee for Conscientious Objectors), *Handbook for Conscientious Objectors, 11th Edition.* Central Committee for Conscientious Objectors: Philadelphia, PA. March, 1971.

Chernus: *American Nonviolence: The History of an Idea.* Ira Chernus. Orbis Books, Maryknoll, New York. 2004.

Church of the Brethren: *Waging Peace: Strategies for Brethren Seeking and Working for Enduring Peace, A Six-Session Study/Action Guide.* Brethren Witness Office, Church of the Brethren General Board. 2002.

Church of the Brethren: *How the Draft Would Work and Conscientious Objection*, by John Hartsough, Manchester, Indiana. April, 2006.

Church of the Brethren: It Really is a Matter of Conscience: Conscientious Objector Resource Packet. 2005.

Craigie: *The Problem of War in the Old Testament.* Peter C. Craigie. William B. Eerdmans Publishing Company, Grand Rapids, Michigan. 1978.

Day: *Dorothy Day: Selected Writings.* Robert Ellsberg, Ed. Orbis Books, Maryknoll. 2001.

Day: *The Long Loneliness.* Dorothy Day. Harper and Row, Publishers, Inc.: New York. 1952.

D'Emilio: *Lost Prophet: The Life and Times of Bayard Rustin.* John D'Emilio. The University of Chicago Press. Chicago. 2003.

Doss: *The Conscientious Objector: A True Story of An American Soldier* (video tape and DVD of Desmond T. Doss). Georgia-Cumberland Association www.desmonddoss.com. 2004.

Dyer: *War.* Gwynne Dyer. Crown Publishers. New York. 1985.

Ellul: *The Presence of the Kingdom.* Jacques Ellul. Helmers and Howard: Colorado Springs, CO. 1967, 1989.

Eisenhower: *Farewell Address.* Dwight D. Eisenhower. Eisenhower Library and Museum: Abilene, KS. http://www.eisenhower.archives.gov/farewell.htm.

Fager: *A Quaker Declaration of War.* Chuck Fager. Presented at Illinois Yearly Meeting, 7th Month 30, 2003.

Ferguson: *War and Peace in the World's Religions*, John Ferguson. Oxford University Press, New York. 1978.

FGC, Clark: *Lives that Speak: Stories of Twentieth Century Quakers.* Marnie Clark, Editor. Quaker Press of Friends General Conference: Philadelphia, PA. 2004.

FGC, Torell & Carlton: *Raising Conscientious Objector Consciousness among Our Youth.* Curt Torell and Alice Carlton. Quaker Press of Friends General Conference: Philadelphia, PA. 2003. (or download from www.FGCQuaker.org).

Fisher: *Religious Liberty in America: Political Safeguards.* Louis Fisher. The University Press of Kansas. Lawrence, Kansas. 2002.

Gandhi: *Non-Violent Resistance (Satyagraha).* M. K. Gandhi. Schocken Books, New York. 1951, 1961.

Gandhi: *The Words of Gandhi.* Selected by Richard Attenborough. New Market Press: New York. 1982.

Gioglio: *Days of Decision: An Oral History of Conscientious Objectors in the Military during Vietnam War.* Gerald R. Gioglio. The Broken Rifle Press, Trenton, NJ. 1989, 1993.

Ground Truth, The: DVD by Focus Features, LLC. Universal Studies Home Entertainment, Universal City, CA 91608. www.thegroundtruth.net. 2006.

Harris and Morrison: *Peace Education.* Ian Harris and Mary Lee Morrison. McFarland & Company, Inc. Publishers. Jefferson, North Carolina, and London. 2003.

Hartscough: *How the Draft Would Work and Conscientious Objection.* John Hartscough. Church of the Brethren, Selective Service, and War. April 2006.

Hauerwas: *The Peaceable Kingdom: A Primer in Christian Ethics.* Stanley Hauerwas. University of Notre Dame, Notre Dame, Indiana. 1984, 2002.

Hoh: *Insulting America's Sacred Idols: Helping Veterans Recover From Moral Injury.* Matthew Hoh. 7/30/15. http://www.huffingtonpost.com/matthew-hoh/insulting-americas-sacred_b_7905696.html.

Hopkins: *Men of Peace: World War II Conscientious Objectors.* , Mary R. Hopkins, ed.: Producciones de la Hamaca, Caye Caulker, Belize. 2010.

Jafri: *The Islamic View of War.* Maqsood Jafri. Islamic Research Foundation International, Inc., at www.irfi.org/articles/articles_201_250/islamic_view_on_war.htm. 8/1/07.

Jewitt: *Jesus Against the Rapture: Seven Unexpected Prophecies.* Robert Jewett. The Westminster Press, Philadelphia, PA. 1979.

King: *A Testament of Hope, The Essential Writings and Speeches of Martin Luther King, Jr.* Edited by James M. Washington. Harper: San Francisco, CA. 1986.

King: *Stride Toward Freedom.* Martin Luther King, Jr. Harper & Row, Publishers: New York. 1958, 1964. (Contains his "Six Characteristics of Nonviolence")

King: *Where Do We Go From Here: Chaos of Community?* Martin Luther King, Jr. Beacon Press: Boston, Mass. 1967, 1968.

Lamoreau: *Waging Peace: A Study in Biblical Pacifism.* John Lamoreau and Ralph Beebe. Barclay Press. Newberg, Oregon. 1980.

Macgregor: *The New Testament Basis of Pacifism.* G. H. C. Macgregor. Fellowship Publications, Nyack, New York. 1954.

Mayer: *The Pacifist Conscience.* edited by Peter Mayer. Henry Regnery Company: Chicago, Illinois. 1966, 1967.

McSorley: *The New Testament Basis of Peacemaking.* Richard McSorley. Center for Peace Studies, Georgetown University. Washington, D.C. 1979.

Mehl-Laituri: *Reborn on the Fourth of July: The Challenge of Faith, Patriotism, & Conscience.* Logan Mehl-Laituri. InterVarsity Press, Downers Grove, IL. 2012.

Meltzer: *Ain't Gonna Study War No More: The Story of America's Peace Seekers.* Milton Meltzer. Random House, New York. 1985, 2002.

Merton: *Faith and Violence: Christian Teaching and Christian Practice.* Thomas Merton. University of Notre Dame Press: Notre Dame, Indiana. 1968.

Methodist Church: *Conscientious Objectors and the Draft.* Published by the General Board of Church and Society of The United Methodist Church in cooperation with the Center on Conscience & War. 2002.

Mother Theresa: *Mother Theresa: In My Own Words.* Mother Theresa. Gramercy Books, Division of Random House Value Publishing, New York. 1997.

Mother Theresa: *Simple Path.* Mother Theresa. Ballantine Books, Division of Random House, Inc., New York. 1995.

Nardin: *The Ethics of War and Peace: Religious and Secular Perspectives.* Edited by Terry Nardin. Princeton University Press, Princeton, NJ. 1996.

Schlissel: *Conscience in America: A Documentary History of Conscientious Objection in America, 1757-1967.* Edited by Lillian Schlissel. E. P. Dutton & Co, Inc. New York. 1968.

Seeley: Choosing Peace: *A Handbook on War, Peace, and Your Conscience.* Robert A. Seeley. Central Committee for Conscientious Objection, Philadelphia, PA. 1994.

Seeley: *A Handbook of Non-Violence, including Aldous Huxley's Encyclopedia of Pacifism.* Robert Seeley and Aldous Huxley. Lawrence Hill, Co./Lakesville Press. Westport, CT. 1986.

St. Augustine: *The Political Writings of St. Augustine.* Edited by Henry Paolucci. Regnery Publishing, Inc. Washington, DC. 1962.

Tolstoy: *On Civil Disobedience and NonViolence.* Leo Tolstoy. Bergman Publishers: New York. 1967, 1968.

Useem: *Conscription, Protest and Social Conflict: The Life and Death of a Draft Resistance Movement.* Michael Useem. Wiley Publishing, New York, New York. 1973.

Yoder: *For the Nations: Essays, Evangelical and Public.* John Howard Yoder. Wipf and Stock Publishers, Eugene, Oregon. 1997.

Yoder: *The Christian Witness to the State.* John Howard Yoder. Herald Press, Scottdale, PA & Waterloo, Canada. 1997.

Yoder: *The Original Revolution: Essays on Christian Pacifism.* John Howard Yoder. Herald Press, Scottsdale, PA. 1977.

Yoder: *The Politics of Jesus.* John Howard Yoder. William B. Eerdmans Publishing Company, Grand Rapids, Michigan. The Paternoster Press, Carlisle, UK. 1972.

Yoder: *What Would You Do?* John Howard Yoder. Herald Press, Scottsdale, PA. 1983.

Yoder: *When War Is Unjust: Being Honest in Just-War Thinking.* John Howard Yoder. Wipf & Stock Publishers, Eugene, Oregon. 1996.

Yusuf: *The Meaning of the Holy Qur'ān.* 'Abdullah Yūsuf Ali. Amana Publications, Beltsville, Maryland. 11th edition, 2006. Used for English translations of Qur'ān.

Zinn: *A People's History of the United States.* Howard Zinn. Harper Collins Publishers, New York, New York. 2005.

"They treat soldiers like tires. They put them on and use them up, and when they don't function any more they throw them away and get new ones."
- Mother of a wounded combat veteran, from GI Rights Hotline

POWERPOINT SLIDE PRESENTATION HARDCOPIES

Accompanies PowerPoint Slide Presentation, *Conscientious Objection: Is This for You?* which can be downloaded at www.quakerhouse.org)

Slide 1

Conscientious Objection:
Is This for You?

Discerning and Documenting a CO Claim at Selective Service Registration

A PowerPoint Presentation, with Activities and Reference Handouts
Curt Torell, Quaker House Board Member and Treasurer
Lynn and Steve Newsom, Quaker House Co-Directors
© Copyright Quaker House, September 1, 2016

September 2016

See *Read Me First*

Slide 2

This is an **Overview**
(See the Teacher's Guide for Details)

- Information about the Selective Service System (SSS), draft, & conscientious objection (CO) as well as how to discern and document a CO claim & **letter**
- Activities and exercises including a simulation, filing a CO application, & role-playing before a "Mock Draft Board"
- Reactions, explorations, discussion, & action plans

See *Agenda #1, 2, or 3*

Slide 3

Why Go Through the Effort?

1. Conscientious Objection to War:

   To safeguard young people in case a draft is ever reinstated

   Preparing for an event that may never happen vs. NOT preparing for that event, and it does happen

2. Conscientious Commitment to Peace:

   To promote the testimony of peace & nonviolence as teens become adults

   Discerning and articulating a CO stance that has both immediate and long-range benefits

   See *Long-Range Benefits of Writing CO Letters*

Slide 4

Context and Disclaimers

✓ Being a CO comes from a deep, inner belief or leading. It is not simply a way to get out of the draft or to avoid life-threatening situations.
✓ Others feel it is their patriotic duty to join the Armed Services. We do not wish to diminish their decision.
✓ This presentation is based on prior experience, case law (when the draft existed), and current Selective Service System (SSS) law. Everything could change.
✓ SSS currently does not grant CO status. Only a draft board would and only if a draft is reinstated. But these steps may help.
✓ Claiming a CO exemption is not easy. These steps are NO GUARANTEE one will be granted. That will depend upon the applicant and the draft board.

Slide 5

Three Criteria for Being a CO
(Conscientious Objector)

1. Conscientiously opposed to participating in **any and all war,**
2. Based on **moral, ethical, and/or religious** beliefs (and training), and
3. Must be **sincere or deeply held** (or play a significant role in one's life).

See *Overview of Selective Service and Conscientious Objection*

Slide 6

Opening Exercises:

- View video tape interviews **OR**
- Pick one of these exercises:
  ➢ Could You Chant This at Boot Camp then Do It Later? Or Cadences and Jody Calls
  ➢ Meaningful or Inspiring Quotes
  ➢ Could You – Would You? Some Real-Life Decisions in the Military
- If more time is allotted, also use the Violence vs. Nonviolence Brainstorming Exercise.

See *Exercises* as listed

Slide 7

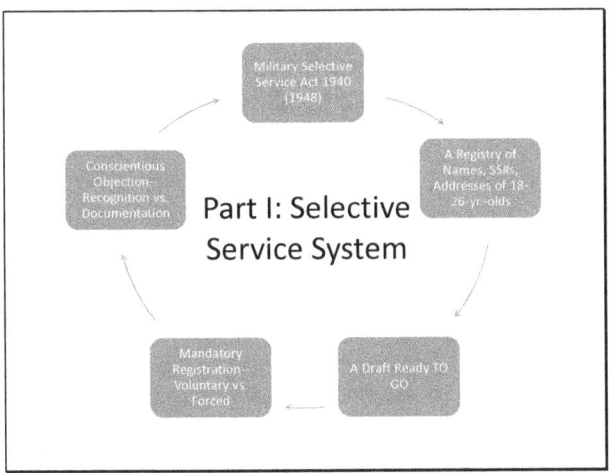

Part I: Selective Service System

- Military Selective Service Act 1940 (1948)
- A Registry of Names, SS#s, Addresses of 18-26-yr-olds
- A Draft Ready TO GO
- Mandatory Registration—Voluntary vs Forced
- Conscientious Objection—Recognition vs. Documentation

Slide 8

The Military Selective Service Act

- To deliver manpower to Armed Forces
- A bureaucratic organization complete with personnel, a set of regulations, rules, definitions, and procedures
- A registry of names and contact info
- Administers "Alternative Service"
- "The purpose of registration is, in itself, a form of participation in war" (*Rostker v. Goldberg*, U.S. Supreme Court, 1981)

President Franklin Roosevelt signed the Military Selective Service Act

Courtesy of Selective Service Teacher's Guide; https//www.sss.gov

Slide 9

The Selective Service System: A Draft Ready To Go

- *In Non-Draft Times*

   A registry that holds the name, address, birthdate, and social security number of young men (possibly young women in the future) eligible and ready for military induction

- *In Draft Times*

   A federal system/procedure that drafts young men (and perhaps women) into the military. Includes a lottery selection, induction notices, re-classifications or deferments, local draft boards, and procedures right up to induction

Slide 10

Selective Service Registration Law & Threats (*Real, but not used now*)

➤ **With few exceptions, all 18-year-old men** in the U.S. (and maybe women in the future) must register within 30 days of their 18th birthday.

➤ Failure to register is a felony, with a fine of up to $250,000 and/or 5 years in jail.

➤ Selective Service law has no procedure for filing a claim as a CO at registration time.

See *Overview of Selective Service and Conscientious Objection*

Slide 11

What Actually Happens!
Solomon & Thurmond Amendments

- Few prosecutions sought within the past 30 years.
- Rather than fines and jail, those who do not register suffer subtle, hidden penalties, ineligibility, and missed opportunities: a state a driver's license, federal or state aid for college & medical students, federal or state jobs & training, & citizenship to immigrants.

See the Appendix for *More on Selective Service* and *Registration Linked to State Driver's License & Other Opportunities*

Slide 12

What If I Don't Register?
Federal Consequences

✓ No Federal grants or loans
✓ No Federal job training programs
✓ No Federal employment
✓ No U.S. citizenship for immigrants

Above slide courtesy of *Selective Service Teacher's Guide*

Slide 13

What If I Don't Register?

State consequences: your driver's license plus "Solomon & Thurmond" penalties

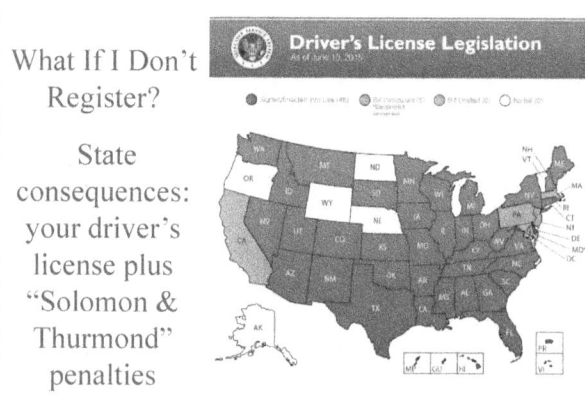

Driver's License Legislation
As of June 10, 2015

See Appendix: *Registration Linked to State Driver's License; Other Opportunities; California Legislature passed but Gov. Brown vetoed, saying it was not necessary.*

Slide 14

What If I Am 26 or Older and Haven't Registered?

Once you reach age 26, it's too late to register!

Even though you may not be prosecuted, you may be denied student financial assistance, federal job training, most federal employment, and citizenship for the undocumented <u>FOREVER</u> unless you can "show a preponderance of evidence" convincing the agency providing the benefit you are seeking, not Selective Service, that your failure to register "was not knowing and/or willful."

Slide 15

Ways SSS Suggests to Register

- U.S. Postal Service form (only way to indicate a CO claim)
- On-line through Agency website
- Reminder postcard from Agency
- Telephone, if card & PIN received in mail
- At a participating High School
- U.S. Embassy
- While filling out Federal student aid or job training form
- Visa application or Immigration/Naturalization form

*Note: SSS does not mention automatic registration in over 46 states/territories when applying for a state driver's license!

Slide 16

SSS: Same Yet Different from Before

- Still a mandated <u>Federal Law </u>for 18-yr.-old males
- Still <u>the precursor to a draft</u> that is ready to conscript and mobilize an expanded Armed Forces
- Still <u>a civilian agency</u>, separate from DoD or Pentagon, falling under Executive Branch
- BUT, <u>"fairer," more equitable</u>, less preferential treatment, fewer deferments. Boards will have consistent standards and training
- Shifted from applicant initiated to <u>automated</u>, hidden systems Denial of state/federal programs and state driver's license
- Registration is more <u>efficient, effortless, seamless, invisible</u>
- <u>No way to indicate a CO claim</u>; can only be done with draft
- Agencies <u>electronically cross-reference & data-share</u> registration (State Dept. of Motor Vehicles, Education, Labor, Citizenship and Immigration, I.R.S, U.S. Postal Service, JAMRS, etc.)

Slide 17

No Draft Now, BUT...
Reaching the "Tipping Point:"
An End to the All Volunteer Force

- "Endless wars" that truly never end
- Service members, through stop-loss orders and repeated deployments, suffer from physical and psychological wounds
- A global battlefield encompassing every nook and cranny of our nation
- Heightened security and protection at home as well as abroad
- Future wars i.e., with ISIS, the greater Middle East, Iran, North Korea, China
- Universal Service and Training Acts
- Next draft could include women or specialty skills like doctors, linguists, and tech geeks

Slide 18

The Draft Sequence

1. Congress and President authorize a draft.
2. The lottery is held, matching birthdates randomly with sequence numbers (1-366).
3. Components of SS agency are activated including Local and Appeal Boards.
4. Physical, mental, moral examinations are given.
5. Induction notices are sent to those who passed.*
6. Registrants requesting CO re-classification have within 10 days to file paper work; Boards decide.
7. First draftees are inducted. (<2 weeks or 6 months)

From http://www.sss.gov/PDFs/TeachersGuideBook.pdf (in revision)

Slide 19

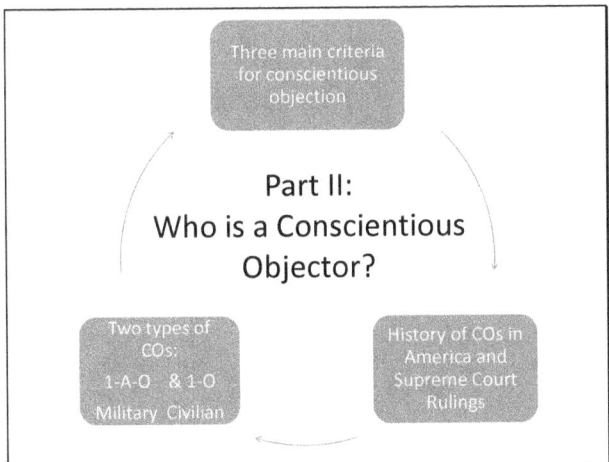

Part II:
Who is a Conscientious Objector?

Three main criteria for conscientious objection

Two types of COs:
1-A-O & 1-O
Military Civilian

History of COs in America and Supreme Court Rulings

Slide 20

Three Criteria for Being a CO
(Conscientious Objector)

1. Conscientiously opposed to participating in **any and all war**,
2. Based on **moral, ethical, and/or religious** beliefs (and training), and
3. Must be **sincere or deeply held** (or play a significant role in one's life).

See *Overview of Selective Service and Conscientious Objection*

Slide 21

A History of COs in America

- American Revolution: Some colonial legislatures exempted COs based on religious affiliation
- Civil War: Still on religious affiliation, a CO could pay $300 to a "Slave Fund" in lieu of conscription.
- WW I: Based on religious affiliation; COs were part of the military and served noncombatant duty; eventually alternative service was an option. COs were not treated well, some imprisoned or abused.
- For 150 years, church membership vs. individual conscience was discussed but never really resolved.
- WW II: <u>Civilian</u> draft board decided deferment, but by religious training or belief (not religious affiliation), and must have a belief in a Supreme Being.

See *COs and Selective Service in America (1656 to Present)* in the Reference Handouts as an outline & as a long narrative in the Appendix.

Slide 22

Key U.S. Supreme Court Rulings Since World War II

1. Seeger, 1965: The Court struck down the "belief in a Supreme Being" clause saying within *religious training and belief* would come "all sincere beliefs ... based upon a power or being, or upon faith, to which all else is subordinate or upon which all else is ultimately dependent," OR, "does the claimed belief occupy the same place ... as an orthodox belief in God...?"

2. Welsh, 1970: "Spurred by *deeply held moral, ethical, or religious beliefs*, (that) would give them no rest or peace if they...become a part of an instrument of war."

3. Gillette, 1971: Not political or selective reasons, or an unjust war. It "must amount to conscientious opposition to participating personally *in any war and all war*."

See *U.S. Supreme Court Rulings, Congressional Legislation, and Law*

Slide 23

Two Types of COs

In the Military	*Not in the Military*
Joins the military but does noncombatant training and service	Has nothing to do with the military system; stays in civilian jurisdiction
Does not carry or use a weapon, even in combat situations	Must do equivalent time of **alternative service*** (outside of military.
Might be assigned as a medic, chaplain, pot scrubber	Might work in a mental hospital, prison, police force
Classified as 1-A-O	Classified as 1-O

*Work of national importance under civilian direction.

See *Overview of Selective Service and Conscientious Objection*

Slide 24

Desmond T. Doss

- 7th Day Adventist
- Worshipped on Sabbath, or 7th day
- Refused to carry a weapon
- Classified I-A-0, or noncombatant, as defined by President Roosevelt
- Served as Medic Pfc. in World War II in Philippines, Guam & Okinawa
- In one battle spanning 23 days, he saved 75 wounded G.I.s under intense enemy fire
- 1st CO to receive the Medal of Honor from President Truman
- CD/Video at www.desmonddoss.com

Slide 25

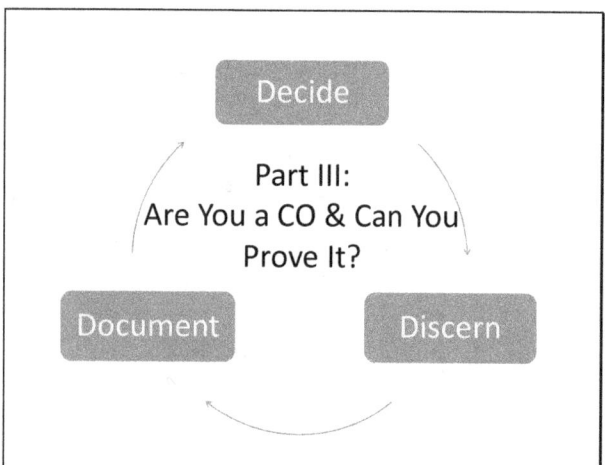

Part III:
Are You a CO & Can You Prove It?

Decide

Document

Discern

Slide 26

Discerning and Deciding: Suggestions to Get Started

1. What do you believe about your own personal participation in war?
2. Can you articulate those beliefs?
3. Can you describe what led you to those beliefs?
4. Can you document or produce evidence that demonstrates those beliefs and how you achieved them?

Slide 27

Scripture vs. The Military Enlistment Document

Hebrew, Christian, & Islamic Scripture

i. Can you kill, or be part of the killing, of another human being? (*You shall not kill; Love your neighbor; Take no life which Allah hath made sacred; Turn off evil with good.*)

ii. Can you subordinate or give up your obedience to God and place it in the hands of another, i.e., a commanding officer? (*You shall have no other gods before me; No one can serve two masters; Therefore serve me, and Me alone; So invoke not anyone along with Allah.*)

Enlistment Document

i. Military Enlistment/Re-Enlistment Document, Section 9: *Many laws, regulations, and military customs will govern my conduct and require me to do things a civilian does not have to do.*

ii. Sections 9a(1) & 9b, of the same. *You will be required to obey all lawful orders and perform all assigned duties and these laws, and regulations...may change without notice to me.*

See *Excerpts from Military Enlistment Document; Hebrew, Christian, Islamic Scriptural Passages*

When God says, "Do not kill" and your command says "Kill," who do you obey?

Slide 28

Exercise: Worksheet Form 22

- Take 10 minutes and put yourself in a CO's shoes.
- Would you be 1-A-O or 1-O?
- Then answer the three questions listed on the form.
- Come back, report on one question, and discuss.
- Tri-fold the Worksheet.

See Exercise: *Worksheet Form 22*
HO: *Suggestions to Build Documentation & Worksheet Form 22 Tips*

Slide 29

How do you register as a CO?

- Selective Service law recognizes conscientious objection as a deferment.
- However, documentation for a CO claim does not exist at registration time.
- Therefore, the registrant needs to devise his or her own documentation as a basis for a claim.

Slide 30

Three Fundamental Ways to Document a CO Claim

1. Write and present a "CO letter" to your faith or support community.
2. Using the Postal Service form, write in a request for a CO claim, and get it witnessed. Then, when your registration card is returned, write on the return portion, "You did not indicate my preference for a CO classification."
3. Gather "Letters of Support."

Tri-fold and send copies to yourself.

See *Three Fundamental Ways to Document a CO Claim*

Slide 31

Letters to Your Faith or Support Community Asking for Recognition and Documentation

- A "generic" sample letter with some main (legal) points to include
- Some specific, real-life examples

See *A Template or Generic Letter Documenting a CO Claim* AND *Two Sample CO Letters*

Slide 32

Some CO Letter Starters...

1. The legal requirements or three criteria for a CO:
   - Against personal participation in any and all war.
   - Based upon moral, ethical, and/or religious training and belief.
   - Sincere; deeply held; documented.
2. Personal statements of conviction and/or belief. Rely on Worksheet Form 22 (& Tips) as a start.
3. Measure yourself against the Supreme Court interpretations of conscientious objection.
4. Ask your faith or support community for help and to hold your concerns institutionally (minutes, lockbox).

See *Suggestions for Faith and Support Communities*

Slide 33

Register on-line (http://www.sss.gov) Author's Note: Registering on-line does not allow additions. Do not register on-line, or complete this form.
SELECTIVE SERVICE SYSTEM REGISTRATION FORM.
DATE OF BIRTH (MM-DD-YYYY)   SEX (Mark with "X")   SOCIAL SECURITY ACCOUNT NUMBER

1⇒   2⇒ ☐ Male ☐ Female   3⇒

***Note: I am a conscientious objector. Martin Luther King, Jr., January 15, 1953. (Signed and Dated)
LAST NAME

4⇒
FIRST NAME & MIDDLE NAME

I, Martin Luther King, Sr., Senior Minister at Ebenezer Baptist Church, witness Martin's conviction. (Signed and dated)
(CURRENT MAILING ADDRESS STREET ADDRESS & APARTMENT NUMBER)

5⇒
CITY   STATE   ZIP CODE

I, Howard Thurman, long-time mentor of Martin, witness his conviction as a CO. (Signed and dated)
TODAY'S DATE (MM-DD-YYYY)

6⇒   7⇒ _____
SIGNATURE

See *Sample Selective Service System Registration Form*

Slide 34

Change of Information Form

See *Change of Information Form and a Suggested Reply*

Slide 35

Letters of Support (from others)

- Gather two, three, or maybe more.
- Get from "respected" people; use a cross- section.
- Should attest to CO's *sincerity and integrity.*
- Person is familiar with the CO's position, but doesn't have to agree.
- Start collecting now, especially because contacts tend to fade through early adulthood transitions from high school, college, and jobs.

See *Letters of Support*

Slide 36

DOCUMENT
DOCUMENT
DOCUMENT

- **Keep a CO folder**. Include copies of registration forms, CO letters, worksheets, dated workshop agendas, correspondence from SS, readings, journals, homework assignments, movies, songs, discussions, activities, volunteer work, etc.
- Refer to your faith or support community's records and minutes, letters of support, etc.
- Tri-fold important papers: Copy, fold in thirds, send to self and KEEP, unopened.

See *Suggestions to Build Documentation & Worksheet Form 22 Tips*

Slide 37

A Checklist of Procedures...

☑
☑
☑
☑

- For the 18-year-old's CO folder
  - ❑ Worksheet Form #22
  - ❑ Workshop handouts, signed and dated
  - ❑ SS Registration Form; Correction letter
  - ❑ Letter to one's support or faith community
  - ❑ Letters of support from others
- For the Faith or Support Community
  - ❑ Clearness or Support Committee
  - ❑ Official records and/or minutes
  - ❑ Witness SS Registration Form
  - ❑ Store records in a safe place (or use a national registry or other outside agency)

See Suggestions to Build... AND Suggestions for Faith and Support...

Slide 38

Can you "defend" your position?

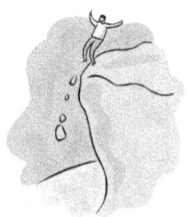

Role-play a Mock Draft Board
A witness of conscience vs. fear
Not a "test" but a "testimony"

See Exercise: Sample Questions a Draft Board Might Ask

Slide 39

Did We Miss Anything?

- All materials, PowerPoint, handouts, and interview tapes can be downloaded or a hard copy purchased from 910-323-3912 www.Quakerhouse.org
- You can purchase a hard copy of *Raising Conscientious Objector Consciousness among Our Youth* from Friends General Conference (www.FGCQuaker.org) or get a free PDF download at: http://criticalconcern.com/swords-plowshares/co-consciousness.pdf.
- See also www.afsc.org/youthmil and www.centeronconscience.org

See Teacher's Resource Guide for additional materials

Slide 40

Contact Information for Quaker House

- Lynn & Steve Newsom, Co-Directors
- www. quakerhouse.org
- Email = qpr@quaker.org curtnpatty@aol.com
- Phone = 910-323-3912
- Curt Torell, Board member/Treasurer (and Clerk for NC Choices for Youth)
- Email = curtnpatty@aol.com

Slide 41

Let's Review: The Final Exam

1. What are the three criteria for being a CO?
2. What's the difference between Class 1-A-O and Class 1-O?
3. What are some types of documentation that show your convictions, leadings, inclinations?
4. What is "tri-folding"?
5. Where can I get copies of these materials?
6. Feedback questions on the presentation:
   - ✓ What was most helpful to you in this workshop?
   - ✓ Did this meet your expectations? Why/why not?
   - ✓ How could it be improved or help you better?

Slide 42

Wrapping Up

1. Get your agenda signed and dated. Add it to your CO documentation folder.
2. Remember to photocopy your Worksheet Form 22, tri-fold, stamp, self-address, and send to yourself.
3. Read the handouts referenced throughout the PowerPoint or found in the Teacher's Resource Guide.

"War is not the answer."
Martin Luther King, Jr. from *A Time to Break Silence* speech, April 4, 1967, Riverside Church, N.Y.C

> # Conscientious Objection:
> ## Is This for You?
>
> *Discerning and Documenting a CO Claim at Selective Service Registration*
>
> A PowerPoint Presentation, with Activities and Reference Handouts
> Curt Torell, Quaker House Board Member and Treasurer
> Lynn and Steve Newsom, Quaker House Co-Directors
> **© Copyright Quaker House, September 1, 2016**
>
> *September 2016*
>
> See *Read Me First*

INTRODUCTION SLIDES:

Check the ***Read Me First*** word document for information about this PowerPoint. The lecture notes and resource materials are comprehensive. Review them first and highlight essential points.

Thank the organizers and participants for the opportunity to present this topic. Refer them to downloadable materials from www.quakerhouse.org, including the PowerPoint presentation and its Notes Pages, agendas, resource materials, and interview DVDs.

Mention that the topic of conscientious objection and documenting one's position is not a pressing issue now, because we have no draft. Yet for teens particularly, it is important to lay a foundation, both in developing beliefs and in establishing documentation at the time of Selective Service registration.

Facilitators could hand out file folders for each participant to keep all of his or her own documentation. See the list of handouts in ***Agenda #1: Handouts and Topics They Reference***. Have each person label the folder, "CO (Conscientious Objector) file."

Go through the PowerPoint quickly, especially if people have it as a handout too, so that they can follow along. Time is best spent exercises, discussion, and the articulation of CO claims and beliefs.

> ## This is an **Overview**
> (See the Teacher's Guide for Details)
>
> - Information about the Selective Service System (SSS), draft, & conscientious objection (CO) as well as how to discern and document a CO claim & **letter**
> - Activities and exercises including a simulation, filing a CO application, & role-playing before a "Mock Draft Board"
> - Reactions, explorations, discussion, & action plans
>
> See *Agenda #1, 2, or 3*

Refer to the one page word document, ***Agenda #1: A Broad Overview, One 1-Hour 45-Minute Basic Workshop***. The workshop is comprehensive in both information and scope. Some instructive portions can be skipped and referred to later in the handouts. The presentation uses a full variety of learning styles to encourage thought, reaction, exploration, and discussion to start articulating one's beliefs. This is the first step for participants to document their beliefs and create an action plan for a CO claim.

***Agenda* #1** shows the order and times. The PowerPoint Notes Pages, reference handouts, and Agenda #1 Annotated for Facilitators Version provide detail. If time permits, devote more to exploration of beliefs, role-plays, and responses to the forms.

For this slide, say, "After this introduction, we'll do an opening exercise to get you thinking about what a CO is. Then, cover Selective Service System (SSS) and the draft. Later, we'll review some history and court definitions about conscientious objection followed by some more exercises. At the end of this, you'll have a better understanding of whether you might be a CO (or not), and why."

Ask the group what their expectations are for the workshop. Use their responses to adapt the session according to their needs.

Why Go Through the Effort?

1. <u>Conscientious Objection to War</u>:

   To safeguard young people in case a draft is ever reinstated

   Preparing for an event that may never happen vs. NOT preparing for that event, and it does happen

2. <u>Conscientious Commitment to Peace</u>:

   To promote the testimony of peace & nonviolence as teens become adults

   Discerning and articulating a CO stance that has both immediate and long-range benefits

   See *Long-Range Benefits of Writing CO Letters*

With no draft, why is this workshop and process important? See ***Handout: Long-Range Benefits of Writing CO Letters.***

1. **<u>A Safeguard</u>:** In statistical hypothesis testing, a **type I error** is the incorrect rejection of a true null hypothesis, while a **type II error** is the failure to reject a false null hypothesis. Simply stated, a type I error is detecting an effect that is not present or <u>rejecting it when it is in fact true</u>, while a type II error is failing to detect an effect that is present <u>or accepting an effect that is actually false</u>.

Borrowing from that analogy, a type I error is preparing for something that does not happen vs. a type II error which is not preparing for it but then it does happen. In this case, <u>we advocate preparing for a draft even though it may not happen, instead of not preparing for a draft, and then it does.</u>

Another analogy is building a tornado shelter that, fortunately, you never have to use vs. NOT building the shelter and being struck by a tornado.

In both cases, which is the better route and which error would you choose?

2. **<u>A Testimony to Peace</u>:** Many teens who write CO letters find long-range benefits that frame their views on violence in later years. Some say it was because of their faith community's focus on non-violence and awareness of what a CO is that prompted them to make such a conviction. "When I saw the definition of a CO, I realized I wanted to claim it," said one of the CO Letter Writers. See Handout mentioned above for other examples.

Slide 4

Context and Disclaimers

✓ Being a CO comes from a deep, inner belief or leading. It is not simply a way to get out of the draft or to avoid life-threatening situations.

✓ Others feel it is their patriotic duty to join the Armed Services. We do not wish to diminish their decision.

✓ This presentation is based on prior experience, case law (when the draft existed), and current Selective Service System (SSS) law. Everything could change.

✓ SSS currently does not grant CO status. Only a draft board would and only if a draft is reinstated. But these steps may help.

✓ Claiming a CO exemption is not easy. These steps are NO GUARANTEE one will be granted. That will depend upon the applicant and the draft board.

Read this slide (or have it read). Add that the intent is not to make everyone a CO. Such a conviction is an individual, deeply held belief. Nor does this workshop challenge anyone's commitment in how to serve one's country. The workshop simply creates an awareness of what a CO is and lays a foundation if a person is so inclined. Such a conviction grows and matures, often gradually and slowly. It is a process that needs nurturing and guidance along the way. Elaborate further if needed:

1. *Being a CO comes from a deep, inner leading. It is not simply a way to get out of the draft or to avoid life-threatening situations.* Simply put, a CO refuses to participate personally in war and/or to kill another human being through the act of war. At the same time, for an 18-year-old, this conviction usually is only blossoming and requires patient nurturing.

2. *While shunning violence, those young men and women who serve in the Armed Services and are willing to put themselves in harm's way should be held in the Light.* Many young adults join the armed forces through their sense of patriotic duty to serve their country, some as a way towards citizenship, and others simply for economic relief. Few have ever heard the phrase "conscientious objector." While the presentation is on conscientious objection, we do not wish to demean other choices.

3. *A new law could change everything.* While the Selective Service System exists and is operational, a new draft could change established procedures. Materials presented here are based on current and past practices, and today's more conservative U.S. Supreme Court may interpret regulations differently. So these suggestions, while based upon precedent and collective wisdom, are merely a conjecture and a guide.

4. *Currently, Selective Service registration has no place to indicate a CO status.* In fact, a CO status is granted ONLY after one gets an induction notice, files for a CO re-classification (possibly within nine days), appears before a draft board with supportive testimony, and is accepted hopefully by the Board. That doesn't mean to wait until then to start documenting a claim. It should start now!

5. *The process of documentation presented in this workshop is NO GUARANTEE for a CO classification. It likely will be difficult, and it might force one to decide on jail or other alternatives.* In the end, a local draft board will make a decision on one's CO request based upon the most current U.S. law, precedent, and the content and sincerity of one's claim.

Three Criteria for Being a CO
(Conscientious Objector)

1. Conscientiously opposed to participating in **any and all war,**
2. Based on **moral, ethical, and/or religious** beliefs (and training), and
3. Must be **sincere or deeply held** (or play a significant role in one's life).

See *Overview of Selective Service and Conscientious Objection*

Refer to **Handout:** *Overview of Selective Service and Conscientious Objection*.

This is the most important slide or lesson from the workshop. Remind participants that this is on their "final exam."

- *Any and all war* is pretty clear. It is not just for political or situational reasons, like against a particular war. For a CO, no war is "just" or could fit into the religious doctrine or "just war" theories of theologians. Secondly, the focus is *any and all war* as we know it <u>now</u>. A person does not have to answer if he or she would have fought in WW II. One can't say what one might do in another period.

- *Moral, ethical, and/or religious* gives latitude of expression. While beliefs are hard to prove, put into words, or even crystallize fully, this must be done. See the handout on Supreme Court rulings for clarifications.

- *Deeply held* means sincere or, in legal terms, it means documented. This is why starting now is essential. Suppose you suddenly got drafted, had no prior documentation, but decided to claim CO status. The first question the draft board would ask is, "Why are you making a CO claim now? Do you just want to get out of the draft?" Prior documentation demonstrates a sincere track record, and it is a main reason for this workshop.

Opening Exercises:

- View video tape interviews **OR**
- Pick one of these exercises:
  - ➢ Could You Chant This at Boot Camp then Do It Later? Or Cadences and Jody Calls
  - ➢ Meaningful or Inspiring Quotes
  - ➢ Could You – Would You? Some Real-Life Decisions in the Military
- If more time is allotted, also use the Violence vs. Nonviolence Brainstorming Exercise.

See *Exercises* as listed

Pick one of these **Exercises** for an opening activity. Note the differences and depth of each one.

Could You Chant This at Boot Camp Then Do It Later is the most experiential and takes the least amount of time. It is recommended, because it is short and gets participants physically active at the beginning of the workshop. Many participants don't believe that service members chant these words during boot camp. But they do! More examples are found in ***Cadences and Jody Calls***.

Meaningful or Inspiring Quotes is more academic and cerebral. Participants may want to share their own quotes.

Could You – Would You leads the participants through levels of military actions from the least damaging to the most cataclysmic. The first few examples are from recruiting materials.
Consider asking the group which exercise they would prefer. Set aside time to debrief, esp. for the cadences. These can elicit strong feelings and reactions. Excuse anyone who has difficult participating.

If more time is allotted, also use the ***Violence vs. Nonviolence Brainstorming*** exercise. This is an excellent way to get the group to think about these concepts.

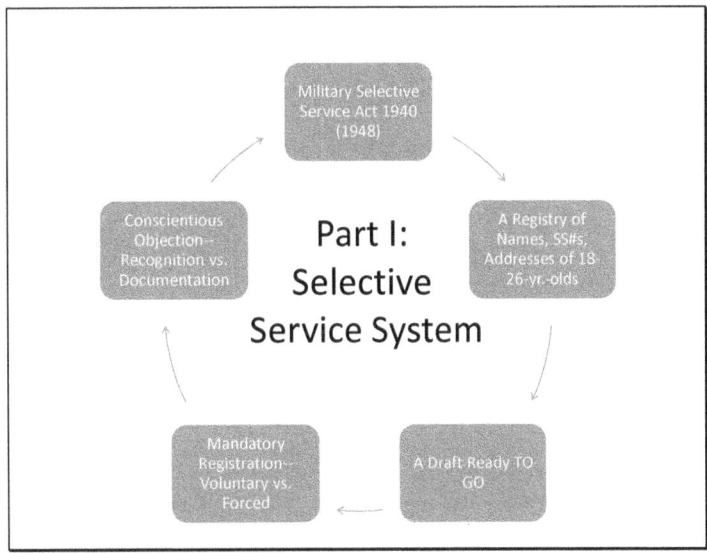

SELECTIVE SERVICE SYSTEM

This section gives a brief overview of the Selective Service System: how it came to be (the Law), what it is (a registry), how it is related to the draft (its precursor), how registration is handled (alternative methods and penalties for nonregistration), and how conscientious objection is acknowledged in the law (but with no means to document a claim at Selective Service registration time).

GO THROUGH THIS SECTION QUICKLY. This is background information only, but understanding the Selective System is fundamental, and Selective Service drives this whole process. It is the LEGAL framework for documentation, CO claims, and successful re-classification. If participants have copies of the PowerPoint presentation, you can go more quickly.

THE LAW

The Military Selective Service Act

- To deliver manpower to Armed Forces.
- A bureaucratic organization complete with personnel, a set of regulations, rules, definitions, and procedures.
- A registry of names and contact info.
- Administers "Alternative Service."
- "The purpose of registration is, in itself, a form of participation in war" (*Rostker v. Goldberg*, U.S. Supreme Court, 1981).

President Franklin Roosevelt signed the Military Selective Service Act

Courtesy of Selective Service Teacher's Guide; https//www.sss.gov

Despite the attempt by several members of Congress in the 1990s to eliminate it, the Selective Service System is alive and well, in fact, it is doing quite well. It's operational, fully funded, renewed by Congress, and evolving in a changing technological world to meet its intended mission, i.e., to draft young men (perhaps women in the future) into the Armed Forces.

The MSSA or Military Selective Service Act 1948 (Title 50 U.S. Code, appendix 451-471) was a revamping of previous laws (The Selective Service Act of 1917, The Selective Training and Service Act of 1940, and the Selective Service Act of 1948). It has been amended several times since that time.

The Act set up the current Selective Service System giving it a twofold mission: (1) to deliver manpower to the Armed Forces in time of emergency, and (2) to administer an Alternative Service Program for Conscientious Objectors.

Notes: This slide was adapted from the Selective Service official website. The MSSA, as published in 50 U.S.C. App. 451 et seq., amended July 2003 and with notes and the legislative history of amendments can be found at http://uscode.house.gov/usc.htm.

The Selective Service System: A Draft
Ready To Go

- *In Non-Draft Times*
    A registry that holds the name, address, birthdate,
    and social security number of young men
    (possibly young women in the future) eligible and
    ready for military induction
- *In Draft Times*
    A federal system/procedure that drafts young men
    (and perhaps women) into the military. Includes a
    lottery selection, induction notices, re-
    classifications or deferments, local draft boards,
    and procedures right up to induction

The current SSS is based on the Selective Service Act of 1948. Its mission was "to be prepared to supply manpower to the Armed Forces adequate to ensure the security of the U.S. during a time of national emergency" (Selective Service Home page, Library of Congress). See next slide on who must register.

The SSS is already in place with two different systems, depending on emergency need. One provides an inductee force in less than two weeks (*RIMS*), the other (*RIPS*) in six months. More on *RIMS* and *RIPS* later (see slide titled *No Draft Yet, BUT...*).

Under current Selective Service law, classification as a CO cannot be done at the time of SS registration. The official process happens only AFTER a draft is reinstated and a person receives an induction notice (see later materials). However, we feel this is too late. Discerning, articulating, and documenting beliefs takes time. It should begin prior to and through the actual registration process (outlined later).

> ## Selective Service Registration Law & Threats (*Real, but not used now*)
>
> ➤ **With few exceptions, all 18-year-old men** in the U.S. (and maybe women in the future) must register within 30 days of their 18th birthday.
> ➤ Failure to register is a felony, with a fine of up to $250,000 and/or 5 years in jail.
> ➤ Selective Service law has no procedure for filing a claim as a CO at registration time.
>
>
>
> See *Overview of Selective Service and Conscientious Objection*

See Handout: Overview of Selective Service & Conscientious Objection.
"Since 1980, a total of 20 people have been prosecuted for failure to register. The last indictment was on January 23, 1986. Almost all of those prosecuted were conscientious objectors to the draft who publicly asserted their non-registration as a religious, conscientious or political statement" (Center on Conscience and War). Prosecution of non-registrants by the Federal Government was intended to scare everyone into compliance. But it backfired because non-registrants appealed to a higher, moral law, and that got media attention. In traditionally conservative and religious areas, it made teens think about what registration really meant.

(Refer to a sample SS Registration form from the Post Office or *Selective Service: Who Must Register* in the Appendix.) Almost every male who turns 18 (and maybe women in the future) must register EXCEPT those already in some form of the military, those confined (prison, hospitalized, institutionalized), or lawful non-immigrants on visas. The Selective Service Form even says "Undocumented (illegal) aliens" (their term) must register, yet the "Privacy Statement" on the back of the form that says it shares information with the U.S. Immigration Department! Information is also shared electronically between State Driver's License Bureaus, the U.S. Postal Service, and other agencies.

While failure to register has not been pursued, other pressures have been used. Threatening letters are sometimes sent as reminders to those who inadvertently miss the registration deadline. The biggest consequence is the denial of opportunities covered in the next slide.

It's a good idea for young **women** to document their beliefs, even though they are not yet called into SS registration. They may be subject to a future draft, and it also shows solidarity with young men.

Author's Note: Advising someone NOT to register for Selective Service (a felony) is itself a felony, because it is a felony to encourage someone to commit a felony. However, informing someone that failure to register is a felony is legal. Note this distinction.

What Actually Happens!
Solomon & Thurmond Amendments

- Few prosecutions sought within the past 30 years.
- Rather than fines and jail, those who do not register suffer subtle, hidden penalties, ineligibility, and missed opportunities: a state a driver's license, federal or state aid for college & medical students, federal or state jobs & training, & citizenship to immigrants.

See the Appendix for *More on Selective Service* and *Registration Linked to State Driver's License & Other Opportunities*

As a result of the backfire of prosecutions and its negative publicity, the federal government enacted punitive legislation and policies to coerce people to comply. These more widespread, subtle effects are due to the **Solomon and Thurmond Amendments**—riders on legislative appropriation bills during the 1990s. **Solomon** prevents non-registrants from receiving federal aid to colleges and medical schools and from participating in federal job-training programs. **Thurmond** prevents them from obtaining employment with any federal executive agency, i.e., most federal jobs. Not surprisingly, Selective Service does not refer to these as "penalties," but rather "benefits and programs linked to registration" (See SS website).

States reflect similar penalties. Some refuse admission and/or financial aid to state-supported educational institutions. In the past few years, almost all states/territories linked registration to obtaining driver's licenses or for state IDs. (See next slides.)

SSS is most interested in registration rates, not prosecution. They want 100% compliance.

The Fund for Education and Training assists teens who for reasons of conscience do not comply with the law requiring registration (see http://www.centeronconscience.org/event-schedule/fund-for-education-and-training.html).

Men (and potentially women in the future) who are not registered with Selective Service may not qualify for the following: Federal (or state) employment, Pell Grants, Supplemental Education Opportunity Grants, Federal College Work-Study, Federal Perkins Loans, Federal Family Education Loans, and Federal Direct Student Loans. Men may also be disqualified for benefits associated with the Workforce Investment Act (WIA). Failure to register may also affect citizenship for undocumented immigrants (see slide after next).

Author's note: Currently, women are exempt from this penalty. Is this discriminatory?

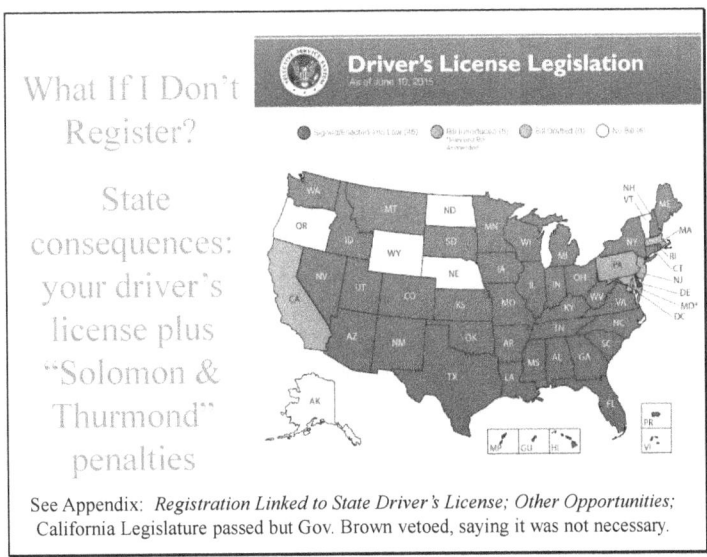

See Appendix: *Registration Linked to State Driver's License; Other Opportunities;*
California Legislature passed but Gov. Brown vetoed, saying it was not necessary.

See ***Handout: Registration Linked to State Driver's Licenses and Other
Opportunities*** in the Appendix for a detailed explanation and listing of state
restrictions.

Now, almost all states link Selective Service registration when applying for a
State driver's license; many make it mandatory. In other words, in many
states a driver's license will be DENIED if you refuse to register with
Selective Service. In 2000, Delaware was the first state to pass such a law.
As a result, their SS compliance rate jumped to <u>nearly</u> 100%. Despite its
central importance, the SS website <u>Teacher's Guide</u> does not even mention the
association of registration with a driver's license. This is a subtle caveat that
many young men, anxious to get their driver's license, do not fully realize.
It's another way that Selective Service is hidden, despite the enormity of its
impact should a draft be reinstated.

Also, many states begin the driver's license process well before a teen turns
18. Though they do not forward an applicant's information to Selective
Service until the age of 18, the permission to do so is given when the teen is
still legally a minor. (Author's note: this is another discriminatory burden on
males.)

Slide 14

What If I Am 26 or Older and Haven't Registered?

Once you reach age 26, it's too late to register!

Even though you may not be prosecuted, you may be denied student financial assistance, federal job training, most federal employment, and citizenship for the undocumented <u>FOREVER</u> unless you can "show a preponderance of evidence" convincing the agency providing the benefit you are seeking, not Selective Service, that your failure to register "was not knowing and/or willful."

This is a little known fact: Once a male reaches the age of 26, he cannot register. This affects all subsequent applications for federal/state employment, financial aid, even citizenship. Failure to register may have lifetime consequences. And the appeal goes before the agency granting the benefit, not Selective Service.

Imagine the bind Selective Service registration puts on undocumented persons. Registration puts them in a federal data bank shared with other agencies including Immigration. Yet, bypassing registration could jeopardize an application for U.S. citizenship.

The following is from http://immigration.lawyers.com/general-immigration/us-immigration-laws-and-the-selective-service.html:

> What about non-US citizens? If you're required to register and don't, then you may be barred forever from becoming a US citizen. As part of the naturalization process, the procedure that allows foreign nationals to become US citizens, you need to establish your good moral character. The USCIS will look carefully at your actions and behavior during the five-year period before you filed your application for naturalization. If the USCIS finds that you didn't register during that five-year period, there's good chance that your application will be denied. Your failure to register may show a lack of good moral character.
>
> So, generally, if you're a man and between the ages of 18 and 25, you're legally required to register. If you're thinking about applying for citizenship, or there's a chance that you may apply sometime before your 32nd birthday, you should register so that you don't jeopardize your chances of becoming a citizen.
>
> Your 32nd birthday is critical because you have to register if you're 26 years old, and the USCIS will look back five years. So, if you're 31 at the time you apply and you didn't register, your application may be denied. If you're 32 years old, the USCIS will focus on your conduct up to the age of 27, at which age you had no obligation to register.

Ways SSS Suggests to Register

- U.S. Postal Service form (only way to indicate a CO claim)
- On-line through Agency website
- Reminder postcard from Agency
- Telephone, if card & PIN received in mail

- At a participating High School
- U.S. Embassy
- While filling out Federal student aid or job training form
- Visa application or Immigration/Naturalization form

*Note: SSS does not mention automatic registration in over 46 states/territories when applying for a state driver's license!

Selective Service has taken a more pro-active role in registration using a range of technological resources making it easier and more efficient. These are the methods suggested from the official Selective Service website. However, they do NOT mention that most states automatically register men when applying for a driver's license.

Using the Internet, college loan, or driver's license as a method to register does not give an opportunity to show, upon first contact with Selective Service, that a person is a CO. Remember it is only a preliminary statement to SSS, not an official claim. So, use the written form from the post office and the procedure described later in the workshop.

Author's Note: While it increases registration rates, the new SS registration methods make the process mostly hidden and automatic. It minimizes and disguises the impact of a major commitment in a male 18-year-old's life, AND it denies the opportunity for that person to lay a conscientious objection claim, thus making it more difficult later should a draft begin.

*Author's note: The Selective Service Teacher's Guide does not mention automatic or optional registration in almost all states when applying for a state driver's license. This goes virtually unnoticed! Almost every young male wants a driver's license, so these laws not only push up compliance rates, they are also a subtle yet devious way to force young men to register. The SS website now actually describes getting a driver's license as a benefit from SS registration. *Delaware, the first state to implement these laws in 2000, hit almost a 100% compliance rate in May 2002.*

SSS: Same Yet Different from Before

- Still a mandated <u>Federal Law</u> for 18-yr.-old males
- Still <u>the precursor to a draft</u> that is ready to conscript and mobilize an expanded Armed Forces
- Still <u>a civilian agency</u>, separate from DoD or Pentagon, falling under Executive Branch
- BUT, <u>"fairer," more equitable</u>, less preferential treatment, fewer deferments. Boards will have consistent standards and training
- Shifted from applicant initiated to <u>automated</u>, hidden systems Denial of state/federal programs and state driver's license
- Registration is more <u>efficient, effortless, seamless, invisible</u>
- <u>No way to indicate a CO claim</u>; can only be done with draft
- Agencies <u>electronically cross-reference & data-share</u> registration (State Dept. of Motor Vehicles, Education, Labor, Citizenship and Immigration, I.R.S, U.S. Postal Service, JAMRS, etc.)

Fundamentally, Selective Service is for one main reason—a draft. During the Vietnam War, the draft was questioned over its fairness and preferential treatment. A higher proportion of African-Americans were being drafted. College students were deferred. Many of these inequities were corrected with the Lottery and other changes.

For now, the SSS is like a huge giant quietly sleeping in the background. The policies and changes in Selective Service have been indirect, subtle, and silent making this sleeping giant invisible. These changes include: (1) the shift from an aggressive imposition of fines and jail time to the denial of federal and state programs, benefits, employment, immigration status, and driver's licenses; and (2) the links to automatic registration when seeking state and federal benefits, esp. a driver's license. As a result, few people realize the full magnitude and extent Selective Service registration has.

Data-sharing and cross-referencing use a SS Registrant Information Bank (current SS registrants) and a Suspected Violator Inventory System to check against other state and federal agencies such as State's driver's license bureaus (using the American Association of Motor Vehicles Administrators software), Dept. of Labor's Job Corps Program, Dept. of Education federal student aid, Dept. of State, Immigration Services, Dept. of Defense, address changes by the U.S. Postal Service; and JAMRS. JAMRS (Joint Advertising and Marketing Research & Studies) contains information from private information brokers, individuals, and government agencies including personal information form ASVAB (Armed Services Vocational Aptitude Battery) administered in most high schools. (See Brennan Center for Justice, *Automatic Registration in the United States: The Selective Service Example*, listed in bibliography.)

No Draft Now, BUT...
Reaching the "Tipping Point:"
An End to the All Volunteer Force

- "Endless wars" that truly never end
- Service members, through stop-loss orders and repeated deployments, suffer from physical and psychological wounds
- A global battlefield encompassing every nook and cranny of our nation
- Heightened security and protection at home as well as abroad
- Future wars i.e., with ISIS, the greater Middle East, Iran, North Korea, China
- Universal Service and Training Acts
- Next draft could include women or specialty skills like doctors, linguists, and tech geeks

We are in a state of "endless wars," a never-ending war on terrorism. During the Iraq and Afghanistan Wars a type of "back door" draft was used to keep service members from ending their tour. This included stop-loss orders, extensions of contracts, calling up both active and inactive reserves, etc. In essence, military personnel already in service were being "re-drafted" back into the military at the end of their assigned duty. The Military Enlistment Document, Section 10b says, "In a time of war, my enlistment may be extended without my consent for the duration of the war and for six months after its end." Some in the Pentagon say our armed forces are broken. Repeated deployments; signature wounds of PTSD, TBI, and Moral Injury; high suicide rates; deaths & severe injuries all plague the services. As of 2016, our nation is in a relative lull of fighting. Troops are being withdrawn from Afghanistan and Iraq, drones purportedly substitute for boots on the ground, and Special Forces operate selectively and in secret. But what if we engage in other arenas – ISIS, Syria, the Ukraine, Iran, North Korea, China? Will the next President after Obama be more aggressive? What if we have more tragedies like at the 2014 Boston Marathon, 2015 San Bernardino, 2016 Orlando, or other threats to our everyday life?

A specialty draft for doctors & computer technicians is considered.

NY Congressman Rangel proposed a draft so that the sacrifice for service could be spread among all economic and racial groups AND so that the wider public might voice louder objections to a draft, much as they did during the Vietnam War. A Universal Training and Service Act, requiring all young adults to give two years of service to their country, could convert easily to a military draft. Would this end up being another "back door" draft? Would COs be part of the military and subject to military laws?

Slide 18

```
┌────────────────────────────────────────────────────┐
│                                                      │
│              The Draft Sequence                      │
│                                                      │
│   1. Congress and President authorize a draft.       │
│   2. The lottery is held, matching birthdates        │
│      randomly with sequence numbers (1-366).         │
│   3. Components of SS agency are activated including  │
│      Local and Appeal Boards.                        │
│   4. Physical, mental, moral examinations are given. │
│   5. Induction notices are sent to those who passed.*│
│   6. Registrants requesting CO re-classification have│
│      within 10 days to file paper work; Boards decide.│
│   7. First draftees are inducted. (<2 weeks or 6 months)│
│   From http://www.sss.gov/PDFs/TeachersGuideBook.pdf (in revision)│
└────────────────────────────────────────────────────┘
```

- A crisis may require conscription to meet military manpower needs. Congress passes and the President signs legislation to activate the draft.
- A lottery based on birthdays assigned to numbers 1-366 determines the order in which registered men are called for service. The first to be called for examination and induction, based on that lottery, would be men whose 20th birthday falls during the calendar year of the draft, followed if needed by those aged 21, 22, 23, 24, and 25. Eighteen-year-olds and men turning 19 during that year would probably not be drafted. The lottery is separate for each age group and is redone annually.
- The Selective Service activates its field structure then orders its State Directors, Reserve Force Officers, and Board Members to report for duty. Local and Appeal Boards are activated; they decide claims for certain classifications that would exempt or defer a young man from service. Local and Appeal Board members are U.S. Citizens at least 18 years of age, never been in the military, uncompensated volunteers, as representative as possible of the racial and national origin of registrants in the area served, serve up to 20 years, required to be fair and unbiased in the decisions they render, and receive standardized training and procedures to minimize bias and to apply the law fairly across all Local Boards. Though not currently active, local boards do exist and citizens are named to them.
- Registered men turning 20 that year, whose birth dates drew low lottery numbers, are ordered to report for a physical and mental examination at the nearest Military Entrance Processing Station (MEPS) to determine if they are fit for service.
- Induction orders are sent to those who passed their physical and mental exams.*
- Those who pass the military exam will have within ten days to file a claim for deferment or exemption. If no claim is filed or it is denied, they will be ordered for induction when their lottery number is reached. Postponements may be granted for certain reasons after an induction order is issued. Local Boards would start processing registrants' claims.
- Within 193 days from a crisis, Selective Service must deliver the first draftees. However, SS does have a system (RIMS) that could shorten this process (see below).

* The procedures as posted on the Selective Service website have some ambiguity. The most recent reference (https://www.sss.gov/About/Sequence-of-Events) says "Once he is notified of the results of the evaluation, a registrant will be given up to 10 days to file a claim for exemption, postponement, or deferment." Later, it says, "Those who pass the military evaluation will receive induction orders. An inductee will have 10 days to report to a local Military Entrance Processing Station for induction." John Hartscough from Church of the Brethren describes this process and its lack of clarity in *How the Draft Would Work and Conscientious Objection*. "Potential inductees, chosen through the lottery system, would be sent SSS Form 252 'Order to Report for Induction.' This form orders the inductee to appear at the nearest Military Entrance Processing Station (MEPS). Since there is no way provided for a Conscientious Objector to War (CO) to state his belief on SSS Form 1, **the first time a CO can make his position known to SSS is after receiving SSS Form 252** (underline and bold not in original). Within ten days following the receipt of SSS Form 252, and only within that ten-day period, the CO must contact his local board and request SSS Form 8, 'Claim for Reclassification.' The CO will return SSS Form 8, indicating a desire to be reclassified as a CO. SSS will then send SSS Form 22, 'Claim Documentation Form Conscientious Objector.' All documentation supporting the CO position must be included with the return of Form 22 to SSS local boards. … There are variations to this induction plan depending on which Procedures Manual is followed by SSS. It could be that the ten-day period for reclassification would occur after the physical examination at the MEPS. The CO will need to consider counseling with someone knowledgeable with SSS rules upon receipt of an induction notice in order to determine which Procedure Manual is being used. The CO should not depend on SSS to provide the necessary information and details surrounding timing of the request for reclassification, nor the consequences of not reporting to the MEPS. The CO who waives his MEPS exam waives his right to any other claims for reclassification in the future. SSS is trying to get all COs to take the physical exam."

Local Draft Boards decide CO claims (and other non-administrative deferments). Everyone is classified originally as I-A (available for unrestricted military service) or eligible to be inducted. Those who fail their physical are reclassified as 4-F (registrants not acceptable for military service). Other deferments decided by the Local Draft Board include 2-D (studying or preparing from ministry), 3-A (unreasonable hardship to dependents), and 4-D (minister of religion). Under current draft law, a college student can have his induction postponed only until the end of the current semester. A senior can be postponed until end of academic year.

The SSS actually has two systems in place if a draft becomes necessary. The first, *RIMS (Registrant Information and Management System)*, could be used in a national emergency to conscript tens of thousands of draftees into boot camp in less than two weeks. A potential inductee would be sent an induction notice and have less than ten days to contact a draft board and request a claim for CO reclassification. *RIPS (Registrant Integrated Processing System)* would take effect in a non-emergency draft and take about six months (193 days).

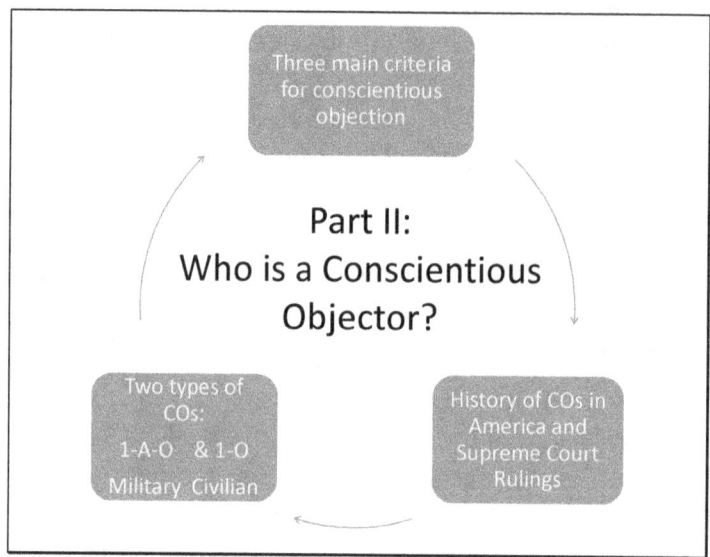

CONSCIENTIOUS OBJECTION

This section will define conscientious objection. After looking at the three main criteria (which will be on the "final exam"), a brief history of COs in America will show how the government struggled with the classification. Then, some U.S. Supreme Court rulings will provide distinctions helpful in articulating and defending a claim. The last section will look at the two types of COs—those who serve in the military, 1-A-O, and those who do not, 1-O. With these clarifications in mind, participants can begin to decide, discern, and document a CO position.

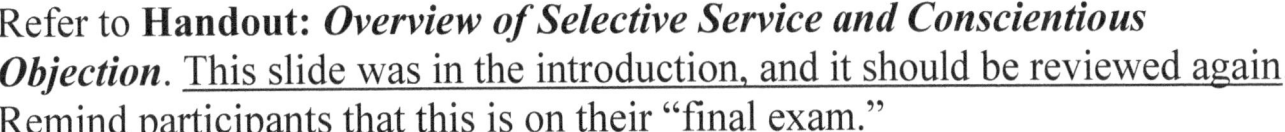

Three Criteria for Being a CO
(Conscientious Objector)

1. Conscientiously opposed to participating in **any and all war,**
2. Based on **moral, ethical, and/or religious** beliefs (and training), and
3. Must be **sincere or deeply held** (or play a significant role in one's life).

See *Overview of Selective Service and Conscientious Objection*

Refer to **Handout:** *Overview of Selective Service and Conscientious Objection*. This slide was in the introduction, and it should be reviewed again. Remind participants that this is on their "final exam."

- *Any and all war* is pretty clear. It is not just for political or situational reasons, like against a particular war. For a CO, no war is "just" or could fit into the religious doctrine or "just war" theories of theologians. Secondly, the focus is *any and all war* as we know it <u>now</u>. A person does not have to answer if he or she would have fought in WW II. One can't say what one might do in another period.

- *Moral, ethical, and/or religious* gives latitude of expression. While beliefs are hard to prove, put into words, or even crystallize fully, this must be done. See the handout on Supreme Court rulings for clarifications.

- *Deeply held* means sincere or, in legal terms, it means documented This is why starting now is essential. Suppose you suddenly got drafted, had no prior documentation, but decided to claim CO status. The first question the draft board would ask is, "Why are you making a CO claim now? Do you just want to get out of the draft?" Prior documentation demonstrates a sincere track record, and it is a main reason for this workshop.

A History of COs in America

- American Revolution: Some colonial legislatures gave exemptions based on religious affiliation.
- Civil War: Pay $300 to a special "Slave Fund" in lieu of conscription, but still largely on religious affiliation.
- WW I: Based on religious affiliation; COs were part of military and served noncombatant duty; eventually alternative service an option. COs were not treated well. Some imprisoned or abused.
- For 150 years, church membership vs. individual conscience was discussed but never really resolved.
- WW II: <u>Civilian</u> draft board decided deferment; by religious training or belief (not religious affiliation). Must have a belief in a Supreme Being.

See *COs and Selective Service in America (1656 to Present)* in the Reference Handouts as an outline & as a long narrative in the Appendix.

Early debates and amendments never fully codified a precise definition or basis for a CO claim and alternated between the individual conscience vs. a peace church membership. In fact, James Madison endorsed that conscientious objection be part of the Bill of Rights, but it did not carry the vote of the Continental Congress.

The World War I Supreme Court case (Arver v. US - 1918) on the legality of a draft (245 U.S. 366) simply asserted that conscription was obvious and practical if the Constitution gave the authority to raise a military, that it was based on precedent by previous U.S. wars and practices of other nations, and that "the very conception of a just government and its duty to the citizen includes the reciprocal obligation of the citizen to render military service." The case only briefly addressed noncombatant COs, their 1st Amendment rights (freedom of religious expression), or involuntary servitude. The Court felt it was "too ridiculous a claim to even comment on," "too wanting in merit to require further notice," "its unsoundness is too apparent to require us to do more," and "we are constrained to the conclusion that the contention to that effect is refuted by its mere statement." (Justice White).

The 1917 Draft Law provided exemption only to those who were members of a "well-organized religious sect or organization…whose existing creed or principles (forbid) its members to participate war in any form."

WW I conscripts who refused to wear a uniform, bear arms, perform basic duties, or submit to military authority were court-martialed. Some convicted objectors were sentenced to 20 years. Military tribunals tried men found to be insincere: 17 were sentenced to death, 142 to life imprisonment, and 345 to penal labor camps (See Schlissel, p. 131; *Conscription in the US*, Wikipedia, ref. #15; and other references). Only Amish, Mennonites, Quakers, and Church of Brethren were given CO exemptions. In other words, the government and military had no sympathy or patience for those who felt conscription was against a person's Constitutional rights or that conscientious objection was a religiously justified position. Their opinion reflected the prevailing culture of the time.

See **Appendix, *COs and Selective Service in America (1656 to present)***

> # Key U.S. Supreme Court Rulings Since World War II
>
> 1. Seeger, 1965: The Court struck down the "belief in a Supreme Being" clause saying within ***religious training and belief*** would come "all sincere beliefs ... based upon a power or being, or upon faith, to which all else is subordinate or upon which all else is ultimately dependent," OR, "does the claimed belief occupy the same place ... as an orthodox belief in God...?"
>
> 2. Welsh, 1970: "Spurred by ***deeply held moral, ethical, or religious beliefs***, (that) would give them no rest or peace if they...become a part of an instrument of war."
>
> 3. Gillette, 1971: Not political or selective reasons, or an unjust war. It "must amount to conscientious opposition to participating personally ***in any war and all war.***"
>
> See *U.S. Supreme Court Rulings, Congressional Legislation, and Law*

See **Handout:** *U.S. Supreme Court Rulings, Congressional Legislation, and Law.* The whole handout is worth reading.

These cases clarify and refine conscientious objection. Read bold portions from the Handout. In some cases, these rulings narrow the definition; in other cases they broaden it. The 1955 Sicurella v. U.S. case ruled in favor of a CO who said violence may sometimes be justified in self-defense, the defense of your family, or to protect a friend from attack. In Seeger, the Court struck down the requirement that a CO must affirm belief in a **Supreme Being** and must derive his (or her) CO claim from that belief, thus significantly broadening the legal definition of who would qualify as a CO.

Mohammad Ali, the greatest heavyweight boxer of all time, claimed, when presented with an induction notice, that he was a CO. His conviction was based upon his religious training and belief as a Muslim. His local draft board denied his request (based upon the FBI's secret recommendation to them), but when called at his induction hearing to take "that step forward" and become part of the military, Ali refused. The result was denial of his boxing license and possible imprisonment. Several years later, the Supreme Court reviewed his case, acknowledged that his conviction against war was based on religious training and belief, overturned the draft board's denial, and gave him his CO status. His license was reinstated, and he continued to box. Only recently has this case been declassified.

See also these other Supreme Court cases: Goldman v. Weinberger, 475 U.S. 503 (1986); Rostker v. Goldberg, 453 U.S. 57 (1981); Parker, Warden, et al. v. Levy, 417 U.S. 733 (1974); Johnson v. Robinson, 415 U.S. 361 (1974); Gillette v. United States, 401 U.S. 437 (1971); Clay, aka Ali v. United States, 403 U.S. 698 (1971); Welsh v. United States, 398 U.S. 333 (1970);United States v. Seeger, 380 U.S. 163 (1965); Sicurella v. United States, 348 U.S. 385 (1955); Myers v. United States, 272 U.S. 52 (1923, 1925, 1926); Selective Draft Law Cases, 245 U.S. 366 (1917).

```
┌─────────────────────────────────────────────────┐
│                Two Types of COs                  │
│                                                  │
│    In the Military         Not in the Military   │
│                                                  │
│  Joins the military but does   Has nothing to do with the │
│    noncombatant training       military system; stays in  │
│    and service                 civilian jurisdiction      │
│  Does not carry or use a       Must do equivalent time of │
│    weapon, even in combat      alternative service*       │
│    situations.                 (outside of military.      │
│  Might be assigned as a        Might work in a mental     │
│    medic, chaplain, pot        hospital, prison, police   │
│    scrubber                    force                      │
│  Classified as 1-A-O           Classified as 1-O          │
│                                                  │
│    *Work of national importance under civilian direction. │
│                                                  │
│  See Overview of Selective Service and Conscientious Objection │
└─────────────────────────────────────────────────┘
```

Go back to Handout: *Overview of Selective Service and Conscientious Objection.*

Read from the slide or from the handout about 2/3 the way down. Joke again that this also is on their "final exam." The difference between being in the military or not is important. One falls under military jurisdiction; the other under civilian. Which one are you? Part of the military or not?

Examples of alternative service include: relief and rehabilitation in war or disaster areas; technical, agricultural, medical, or educational assistance in poor or developing areas; service in mental hospitals, schools for handicapped, homes for the aged, or similar institutions; or participating in mental or scientific research that might benefit humanity. (see a full list of appropriate placements at the Selective Service site: https://www.sss.gov/About/Alternative-Service/Alternative-Service-Employer-Network.

For those already serving in the military whose beliefs change, getting a CO re-classification is a long and arduous process and may not lead to discharge. The G.I. Rights Hotline, 877-447-4487, provides help for these service members. In today's all-volunteer force, a CO is not popular in the military and is seen as a liability because the person will not fight. This was not always the case. As a transition, ask, "Does anyone know who Desmond T. Doss was?"

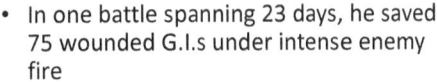

Desmond T. Doss

- 7th Day Adventist
- Worshipped on Sabbath, or 7th day
- Refused to carry a weapon
- Classified I-A-0, or noncombatant, as defined by President Roosevelt
- Served as Medic Pfc. in World War II in Philippines, Guam & Okinawa
- In one battle spanning 23 days, he saved 75 wounded G.I.s under intense enemy fire
- 1st CO to receive the Medal of Honor from President Truman
- CD/Video at www.desmonddoss.com

Doss called himself a **"Conscientious Cooperator,"** not a "Conscientious Objector."

The video tells his story, includes interviews and recollections of how he affected his fellow soldiers, shows their emotional scars resulting from war, and highlights the misunderstanding and abuse he received during training and early combat. Yet soldiers saw his dedication and courage while in combat, and they quickly respected his convictions, integrity, and courage. See *The Conscientious Objector: A True Story of an American Soldier* at www.desmonddoss.com.

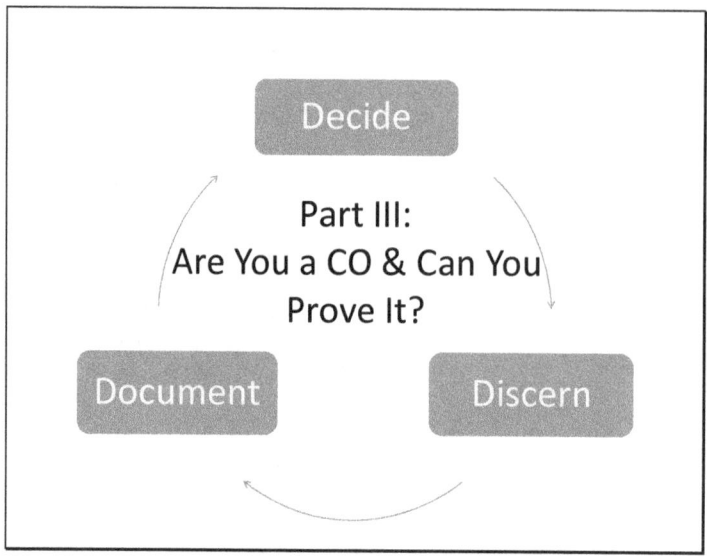

ARE YOU A CO & CAN YOU PROVE IT?

The previous sections provided background information about Selective Service, the draft, and conscientious objection. The rest of the workshop presents methods to decide, discern, and document a CO claim. It is not easy for anyone to articulate his or her beliefs, but these suggestions will help a person get started.

> Discerning and Deciding:
> Suggestions to Get Started
>
> 1. What do you believe about your own personal participation in war?
> 2. Can you articulate those beliefs?
> 3. Can you describe what led you to those beliefs?
> 4. Can you document or produce evidence that demonstrates those beliefs and how you achieved them?

These fundamental questions reflect two dynamics. What do you believe AND how can you document or demonstrate that?

The first is the most important and requires deep soul-searching. Once this is done, the claimant must articulate, document, and "prove" them. The curriculum is designed to help with both aspects.

Slide 27

Refer to the **Handout:** *Excerpts from Military Enlistment/Re-Enlistment Document*, the Military Enlistment/Re-enlistment Document itself at http://www.dtic.mil/whs/directives/forms/eforms/dd0004.pdfor, or Quaker House's Sgt. Abe Truth & Recruitment materials at www.quakerhouse.org.

This simple, overgeneralized slide portrays basic conflicts or moral/ethical dilemmas: the killing of human beings and the giving up of all personal moral, ethical, and religious decisions. The Scripture on the left (from the Hebrew Bible, the Christian New Testament, and the Holy Koran) corresponds on the right to portions from the Military Enlistment Document. Depending on the group and time, stop and discuss this slide.

#1: Soldiers are trained to dehumanize the enemy so they can kill them. They are trained to kill reflexively—without thinking and upon command. Too many vets, torn between loyalties/values to country and to God, return in emotional turmoil or conflict. How many were taught to love their enemies? Exodus 20:13; Matthew 22:37-39; Mark 12:29-31; Luke 10:27; Qur'an 6:151 & 13:22.

#2: Which is greater: your love of God or love of country? Can you serve two masters? Is the family of God limited to national boundaries? Could you give up all decision-making power, including how you are guided by God, or your own conscience, and put it into the hands of another person? See Exodus 20:3, Matthew 6:24. Qur'an 29:56 & 72:18 (The longer Matthew quote is "No one can serve two masters, for a slave will either hate the one or love the other, or be devoted to the one and despise the other. You cannot serve God and wealth.")

Quaker House, a manifestation of the Friends Peace testimony in Fayetteville, NC, home of Fort Bragg, has a handout called Sgt. Abe, the Honest Recruiter, pointing out some of fine print in the Military Enlistment Document. It also refers to Section 8c about promises made by recruiters, "The agreements in this section and attached annex(es) are all the promises made to me by the Government. ANYTHING ELSE ANYONE HAS PROMISED ME IS NOT VALID AND WILL NOT BE HONORED." Download the Sgt. Abe Document from *www.QuakerHouse.org.* For more scriptural Passages see **Appendix:** *Hebrew, Christian, & Islamic Scripture on Peace & God's Law.*

See also the paragraph about Logan Mehl-Laituri in the Reference Handout, *Scripture vs. Military Document* in the Teacher's Guide that uses this same slide.

Exercise: Worksheet Form 22

- Take 10 minutes and put yourself in a CO's shoes.
- Would you be 1-A-O or 1-O?
- Then answer the three questions listed on the form.
- Come back, report on one question, and discuss.
- Tri-fold the Worksheet.

See Exercise: *Worksheet Form 22*
HO: *Suggestions to Build Documentation & Worksheet Form 22 Tips*

Give everyone a copy of *Exercise: Worksheet Form 22, Claim for Conscientious Objector.* Use this one-page practice version, but refer to the longer, two-page form in the Appendix that defines the difference between 1-A and 1-A-O. Read the instructions on the slide while referring to the Worksheet.

The form asks participants to explain how they arrived at a CO claim. In prior years, Worksheet Form 22 was used by Selective Service as claimants appeared before their Draft Board.

Depending upon the group and their sensitivity to this topic, consider giving longer than ten minutes. Later, the workshop will cover writing a letter to one's faith or support community as another way to document a claim.

At the end of this exercise, demonstrate **tri-folding**, a key method to preserve and date documentation. Take the completed form, photocopy it, and fold it into thirds with the written portion inside and blank side out. Staple it shut, then stamp, self-address, and mail it to yourself. The mailed form will come back with a U.S. Postal Service date over the stamp showing when it was done. Put the copy unopened in the CO folder. Even though beliefs evolve and mature, keeping a record of them shows a history or "paper trail" and underscores sincerity. See #2 in **Handout: *More Suggestions to Build Documentation and Worksheet Form 22 Tips.***

How do you register as a CO?

- Selective Service law recognizes conscientious objection as a deferment.
- However, documentation for a CO claim does not exist at registration time.
- Therefore, the registrant needs to devise his or her own documentation as a basis for a claim.

The "Catch-22" about registration is that the form has no place to indicate a CO claim. Yet, if a draft is reinstated, a person could have as little as nine days to prepare and submit documentation. Such a last-minute effort not only undermines the third criteria for being a CO (sincerity), but it does not give an applicant time to discern such a deep inner conviction or period of soul-searching.

Who do you think a draft board will grant CO status to? The person who gets an induction notice and in nine days rushes to complete required paperwork? Or a young person who says, "When I was 18 and had to register, I made the effort to declare myself as a CO, and here are several pieces of documentation done over the years to prove my sincerity?" That is why this workshop recommends starting this now.

Three Fundamental Ways to Document a CO Claim

1. Write and present a "CO letter" to your faith or support community.
2. Using the <u>Postal Service</u> form, write in a request for a CO claim, and get it witnessed.   Then, when your registration card is returned, write on the return portion, "You did not indicate my preference for a CO classification."
3. Gather "Letters of Support."

Tri-fold and send copies to yourself.

See *Three Fundamental Ways to Document a CO Claim*

Refer to Handout: *Three Fundamental Ways to Document a CO Claim.*

This reference handout outlines three main ways to gather documentation. It also lists other reference handouts that provide greater detail and examples.

Each of the three methods listed above is covered in the subsequent slides.

Letters to Your Faith or Support Community
Asking for Recognition and Documentation

- A "generic" sample letter with some main (legal) points to include
- Some specific, real-life examples

See *A Template or Generic Letter Documenting a CO Claim* AND *Two Sample CO Letters*

Refer to Handouts: *A Template or Generic Letter Documenting a CO Claim* <u>and</u> *Two Sample CO Letters.*

Emphasize the three bulleted items on the "generic" letter. Note that they parallel the three criteria or definitions of a CO.

If time permits, read excerpts from the sample letters. Caution the participants that a person's letter is unique and personal. The examples should in NO way determine another's beliefs or views, nor should they be copied or plagiarized.

Some CO Letter Starters...

1. The legal requirements or three criteria for a CO:
   - Against personal participation in any and all war.
   - Based upon moral, ethical, and/or religious training and belief.
   - Sincere; deeply held; documented.
2. Personal statements of conviction and/or belief. Rely on Worksheet Form 22 (& Tips) as a start.
3. Measure yourself against the Supreme Court interpretations of conscientious objection.
4. Ask your faith or support community for help and to hold your concerns institutionally (minutes, lockbox).

See *Suggestions for Faith and Support Communities*

Writing a CO letter is challenging. On the one hand, articulating one's beliefs can be daunting and using words to describe deep, inner convictions can seem trite. On the other hand, a sincere, personal expression of truth cannot be debated by another person, even a Local Draft Board.

Being honest is most important, and that is distinctively unique and different for each person. No letter has to conform to universal or academic principles. It only has to be an expression of personal beliefs. No one can refute them, especially if they are honest and sincere.

Register on-line (http://www.sss.gov) Author's Note: Registering on-line does not allow additions. Do not register on-line. or complete this form.

SELECTIVE SERVICE SYSTEM REGISTRATION FORM

DATE OF BIRTH (MM-DD-YYYY)　　　　　　　　　　SEX (Mark with "X")　　　　SOCIAL SECURITY ACCOUNT NUMBER

1⇒ ☐☐-☐☐-☐☐☐☐　　2⇒ ☐ Male　☐ Female　3⇒ ☐☐☐-☐☐-☐☐☐☐

*** Note: I am a conscientious objector. Martin Luther King, Jr., January 15, 1953. (Signed and Dated)

LAST NAME

4⇒ ☐☐☐☐☐☐☐☐☐☐☐☐☐☐☐☐

FIRST NAME & MIDDLE NAME

☐☐☐☐☐☐☐☐☐☐☐☐☐☐☐☐

I, Martin Luther King, Sr., Senior Minister at Ebenezer Baptist Church, witness Martin's conviction. (Signed and dated)

CURRENT MAILING ADDRESS: STREET ADDRESS & APARTMENT NUMBER

5⇒ ☐☐☐☐☐☐☐☐☐☐☐☐☐☐☐☐☐☐☐☐☐☐☐☐

CITY　　　　　　　　　　　　　　　　　STATE　　ZIP CODE

☐☐☐☐☐☐☐☐☐☐☐☐☐☐☐☐☐☐ ☐☐ ☐☐☐☐☐

I, Howard Thurman, long-time mentor of Martin, witness his conviction as a CO. (Signed and dated)

TODAY'S DATE (MM-DD-YYYY)

6⇒ ☐☐-☐☐-☐☐☐☐ ☐☐☐☐☐　　7⇒ _____

SIGNATURE

See *Sample Selective Service System Registration Form*

See **Handout:** *Sample Selective Service System Registration Form*, <u>and/or</u> a *U.S. Postal Service Form* (pick up some from a Post Office).

As mentioned earlier, use the Postal Service form in order to write in a claim for conscientious objection. See how this is done in the slide. Get two witnesses, perhaps from one's faith or support community. When completed and signed, photocopy this form twice, tri-fold and send one copy to self, keep the other as a backup, and send the original to Selective Service. This is the first and most basic step in preparing documentation for a CO claim. Use this form even if registration was done automatically through a driver's license bureau or other method. It does not hurt to register twice (this time manually within 30 days of an 18th birthday), especially since the other methods did not permit adding the CO request.

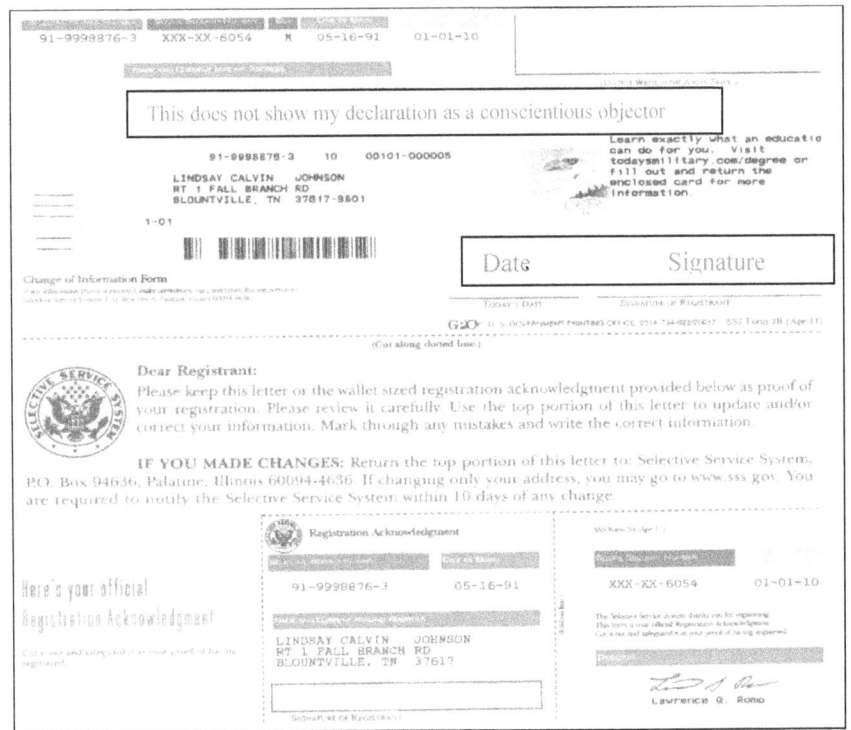

The form above is from Selective Service Site:
https://www.google.com/?gws_rd=ssl#q=%22Lindsay+Calvin+Johnson%22)

Refer to **Handout:** *Change of Information Form and a Suggested Reply.*

This is a nifty way to get dated documentation from Selective Service that demonstrates an attempt to apply for conscientious objection, even though Selective Service has no way of indicating such a claim. Remember to tri-fold, photocopy, and send to yourself every piece of important documentation so that it comes back with a U.S. Postal Service date on it. Otherwise, a Draft Board might accuse the claimant of manufacturing evidence at the last minute.

> ## Letters of Support
> ## (from others)
>
> - Gather two, three, or maybe more.
> - Get from "respected" people; use a cross- section.
> - Should attest to CO's ***sincerity and integrity.***
> - Person is familiar with the CO's position, but doesn't have to agree.
> - Start collecting now, especially because contacts tend to fade through early adulthood transitions from high school, college, and jobs.
>
> See *Letters of Support*

Though often not done during non-draft times, another form of documentation is to collect Letters of Support.

See **Handout:** ***Letters of Support.*** These letters strengthen the extent and sincerity of one's convictions.

Emphasize the last bulleted point above. Some young adults tend not to ask older adults, like teachers, for Letters of Support. But because of transitions from high school to college or a job, young adults often relocate and lose touch with these adults who might have known them well and could have spoken on their behalf. Letters of Support also educate adults who may know little or anything about conscientious objection.

DOCUMENT

DOCUMENT

DOCUMENT

- **Keep a CO folder**. Include copies of registration forms, CO letters, worksheets, dated workshop agendas, correspondence from SS, readings, journals, homework assignments, movies, songs, discussions, activities, volunteer work, etc.
- Refer to your faith or support community's records and minutes, letters of support, etc.
- Tri-fold important papers: Copy, fold in thirds, send to self and KEEP, unopened.

See *Suggestions to Build Documentation & Worksheet Form 22 Tips*

Refer to **Handout:** *Suggestions to Build Documentation and Worksheet Form 22 Tips.*

Talk with participants about other ways that they can articulate or provide documentation of their beliefs. See and expand on the list in the first bullet. Emphasize that the three fundamental forms of documentation on the previous slide are just a start.

Another simple form of documentation is to use the packet of materials provided for this workshop. Have each person write on the front of the PowerPoint or agenda handout, "I, (name), attended this CO workshop on (date) as witnessed by (name of workshop presenter)" then have the presenters sign and date this page. To be thorough, have them go home, photocopy this, tri-fold, and send to themselves, so they have an officially-dated piece of documentation.

Remind them again: document, document, document. Sounds like a "final exam" question, because it is.

A Checklist of Procedures...

- For the 18-year-old's CO folder
  - ❑ Worksheet Form #22
  - ❑ Workshop handouts, signed and dated
  - ❑ SS Registration Form; Correction letter
  - ❑ Letter to one's support or faith community
  - ❑ Letters of support from others
- For the Faith or Support Community
  - ❑ Clearness or Support Committee
  - ❑ Official records and/or minutes
  - ❑ Witness SS Registration Form
  - ❑ Store records in a safe place (or use a national registry or other outside agency)

See *Suggestions to Build...* AND *Suggestions for Faith and Support...*

To impress upon the participants the importance of keeping legal documentation, here is another checklist. Documentation is kept by redundant sources: the claimant (or workshop participant) **and** the claimant's faith or support community. As tedious as it is, the claimant is developing a "paper trail" for future use. Copies of certain documents might also be sent to "Independent" agencies, like CC&W, or a repository, like Peace Abbey. See Handout: ***Sample Letter to Independent Agencies or Repositories*** for mailing and Internet addresses.

Stress that one's faith or support community also has obligations; some are listed in the **Handout: *Suggestions for Faith and Support Communities.***

Some teens may need to introduce conscientious objection, nurture this concept, and build support within their community about their position. Not all faith or support communities will embrace this notion, or they simply may not know what it is. This, in itself, is another way of demonstrating sincerity and confliction about a CO claim.

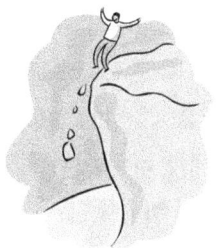

Can you
"defend"
your
position?

Role-play a *Mock Draft Board*
A witness of conscience vs. fear
Not a "test" but a "testimony"

See *Exercise: Sample Questions a Draft Board Might Ask*

Refer to Exercise: *Sample Questions a Draft Review Board Might Ask.*
Also, see the *Annotated Version of Agenda #1* that describes this exercise in detail.

This is a form of affective learning. It puts teens in the position of defending and justifying themselves, though honesty requires no justification. The lesson elicits deep feelings, prompts lively group discussion, and encourages individual soul-searching. The role-plays expose, illuminate, and clarify values; build confidence; and promote resilience in the face of challenges from a future draft board. It is essential to support and nurture this process in a safe, trusting, and open environment.

Set up a role-play with a three-person mock draft review board. The three might be any adults participating, those facilitating the lesson, or a combination of the presenters and younger participants.

Explain that the mock draft board is intended to simulate an experience, almost to the extreme. Its purpose is to bring out both dynamics and content. It is NOT meant to embarrass, offend, or discourage, but rather to illustrate some of the anxiety, urgency, and difficulty of expressing deeply personal views to strangers.

Ask for volunteers to be the CO applicant (or person in the hot seat). Tell them they have two minutes to explain their case. Then immediately start drilling them with questions, starting with perhaps, "Why do you want to be a CO?" As they respond, look for holes (hesitations, inconsistencies, uncertainties, or other weaknesses) and then interrupt them with a challenging question to that effect. To be true to the role-play, some members of the board can be rude and disrespectful, others seemingly nice. The simulation is to challenge, prod, and trick to illustrate how others might have completely different and biased views that might keep someone from expressing who they are.

Use an "angel" (any person) who can come in at any time and whisper help or an answer to the one in the hot seat.

At the end of each role, congratulate the person in the hot seat and "process" what happened. Ask the person in the hot seat: What was this like? How did you feel? What did you feel comfortable with? What was difficult? Where did you need better insight to respond? How did you feel about the draft board members? When done, ask everyone else to give this person a round of applause. Then, turn to the board and ask similar questions. Lastly, ask for the audience's responses.

If time permits, repeat the exercise with new volunteers.

> ## Did We Miss Anything?
>
>
>
> - All materials, PowerPoint, handouts, and interview tapes can be downloaded or a hard copy purchased from 910-323-3912 www.Quakerhouse.org
> - You can purchase a hard copy of *Raising Conscientious Objector Consciousness among Our Youth* from Friends General Conference (www.FGCQuaker.org) or get a free PDF download at: http://criticalconcern.com/swords-plowshares/co-consciousness.pdf.
> - See also www.afsc.org/youthmil and www.centeronconscience.org
>
> See *Teacher's Resource Guide* for additional materials

A six-lesson-plan curriculum, while directed towards Quakers, can be purchased at the FGC (Friends General Conference) website, and it gives more time and space to learn and discern this material. It can be adapted easily to any community. A free PDF can be downloaded from the site mentioned above. It can also be downloaded from https://www.fgcquaker.org/sites/www.fgcquaker.org/files/attachments/Raising %20CO.pdf.

The FGC bookstore has excellent selections on peace-building, nonviolence, and conscientious objection. Other materials can be found at the AFSC (American Friends Service Committee) youth and militarism website at www.afsc.org/youthmil.

Aside from what was used during this PowerPoint, many other handouts, exercises, agendas, PowerPoint Notes Pages, samples of CO letters, video DVDs of CO letter writers, scriptural passages, reference materials, contact information, Internet resources, bibliography, etc. can be found in the Teacher's Resource Guide.

Contact Information for Quaker
House

- Lynn & Steve Newsom, Co-Directors
- www. quakerhouse.org
- Email = qpr@quaker.org
  curtnpatty@aol.com
- Phone = 910-323-3912
- Curt Torell, Board member/Treasurer (and
  Clerk for NC Choices for Youth)
- Email = curtnpatty@aol.com

Feel free to contact Quaker House for questions, suggestions, or other help.

> ## Let's Review: The Final Exam
>
> 1. What are the three criteria for being a CO?
> 2. What's the difference between Class 1-A-O and Class 1-O?
> 3. What are some types of documentation that show your convictions, leadings, inclinations?
> 4. What is "tri-folding"?
> 5. Where can I get copies of these materials?
> 6. Feedback questions on the presentation:
>   - ✓ What was most helpful to you in this workshop?
>   - ✓ Did this meet your expectations? Why/why not?
>   - ✓ How could it be improved or help you better?

Here's the promised final exam. Good news! It's a group exam. Ask the first five questions to the group as a whole.

Option for the presenters: Ask participants to answer the three feedback questions under #6 either out loud or on a blank piece of paper and return them to you. Names on the feedback sheets are not necessary.

Another closing option is to reflect on the introductory exercise. Has this workshop changed your responses or comments to the beginning exercise?

Wrapping Up

1. Get your agenda signed and dated. Add it to your CO documentation folder.
2. Remember to photocopy your Worksheet Form 22, tri-fold, stamp, self-address, and send to yourself.
3. Read the handouts referenced throughout the PowerPoint or found in the Teacher's Resource Guide.

"War is not the answer."
Martin Luther King, Jr. from *A Time to Break Silence* speech, April 4, 1967, Riverside Church, N.Y.C

As participants are dismissed, they can get their agendas signed.

Remind them of their homework, if applicable, i.e., to photocopy the Worksheet Form 22 and send it to themselves.

Have them look at the handouts in their CO folder and answer any questions they have on them.